IMPROVING WRITING
Resources, Strategies, and Assessments

Susan Davis Lenski

Illinois State University

Jerry L. Johns

Northern Illinois University

KENDALL/HUNT PUBLISHING COMPANY
4050 Westmark Drive · Dubuque, Iowa 52002

Books by Jerry L. Johns

Basic Reading Inventory (seven editions)
Secondary & College Reading Inventory (two editions)
Literacy for Diverse Learners (edited)
Handbook for Remediation of Reading Difficulties
Informal Reading Inventories: An Annotated Reference Guide (compiled)
Literacy: Celebration and Challenge (edited)
Spanish Reading Inventory

Books by Jerry L. Johns and Susan Davis Lenski

Early Literacy Assessments & Teaching Strategies (with Laurie Elish-Piper)
Improving Reading: A Handbook of Strategies (2nd edition)
Reading & Learning Strategies for Middle & High School Students (with Mary Ann Wham)
Celebrate Literacy! The Joy of Reading and Writing (with June E. Barnhart, James H. Moss,
    and Thomas E. Wheat)
Language Arts for Gifted Middle School Students

Author Addresses for Correspondence and Workshops

Susan Davis Lenski
Illinois State University
239 DeGarmo Hall
Normal, IL 61790-5330
E-mail: sjlensk@ilstu.edu
309-438-3028

Jerry L. Johns
Northern Illinois University
Reading Clinic—119 Graham
DeKalb, IL 60115
E-mail: jjohns@niu.edu
815-753-8484
Residence:
2105 Eastgate Drive
Sycamore, IL 60178
815-895-3022

Address for Orders

Kendall/Hunt Publishing Company
4050 Westmark Drive
P.O. Box 1840
Dubuque, IA 52004-0810

Telephone for Orders

800-247-3458

Web Site

www.kendallhunt.com

Contents

Preface

Who will use this book?

Practicing teachers, prospective teachers, and professionals who fulfill special resource roles will appreciate the user-friendly approach we have taken in presenting *Improving Writing: Resources, Strategies, and Assessments*. The book is grounded in solid knowledge about writing. It will be used in college and university courses as well as for school district in-services and staff development programs.

What are some of the unique characteristics of this book?

Please note the subtitle—Resources, Strategies, and Assessments. These three topics form the heart of this book, providing teachers with all the background needed to help students improve their writing skills. The variety of strategies, assessment ideas, and resources will meet diverse student needs. Following is a brief outline of the unique features of this book and how these three topics are presented.

RESOURCES	STRATEGIES	ASSESSMENTS

• Reproducible student worksheets
• Transparency masters
• Teacher examples
• Student examples
• Technology Tips referencing specific web sites
• Lists of books
• Lists of web sites
• Appendices
  • Professional organizations and agencies
  • Publishing opportunities
  • Basketball team addresses
  • 549 writing formats
• Reference section
• Index
	• Concise description of writing instruction in Chapter 1
	• Overview of each chapter
	• Boxed teaching goals in Chapters 2–6
	• Background information for teaching goals
	• Step-by-step instruction
	• Expanded instructional ideas
	• Useful, practical activities
		• Teacher self-assessments
		• Student self-assessments
		• Rubrics
		• Practical evaluative ideas
		• Reproducible assessment pages

Is the book easy to use?

Yes! We have published several other books and teachers have complimented us on the organization, content, and presentation.

The organization of *Improving Writing* is similar to our successful and well-received earlier resources for teachers. In short, we have listened to people who teach, plan to teach, or function in various resource roles.

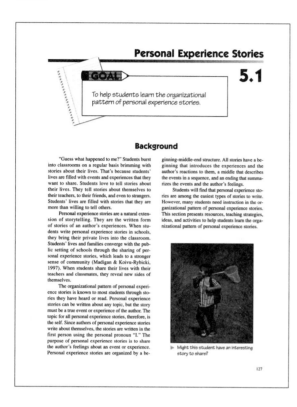

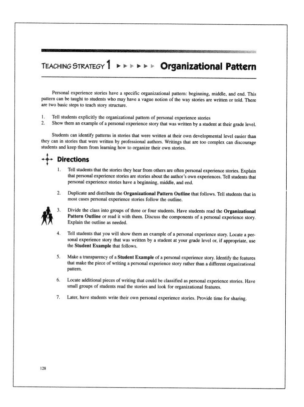

How to use this book

In a few minutes, you can learn to use IMPROVING WRITING.

A **Quick Reference Guide for Teaching and Assessment Goals** appears on the inside front cover.

Choose a specific goal and locate it on the page number listed. Each chapter has four teaching goals arranged in the same basic format:

- Chapter overview
- Numbered section heading (5.1, 5.2)
- Boxed teaching goal
- Background information

- Numbered teaching strategies
- Additional ideas and activities
- Resources throughout
- Assessments throughout

The **teaching goal** for section 5.1 is inside the box.

Background information related to achieving the goal is provided.

Teaching strategies are provided for each goal. They are clearly numbered.

Resources in the form of student examples or overhead masters are given with many of the strategies.

Ideas and activities follow the teaching strategies in many of the sections.

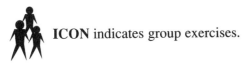 **ICON** indicates group exercises.

Technology Tips are included in the ideas and activities sections that list specific web sites pertinent to strategies introduced. Because the web sites change often, we cannot ensure their accuracy.

The **appendices** provide easy reference to valuable resources in the teaching of writing.

- **Appendix A: Professional Organizations and Agencies** will assist you in locating professional organizations and agencies related to writing.

- **Appendix B: Audiences for Student Writing** lists many places where students can send their work for possible publication. It is an overview of the various journals, but we recommend that you secure and study the actual journals before submitting a student's work.

- **Appendix C: Basketball Teams' Addresses** contains addresses for basketball teams to provide an additional outlet for students' writing.

- **Appendix D: 549 Writing Formats** provides hundreds of writing formats that will help students extend the types of writing that they do.

Word to the wise teacher

 Now it's up to you to use *Improving Writing: Resources, Strategies, and Assessments* to energize and strengthen your writing program. As you use the book, please consider the following invitation.

You're invited

To share an example of student writing (with signed permission),

a teaching idea, or activities that we might be able to use in future editions.

You can find our addresses on the copyright page.

We value your input!

Sue & Jerry

About the Authors

Susan Davis Lenski is an Associate Professor at Illinois State University where she teaches undergraduate and graduate courses in reading and language arts. She also teaches graduate writing courses.

Dr. Lenski brings 20 years of public school teaching experience to her work as a professor and a writer. During her years as a teacher, Dr. Lenski developed a writing program that balances different types of writing activities. She has presented this program to many teachers through staff development programs and graduate courses. As a result of suggestions from practicing teachers, Dr. Lenski has revised and expanded her program, which forms the basis for this book.

As a professor, Dr. Lenski has been actively engaged in research and writing. As an acknowledgment of her professional contributions to reading, Dr. Lenski was inducted into the Illinois Reading Council Hall of Fame. She has presented her work at numerous conferences, has published over 40 articles in state and national journals, and has co-authored six books, including *Improving Reading: A Handbook of Strategies* (with Jerry L. Johns).

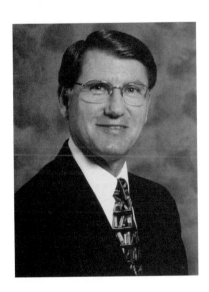

Jerry L. Johns is a Distinguished Teaching Professor at Northern Illinois University. He directs the Reading Clinic and teaches undergraduate, graduate, and doctoral students. He also conducts seminars in writing for publication. As a public school teacher, Dr. Johns taught students from kindergarten through eighth grade and has served as a reading teacher.

Dr. Johns has served on numerous committees of the International Reading Association and was a member of the Board of Directors. He was also president of the College Reading Association and the Illinois Reading Council.

Dr. Johns has been invited to consult, conduct workshops, and make presentations for teachers throughout the United States and Canada. He has also prepared nearly three hundred publications. His *Basic Reading Inventory* and *Improving Reading* (with Susan Davis Lenski) are widely used in undergraduate and graduate classes as well as by practicing teachers. Other recent co-authored books include *Early Literacy Assessments & Teaching Strategies* and *Reading & Learning Strategies for Middle & High School Students*.

Acknowledgments

We take pleasure in thanking the following individuals who shared ideas, compiled resources, edited our writing, and offered support and encouragement during the writing of this book.

Dawn Andermann
Christina Basham
Liz Beardmore
Rachel Becknell
Cheryl Benes
Pam Bloom
Jenny Bolander
Carol Burger
Julie Byrd
Becky Cockrum
Sharon Cuningham
Donna Deatherage
Trina Dotson
Shelley Fritz
Susan Giller
Barb Glover
Robin Gran
Mary Ann Gregg
Wendy Hagenbuch
Jan Herman
Lynda Hootman
Jane Jackson
Annette Johns

Jan Karcher
Sandy Leffler
Fran Lenski
Joyce Madsen
Julie McCoy
Cindy McDowell
M. Kristiina Montero
Marla Moore
Barbara O'Connell
LaShawn Pierce
Laurie Reddy
Rebecca Rhodes
Marilyn Roark
Gretchen Schmidt
Lin Scott
Barbara Short
Kari Tangel
Pamela Tow
Isabelle Townsend
Tammy Tripp
Brenda Vercler
Jill Veskauf
Sally Wallace

Chapter 1

Improving Writing Instruction

"I love being a writer. What I can't stand is the paperwork."—Peter DeVries

Overview

Writing instruction in elementary schools has improved dramatically over the past 25 years. The changes in instruction have been the result of research on the process of writing (e.g., Emig, 1971; Graves, 1975). This research has influenced the way teachers think about writing and how they teach writing in schools. For example, many teachers are now providing students with more frequent authentic writing experiences. And many teachers are helping students learn how to write for real reasons and specific audiences. Teachers are also helping students understand that writing is a process—not just a product.

Although writing instruction has definitely improved over the past two decades, expectations for students' writing have increased even more. Teachers now expect all students to be able to write enthusiastically and competently. National expectations have been defined by national standards—one of which states that students will be able to "employ a wide range of strategies as they write and use different writing process elements appropriately

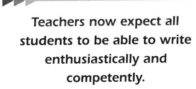

Teachers now expect all students to be able to write enthusiastically and competently.

1

to communicate with different audiences for a variety of purposes" (International Reading Association & National Council of Teachers of English, 1996). In order for students to meet this ambitious standard, teachers will need to spend more time helping students learn the skills, strategies, and subtleties of writing. New ideas about writing instruction can help teachers meet this goal.

▶ What can a teacher do to help this student meet the National Standards?

Writing: A Process, An Art, and A Craft

No matter what kind of writing curriculum or program you currently use, writing instruction in your class can be improved. To improve writing instruction in your class, you need to address all three of the components of writing: the process, the art, and the craft.

▶ The Process

You will need to help students learn that writing is a process. That means that you should help students understand that writing requires planning, drafting, revising, and editing.

▶ The Art

As students experience the stages of writing, you should teach them that a piece of writing is a work of art; it is a creation. Therefore, you need to make room in your writing program for students to experience the magic and mystery of writing. You can do this by organizing the contexts of writing so that students experience the freedom that allows the art of writing to emerge.

▶ The Craft

Writing is also a craft. Writing can be the intentional act of using knowledge about words, sentences, and paragraphs. These skills can be learned through a balanced instructional program that includes a variety of types of writing activities, experiences, and instructional lessons. A balanced writing program can help students learn the many organizational patterns, traditions, rules, and conventions that govern writing.

> ## Five Stages of Writing
> - Prewriting
> - Drafting
> - Revising
> - Editing
> - Sharing

When you address the process of writing in its contexts through a balanced writing program, you are teaching writing as a process, an art, and a craft. Consequently, your writing instruction will be improved.

The Writing Process

To improve writing instruction, teachers need to have a basic knowledge of the writing process. (See Figure 1.) Writing has been described as a recursive process with five stages (Emig, 1971; Graves, 1975). The five stages in the writing process are prewriting, drafting, revising, editing, and sharing.

▶ Prewriting/Planning

Writers begin their writing tasks by prewriting or planning their pieces of writing. During the prewriting stage, writers consider their purposes for writing, determine the forms that their writing will take, and identify their audiences. Writers can choose to outline their ideas during the prewriting stage, they can map their ideas on a graphic organizer, or they can think through ideas in their minds.

Figure 1

The Writing Process

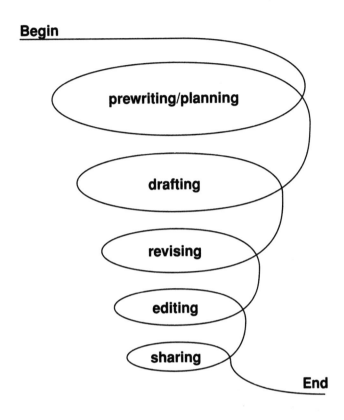

Begin

prewriting/planning

drafting

revising

editing

sharing

End

▶ Drafting

After writers have a plan for writing, they usually write their first drafts. When drafting pieces of writing, writers record their thoughts and ideas, often referring to their writing plans. During drafting, writers might decide to periodically address the conventions of writing such as spelling and word usage, but the primary purpose of the drafting stage is to write down thoughts and ideas.

▶ Revising

After a piece of writing is drafted, writers often begin revising their writing. While revising, writers reread their pieces, looking carefully at the substance of their writings. Writers may rework their writings at this stage, rewriting passages or sentences to make their meanings more clear. Writers may revise their pieces of writing many times. In fact, well-known authors often revise drafts hundreds of times before editing.

▶ Editing

When revision is complete, writers edit their writings. In order for an audience to be able to read and understand a piece of writing, it needs to be written using the conventions of the language in which it is written. Final drafts, therefore, should be edited to conform very closely to Standard English.

▶ Sharing

The final stage in the writing process is sharing the writing with an audience. Writing is meant to be read. Because sharing is a vital component of the writing process, many writers submit their works in some type of published form. In the case of students, publishing could mean a class book, a display, or an electronic file.

▶▶▶ ────────────────

Writing is generally a bit messy.

Recursive Nature of the Writing Process ──── ◀◀◀

Writing is a composing process that is shaped by the decisions writers make as they identify their writing purposes, decide upon forms, and clarify their thoughts and ideas (Dyson & Freedman, 1991). Writing is like cooking soup, designing a web page, or painting a picture. It follows specified steps but allows for spontaneity. The process of writing, therefore, has five stages that are followed in order in some instances or are adapted to fit the contexts of writing. The process of writing is recursive.

Writers know that completing a piece of writing is rarely as neat as many people infer from the writing process. Writing is generally a bit messy. That's because the writing process is recursive. When writing, writers move back and forth between writing stages as necessary. Sometimes a piece of writing takes little or no revision or editing; sometimes writers begin the process by drafting; sometimes writers edit as they write. Therefore, it's important for teachers to realize that the five-stage writing process represents a *model* of writing. Writers often use all five stages, but they will not necessarily follow every stage in order as they write.

Contexts for Writing

The process used for writing is shaped by its contexts (Hayes, 1996). (See Figure 2.) Because the process of writing is embedded with a writer's decisions, every writing event is unique and individual. Writing, however, is shaped by three factors: the social contexts in which writers find themselves, the physical contexts of writing, and the individual contexts consisting of motivation, knowledge, and ability.

┌─────────────────────────────┐
│ **What Factors Shape Writing?** │
│ • Social   │
│ • Physical   │
│ • Individual   │
└─────────────────────────────┘

▶ Social Contexts

Writing occurs in specific social contexts.

CURRICULUM AND LOCAL OR STATE MANDATES. In schools, teachers' writing assignments and students' purposes for writing may be influenced by a curriculum and local or state mandates.

AUDIENCES. Students in schools write for slightly different purposes than do other writers. Students often write for an audience of teachers rather than selecting their own audiences.

WRITING COMMUNITY. Students participate in a different type of social community from most writers. Students in schools are a part of a large community of learners, often 20 to 35 other students. In this community, writing may be highly valued or writing may be neglected. The community of learners may have a high degree of interest and energy, or the class may be quiet and passive. As the leader of the learning community, the teacher may be an enthusiastic writer, or the teacher may dread writing.

All of these factors influence the social contexts of the writing community.

▶ Physical Contexts

A second context for writing is the physical context. Writing occurs in a physical environment and can be influenced by that environment.

CLASSROOM. The physical environment in a classroom could be noisy or quiet; it could be bright or dark; it could be crowded or roomy.

WRITERS' TOOLS. Writers' tools are also a part of the physical context of writing. Some writers work better at a keyboard. Others need a specific type or size of pen. Many writers have other individual preferences: sharp #2 pencils, purple ink, lined paper.

The physical contexts of writing are an important piece in the writing process. In order to compose a piece of text, writers frequently need their physical environments to accommodate their individual writing preferences.

Figure 2

Contexts for Writing

SOCIAL CONTEXTS

- Curriculum
- Local or state mandates
- Audiences
- Writing community

PHYSICAL CONTEXTS

- Classroom
- Writers' tools

INDIVIDUAL CONTEXTS

- Motivation
- Knowledge
- Experiences
- Abilities

Is writing valued or neglected in your classroom?

▶ Individual Contexts

Most of all, writing is individual. The individual contexts for writing consist of the writer's motivation, knowledge, experiences, and abilities. Although writing is influenced by its social and physical contexts, it is primarily an individual process.

MOTIVATION. Writers come to a writing event with their own goals and purposes. Even though the goals and purposes for students' writings are frequently influenced by teachers, writers also have their own agendas.

KNOWLEDGE. In addition to their goals and purposes, writers bring knowledge to each writing event. Students will bring a range of knowledge about other genres and contents. For example, if you were asking students to write fairy tales, some students would have lots of experience hearing and reading fairy tales while others would have less experience with this genre. If students were writing a fictional story set in a forest, students with prior knowledge about the animals, plants, and weather of a forest would have more knowledge about the content than other students would. Therefore, the knowledge about genres and contents that students bring to a writing event influences their ability to write a specific piece.

EXPERIENCES. Students will bring different experiences to writing. Some students have experienced positive, enthusiastic writing programs that have encouraged them to write. Other students may not be so lucky. They may have experienced writing in-struction that is narrowly focused and even punitive. While students who have had positive experiences with writing may not always be the best writers in your class, their experiences with writing are different from students who have had negative writing experiences. These differences in experiences also can influence students' writings.

ABILITIES. Students bring different inherent abilities to writing assignments. Some students are more fluent than are other students. While some students gush words, others struggle to find words to express simple thoughts. Although the ability to write fluently can be learned, students do bring individual talents and abilities to writing assignments.

In conclusion, writers bring *themselves* to each writing event. They bring their attitudes and abilities, their successes and their failures, their enthusiasms and their dislikes. Writing is an individual process that is highly influenced by contexts for writing.

Balanced Writing Instruction

Writing instruction should include many different kinds of writing experiences, activities, and strategies. Teachers can improve their writing instruction by providing students with a balance of instructional activities. Balanced writing instruction takes into account different types of writing students need to learn along with a variety of components that are essential to writing. (See Figure 3.)

One way to describe a balanced writing program is to compare writing instruction to the prepa-

Do your students have the tools they need to begin a writing assignment?

Figure 3

Balanced Writing Instruction

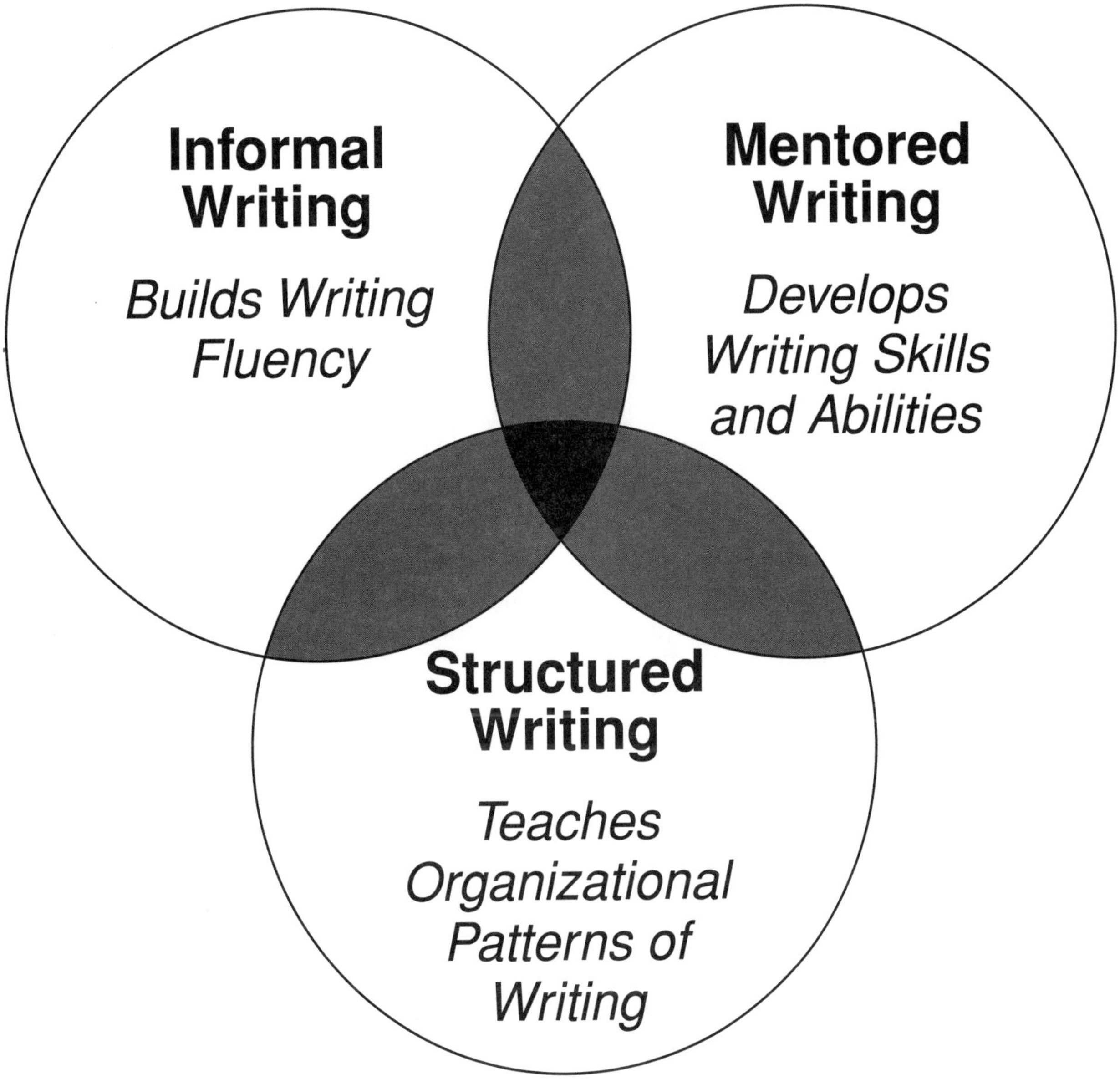

Informal Writing

Builds Writing Fluency

Mentored Writing

Develops Writing Skills and Abilities

Structured Writing

Teaches Organizational Patterns of Writing

Will your students become writing winners?

ration for running a race. When training for a 10k race, for example, runners will not run the same distance at the same speed every day. Instead, they vary their training regime based on their needs. Runners organize their training programs so that they run at a steady pace for a set number of miles several times a week to build a base for improvement. They spend another day or two practicing skills by running on a track, running up hills, or increasing their distances. Finally, runners compete in races to chart their progress. As in running, a writing program should include a variety of activities to improve students' writing abilities.

Generally, there are three types of writing assignments that teachers should consider as they develop a balanced writing program—informal, mentored, and structured.

▶ Informal Writing

Informal writing is the kind of writing that people participate in to discover their thoughts and feelings, to learn new content, or to respond to other pieces of writing. Informal writing provides practice with transforming ideas into words. Using the running analogy, informal writing is like running miles with no stopwatch and no coach. It builds a base of experiences in order to move to the next level of proficiency.

▶▶▶

A writing program should include a variety of activities to improve students' writing abilities.

◀◀◀

Merely assigning informal writing activities to students will not help them learn how to become better writers. Again, comparing writing to running a race, at one time runners believed that if they ran long, slow distances in practice they would become expert runners. On race day, however, these runners found that they ran more slowly than they had intended. Runners need to build their running skills by timing splits and running hills. Teaching students how to write is very similar. If students spend all of their time practicing writing, they will not make as much improvement as if they had a writing coach, or a mentor.

▶ Mentored Writing

When people learn new skills, they generally need others who are more knowledgeable to help them improve in specific areas. Writing is a skill to be learned as well as a craft. Writers, therefore, need writing mentors (Dorn, French, & Jones, 1998). Mentored writing works best as students learn the skills of writing while experiencing the writing process. While students write, they need teachers to help them refine their pieces of writing by helping them set purposes, identify topics, and locate audiences. Teachers can also help students develop their knowledge of the craft of writing by showing them how to develop their own writing styles, by helping them revise their writing, and by assisting with editing. Helping students learn the craft of writing during the writing process is an important function of a balanced writing program.

▶ Structured Writing

The final component of a balanced writing program is teaching the organizational patterns of writing. Writing is governed by rules and conventions. These rules apply not only to the conventions of language but also to the patterns of writing. Writing is often structured in common writing genres:

- personal experience stories
- fictional writing
- expository writing
- persuasive writing

Although most long pieces of writing include passages of more than one organizational structure, teaching students the common organizational patterns of writing helps them understand various ways to organize ideas.

Using the running analogy, once a runner has run lots of miles to build up a running base and has developed running skills by running splits or hills, the runner is ready for a race. Before running a race, however, the runner should become aware of the rules of the race. For example, to begin a race, typically a gun fires or someone shouts "Go." Then the runners take off down the course, heading for the finish line. They are timed as they cross the finish line and are given their race times. Let's say a runner is unfamiliar with the structure of a race. The runner begins when the starting gun fires, but then she notices a stone in her shoe. She thinks back to training sessions when she would take out the stone and begin the run a second time. Think about the absurdity of this runner stopping and yelling, "Wait a minute. I'd like to start again." It wouldn't happen.

The running analogy illustrates the need for teachers to teach students the accepted structures of writing. In addition to giving students practice writing and helping students build their repertoire of skills, teachers also need to teach students the organizational patterns of writing that are accepted in our society.

> ▶▶▶
>
> **Teachers are being encouraged by experts to assess rather than grade writing.**
>
> ◀◀◀

Writing Synergy

All of the components of a balanced writing program work in conjunction with each other to help students write. They can be called synergetic, because each component of a balanced writing program supports and extends other components in a variety of ways. For example, informal writing is a good activity in itself. Participating in informal writing activities can help writers generate ideas and clarify thoughts. In turn, these ideas and thoughts can be the basis for developing writing topics. Another example is that when writers learn the organizational patterns of writing, they can use their knowledge about writing genres to make decisions about writing purposes, forms, and audiences.

> ▶▶▶
>
> **Thinking writers are more strategic writers.**
>
> ◀◀◀

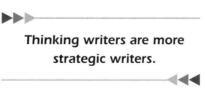

Three Types of Writing Assignments

- Informal
- Mentored
- Structured

Writing activities are synergistic—another reason why a writing program should include a variety of writing activities.

Writing Assessment

As teachers develop a balanced writing program based on knowledge about their students, the writing process, and the contexts of writing, they also need to consider how they will assess writing. Writing used to be graded after students completed a piece of writing. Teachers judged writing by marking the errors and assigning a grade. Currently, however, teachers are being encouraged by experts to assess rather than grade writing (Tchudi, 1997). The assessment standards developed by the International Reading Association and the National Council of Teachers of English (1994) best describe the essentials of writing assessment.

These assessment standards are challenging. While it may be difficult to address all of these standards in a writing program, teachers can periodically implement writing assessments that conform to the standards developed by these two large professional literacy organizations. Through the use of different types of assessments such as self-reports, checklists, and rubrics, teachers can begin assessing writing rather than grading writing.

Thinking Writers

Writing is a thinking process. Writers control the thoughts, images, and words that they produce in print. Thinking writers are able to make decisions about writing, such as what organizational pattern of writing to use, how to organize information, and what works best to express the writers' intents.

Thinking writers are more strategic writers (Collins, 1998). They can determine what to do in different writing situations and can make decisions that facilitate their writing. Thinking writers are not reliant on their teachers for every decision but are able to forge ahead on their own initiative. The goal of writing instruction

1. The interests of the students are paramount in assessment.
2. The primary purpose of assessment is to improve teaching and learning.
3. Assessment must reflect and allow for critical inquiry into curriculum and instruction.
4. Assessment must recognize and reflect the intellectually and socially complex nature of writing and the important roles of school, home, and society in literacy development.
5. Assessment must be fair and equitable.
6. The consequences of an assessment procedure are the first, and most important, consideration in establishing the validity of the assessment.
7. The teacher is the most important agent of assessment.
8. The assessment process should involve multiple perspectives and sources of data.
9. Assessment must be based in the school community.
10. All members of the educational community—students, parents, teachers, administrators, policy makers, and the public—must have a voice in the involvement, interpretation, and report of assessment.
11. Parents must be involved as active, essential participants in the assessment process.

and assessment, therefore, is for all students to be able to take control of writing processes and to become thinking writers.

Conclusion

Writing is a process, an art, and a craft. To improve writing instruction, teachers need to allow students to experience writing so the art of writing can flourish. The art of writing is the creative component that mysteriously happens. It can't be taught, but it can be encouraged by providing an atmosphere that encourages creativity. Teachers can orchestrate an atmosphere of creativity by becoming writing role models and by creating a community of writers in their classrooms. Additionally, teachers can join their own community of learners by becoming involved in a professional organization such as those listed in Appendix A. By becoming members of a professional organization, teachers can join other professionals in learning how to strengthen their instructional writing programs.

Writing is also a craft. Teachers can teach the craft of writing through a balanced writing program

and a variety of lessons. Students need to learn how to discover their thoughts and feelings through writing, to develop the content of their writing, to understand the structures of writing, and to refine language to conform to Standard English. Teachers can provide students with instructional activities that facilitate this type of learning.

The final step in improving writing instruction is to encourage students to become thinking writers. Because writing is a process of decision making, teachers need to organize their instruction so that students have opportunities to make writing decisions. Teachers should avoid teaching writing in a rigid linear progression. They should celebrate the ambiguities and surprises of the writing process. This type of instruction can be uncomfortable. It means that teachers need to teach the craft of writing while celebrating the art of writing. The end result, however, is extremely worthwhile. Teachers can improve their writing instruction so that all of their students are able to use their knowledge about writing to achieve a variety of purposes when communicating with a variety of audiences. Their students then become thinking writers.

Chapter 2

Creating a Writing Community

"I try to leave out the parts that people skip."—Elmore Leonard

Overview

A writing community is a place where both teachers and students write. In a writing community, writing is initiated for real reasons and is produced for real audiences. Ideally, all writers—teachers and students—engage in meaningful writing activities that improve their writing abilities. In order for a writing community to exist, however, the cognitive, affective, social, and physical conditions of writing must be addressed (Hayes, 1996).

WRITING IS A COGNITIVE, OR THINKING, ACTIVITY. As writers write, they think about their writing content, make decisions about words, and try to express their ideas in language. Writers must have a command of language to write, and they must be able to take control over the many decisions they face. Writing, however, is not merely a cognitive activity.

WRITING IS AN AFFECTIVE, OR EMOTIONAL, ACTIVITY. Writing is putting ideas on paper. These ideas are embedded in the thoughts, feelings, and opinions of the writers. Writers lay it all on the line. Therefore, writing has a strong emotional component. In order for writers to be able to set forth their thoughts and ideas in print, they must be motivated. Writers can be motivated to write if they have something to say, if they feel ownership of their writing, and if they feel capable of writing (Spaudling, 1992). Writing is emotional, but writers do not write in a void.

WRITING IS A SOCIAL ACTIVITY.

Because students and teachers write in order to communicate with others, writing is essentially social. The act of writing is social not only because writers are engaged in communication with others. Writers also write in social settings using structures that are socially accepted. All of the conventions of writing, from word choice to the organizational structure of a piece of writing, have been culturally derived over the past centuries. Examples of writing forms that are acknowledged in our culture are essays, poems, and novels. Other less conventional writing forms such as graffiti are also culturally understood. Therefore, all forms of writing are part of a vast network of socially-constructed concepts.

WRITING IS PHYSICAL.

Our emotions and motivations, and even our thinking, are affected by our environment.

- Some writers write in noisy areas; others need dead quiet.
- Some writers need a ritual cup of coffee while writing; others write spontaneously.
- Some writers write early in the morning; others write late at night.
- Some writing workshops in schools are bustling hives of activity; in others, students work quietly at desks or tables.

▶ Does this student have a writing role model?

The physical environment, therefore, is an important component of the writing process.

To build a writing community, teachers need to address all of the various aspects of writing. Teachers should first become writing role models by writing for their own purposes. Teachers need to write with students, write for students, write for themselves, and write outside the school day. Students should know that their teachers are writers. Knowing that teachers are active participants in the writing community can bolster students' affective feelings about writing. Students identify with teachers who are writing role models.

Having teachers as writers in the writing community is fundamental to a strong writing program. Teachers need to encourage students to take part in the writing community by encouraging students to write. Teachers can show the value of writing by writing their own pieces, but they also can structure lessons that make writing fun for students. Teachers need to encourage students to write and to think of themselves as writers.

A writing community is a place where all participants recognize that good writing is a goal for every student (Portalupi, 1999). Teachers guide students to understand what it means to write something well. They need to help students learn the craft of writing. Teachers are mentors in an apprenticeship relationship with students. Teachers need to take into account how different writers benefit from different support systems and different environmental structures.

Finally, a writing community is a caring place. Community members create rituals together, bring their lives into the classroom, and reveal their thoughts and desires (Hindley, 1996). A community is a social place where relationships and interactions are at the heart of learning. All members of a writing community participate in the decision making and the desire to grow as writers. To develop a writing community, teachers need to understand the personal aspects of writing. This chapter contains resources, teaching strategies, and assessment ideas to help you create a writing community.

Becoming a Writing Role Model

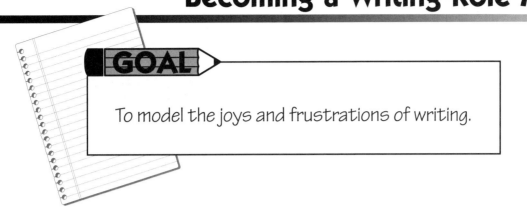

GOAL

To model the joys and frustrations of writing.

2.1

Background

All of us are writers; we really are. We constantly communicate with others through print. Our writing may take the form of letters, lists, messages, notes, memoirs, e-mail messages, or essays. Writing may be as simple as a note to a spouse on the kitchen bulletin board saying, "Went to the library. Back at 6:00. Please put pasta in oven." Or our writing may be as complex as a eulogy read at a funeral. We write to our family, our students, and ourselves. We do write, and we are writers.

Many teachers, however, do not consider themselves to be writers (Brinkley, 1993). Perhaps that's because many teachers do not write beyond the functional level and haven't written a research report or a personal essay since college. And most teachers have not published articles or books. Because most teachers consider these types of formal pieces to be "writing," teachers generally do not think of themselves as writers and do not consider themselves to be positive writing role models for their students.

In the writing classrooms of the twenty-first century, however, teachers must be perceived by their students to be writers. In order for teachers to teach writing in process-writing classrooms, they need to guide students through purposeful activities so that they can construct meaningful texts. But be-

fore teachers can give students input on writing, teachers themselves need to know what it means to dig deeply into their own lives for topics—to feel inspired, to struggle with language, and to feel the exhilaration of finishing a piece of writing (Root & Steinberg, 1996). Teachers need to understand that writing is as much of a mystery as it is a skill to be taught. Teachers need to be writers. After all, would a school hire a Spanish teacher who could not speak Spanish? It follows, therefore, that teachers of writing should write (Rief, 1992).

By experiencing writing and sharing your writing with your students, you can become a positive writing role model. As you think about writing, begin by reflecting on who you are and what you value, write from your heart, and proudly share your work with others, especially your students. The following activities were developed to help you explore your inner world and to develop a strong piece of writing. After each activity is an example of a poem, essay, or letter written by a teacher, an administrator, or a parent who was able to put his or her thoughts and feelings into words so that others could get a glimpse of the layers of their lives. Try one or more of these activities. Experience the joys and frustrations of writing. Be a writing role model for your students. Write!

Teachers need to be writers.

ACTIVITY 1   PICTURE YOURSELF AS A WRITER

Think about writers and imagine what it would be like for you to be a writer. To do this you may want to read a biography of a writer, watch a video of a writer, or go to a place where writers gather, like a coffeehouse. As you learn about writers, look for the parts of your life that overlap the lives of writers. Try to emulate what writers do. For example, many writers go to public places to write. They sit at a table, drink coffee, and observe others. Then they write thoughts and ideas that come to mind. Pretend you are a famous writer and let the words flow as in the example below.

▶ Do you picture yourself as a writing role model?

If I Were a Writer . . .

I would have something profound to say.
People would be able to read my handwriting.
I would know the difference between "If I was . . ."
   and "If I were . . ." and which one is correct.
I would know how to spell "atrocious."
I would have an immense vocabulary
   to bend and twist and weave into glorious works of art.
I would say, "I am a writer." And people would say, "She is a writer."
I would really be free—
I would write.

Marcia Brandt
Fourth-grade Teacher

ACTIVITY 2   WRITE ABOUT YOUR LIFE

Many of us think we have nothing to write about. Jane Austen, however, had some words of wisdom for all writers: write about what you know. Even though your life may be filled with teaching, learning, and caring for others, you have something to say. Think about what you do during the week. Think about how you feel as you prepare for class or drive to school. Think about the responsibilities you have and how you accomplish all that needs to be done. Write about your life as in the following example.

What a Week

Monday through Friday
   Teacher, Student, Wife.
   Patient, calm, and jubilant.
   Classes, notes, and lecture.
   Loving, supportive, and caring.
Saturday
   Household chores.
   Cleaning, yard work, and bills.
   Studying.

Research, reading, and writing.
Keep moving. Keep doing.
Keep that head above water.
Trying, hoping to make it to . . .
Sunday
Day of rest.
Walk the trail.
Bubble bath, manicure.
Reading for pleasure.
Relaxed, revived, rejuvenated.
Ready for another try.
Ready for . . .
Monday.

Carrie Heissler
First-grade Teacher

ACTIVITY 3   WRITE ABOUT A MEANINGFUL EXPERIENCE

You have had experiences in your life that have touched your soul. Think about those experiences that are really important to you. List several ideas that you could write about. As you drive to school or take a walk, relive those experiences. Think about why they were important to you. Remember what happened. Then write about one of them as in the example below.

Relay For Life

Recently, I was asked to write a short article on why I became involved in the Relay for Life. In the spring of 1993, my mom and dad returned home from their winter hibernation in Arizona. My dad was experiencing a scratchy throat and a case of laryngitis. He went to the doctor and was given medication for acid reflux. He was to return if it didn't improve.

My dad returned to the doctor and was then sent to a specialist. By the end of July, he was diagnosed with cancer in the chest wall. A tumor was pressing on one of his vocal chords.

After other tests were done, the doctors learned that the tumor had metastasized to his brain. A helmet had to be made so that his head could be bolted to a table for radiation treatment. He began treatments that lasted six weeks. Complications set in and he was in and out of the hospital. His main concern was that he wouldn't be ready to go back to Arizona by November 1st.

On November 1st, my dad lost his battle to cancer. My mom said, "Well, Charlie, you left without me!"

I was angry that once again cancer had won. Now it involved someone I loved dearly, so I formed a Relay for Life team of family members and friends. My father's name was Charles, but many of his friends called him Charlie. So I named our team "Charlie's Angels." He would have liked that!

I hope in the future, with my help and the help of others at the Relay for Life, that fewer people will lose their battle with cancer. Someday we will have more winners than losers. I have to believe that!

Sandi Armstrong
Kindergarten Teacher

ACTIVITY 4   WRITE ABOUT EVERYDAY THINGS

Things. We all have many things cluttering our closets and our lives. Some of these items have sentimental value; others seem pretty mundane. When we look at some of the things in our lives, we can almost elevate them to a symbolic plane through writing. Think of an everyday item in your house. For example, look at your garden shears or a favorite chair. What meanings could those simple items have for you or for a family member? Jot down some ideas. Then arrange the words in a poem as in the following example.

The Baseball Glove

In a closet a cardboard box sits,
   an old baseball glove lies within.
Retired many years ago the glove,
   has darkened with age.
Hands of youth reach in to lift,
   the glove from its grave.
Nimble fingers retie the glove's laces,
   the leather is softened with oil.
Thump . . . thump . . . thump . . .,
   goes the ball into the pocket.
Baseball dreams,
   are alive again.

Diana Embry
Fifth-grade Teacher

ACTIVITY 5   WRITE A LETTER TO A LOVED ONE

Did you ever wish you could express your feelings to a loved one more fluently? You can. Write a letter. Think about the feelings you have for someone special. As you think about your feelings, picture that person. You can change the time frame of the letter or write the letter in real time. As you write, be specific about your thoughts and feelings and give as many examples as you can. Then send the letter or save it for a special occasion. Your loved one will welcome your letter, but be prepared for tears. The following example is a letter a second-grade teacher wrote to his baby son to be given to him on his sixteenth birthday.

A Letter to My Son on His 16th Birthday

Dear Noah,

Happy birthday, Noah! If you are receiving this on your sixteenth birthday everything went according to plan. Today you are only one year old. I wanted to share some of my feelings and thoughts with you. You will be a man very shortly and going out on your own to start your own life. I wanted you to know how I feel about you and what I hope and pray for your life-to-be.

I guess I'll start at the beginning when we first thought we were pregnant. We ran out and took a pregnancy test. It was positive. I couldn't believe it, so I went out and bought another pregnancy test. We still did not believe it so we bought another one. Three tests, thirty dollars, and three positives. We were going to be parents and we were so excited.

Many things ran through my head as an expectant father. "Will it be a boy or a girl? Will it be healthy? Can we manage and take care of things?" Then something else popped into my mind. Can I be the kind of father I should be, or will I be a horrible dad? I don't know why, but that was my biggest fear. I wanted to be the kind of Dad you could be proud of.

Then you were born. Wow! I will never forget that day or what happened. **My son was born.** As I held you, I felt changed. I was so full of joy and excitement. I remember holding you in my arms and feeling so much love, and knowing how blessed I was. That moment was special, and I wouldn't trade it for anything. I want you to know that.

Now there are some things I want to share with you about leading your life and growing into a man. I truly believe there are things you need in your life to truly be a man. Turning an age doesn't make you a man, but leading your life with character does.

The first part of character is honesty. You measure a man by his honesty. I admire honesty, but as a young man, I did not understand its value. Only after I met your Mom's Dad did I understand what true honesty and character were. He modeled it for me and lived it in his life. The feeling you have when you are known as a man of his word is a treasure to hold onto. As you turn into a man, my hope for you is to be known as a man of his word.

Another element of being a man is integrity, doing the right thing regardless of what is easy or popular. The world and society tell us to take care of ourselves and look out for number one. I cannot think of a more selfish idea. You should take care of yourself, but not at the expense of others. Noah, I won't always be there for the choices you make, but I hope you learn to serve people and be a model of integrity.

Last, but probably the most important of all, is love. Love is many things, not easily defined. Love is a gift and you need to share it. Everything you do should show love. If somebody says or does something wrong to you, turn the other cheek and walk away. Anger puts you on their level, while returning a wrong with kindness shows true character. Let your love shine through your daily actions and words.

As I sit here with my heart breaking, I pray that I have communicated what you need to know. Noah, there is a purpose for your life and I want that purpose to be fulfilled. I hope as you read this letter, all I have written you have seen in me, and it has become part of you. If it has not, please forgive me and realize the importance of what I wrote. I know you will be a great man, father, husband, and person. I love you with all my heart.

Your Dad

Randy Johnson
Second-grade Teacher

"Thanks for the memories. . . ." We love to remember, and we love to hear the memories of others. Think about someone who is special to you and remember. Remember the things you did together, the feelings you had, what the person looked like, where you were. Remember the sounds and the smells. Let your mind run through memories like an old movie. Then write down your memories as in the following example.

For Grandma's 90th Birthday
"I Remember . . ."

Grandma is 90 years old today! To me, she looks the same as she did 20 years ago. When I shut my eyes and remember Grandma, I see snapshots . . .

I see her pretty white hair, always styled and neat.
I see her beautiful hands and ladylike fingernails.
I see an image of a pink or purple dress and matching beads.
I see tables laden with food—cakes, pies, ham, jello.
I see her under a tree at a summer picnic.
I see the old house, the big kitchen table, and a backyard with flowers.

I remember Grandma coming to visit me when I got my first apartment. Her visit made me feel special. She took the time to visit us a lot. I remember her present at every event, whether it was a birthday or a ceremony.

I remember the "new" house and the basement and gatherings with LOTS of food. I always remember lots of food at Grandma's house. I used to think she was the best cook in the entire world.

When I think of Grandma, I think of someone who is patient and gentle. I wish more of those qualities had rubbed off on me. She doesn't talk a lot; she doesn't feel the need to fill the silence with chatter. It's nice just to sit with Grandma. You really don't have to talk the whole time to enjoy time together with her. But she always lets me know she loves me by her actions.

Grandma is a special lady. Whenever I think it's hard to raise children, I wonder how in the world Grandma did it with five boys and three girls—and during very hard times. She must be as strong as steel underneath all that ladylike hair, polished nails, and quiet personality. I am blessed to be part of her legacy and consider myself lucky to have her as my Grandmother and my friend.

Marsha Jay
At-home Mom

At times throughout our lives we stop and reflect on where we are and where we are going. These times of reflection are valuable, but often our reflections are lost to us because we don't write them down. Think about your life. You may be a new teacher, just entering the profession. Think about your childhood and your college years. You are entering a new phase in your life, but remember the one you just passed through. Maybe you are a new parent. Think about your life right now and how your life has changed. Or you may be looking forward to retirement. Before you make that big change, reflect on your years as a teacher. What did you experience? How did you feel? Write some of your reflections as in the following example.

Reflections on My Life

Reflections are truly a mirrored look at oneself. My reflections are not earth shattering. Nor are they awe inspiring. They are simply random thoughts reflecting over 50 years of life.

Half a century plus a few more years have quickly passed in my life. It has been filled with more joy than sadness and more love than hate. It has seen thousands of children reaching toward their horizons and thousands of others whose horizons are unknown.

Everybody told me that reaching 50 was difficult, but nobody told me that the difficult part was not my aging body and mind. It is instead the inner soul that aches with the illnesses and losses of treasured friends and relatives. Nobody said that my circle of support would diminish, that hospitals and doctors would become more important than ever before. And—that all of this is a part of life that we have no control over. We can only sit by, hoping and praying.

School has been a vital part of my life. Starting out as a crying child in kindergarten, I have been through 46 years of school as a student, teacher, and administrator. These years have brought with them innumerable joys and unlimited happiness. There is nothing that compares with the face of a child deep in thought; the smile of a child as a problem is solved; and the excitement of a child facing a new challenge. The stresses placed on the children of today by families and society are incredible, yet these children pour out their hearts and souls to the caring few they find in the stability of the classroom.

Everyone deserves to love and be loved unconditionally. It has been my fortune to have found my love in family and friends. My family has been a foundation of all that I have done. Moving from my nuclear family to a wife and children of my own has been the most challenging yet rewarding aspect of my life. My life would have been incomplete without my wife and children. Through all the stages of development our family grew and grew—not in size but instead in compassion, love, and understanding. Our two adult children are now moving along the road of life while my wife and I bask in their successes and force their failures from our minds. This is the greatest part of aging—seeing the results of past years becoming a positive part of the future.

The fact is that life is a forward moving train—never halting, never slowing, never speeding. The focus of moving from second to second, minute to minute, hour to hour is so much a part of aging that it is completely forgotten.

My life has been joy—the bumps in it often led to happiness but other times were filled with sadness and grief that cannot be described. I have been fortunate to have received from others more than I could possibly have given to them. If all those living had the opportunities of life that have been mine, our world would be paradise—filled with peace, joy, and happiness.

Lawrence Pennie
Elementary School Administrator

From Lenski, S.D. (Ed.). (1997). *A closer look: Writings by teachers.* Bloomington, IL: Illinois Reading Council.

MOVE BEYOND WRITER'S BLOCK

Writer's block is not a myth. All writers experience a time when no words flow, nothing comes. As you try to write, you will also experience writer's block from time to time. Writer's block, however, can be a time for rich ideas. Begin by writing how you're feeling during this time. As you write, ideas may flow as in the following example. But beware. They may not. If you are truly blocked, set your writing down and wait for tomorrow. Just be sure to pick up your writing soon. No one is blocked forever.

Say What?

I'm stuck! Hard to move beyond myself.
I'm stuck!! Hard to really see myself.
I'm stuck!!! Hard to let myself be me.

Write? About what?
What could I possibly say to others . . .
not too personal, not too revealing,
just a hint of deeper realms . . .

Struggle—
Where do the thoughts go when you need them?
Insecurity finds me comparing what I say
with what others think I should, or could, be saying.

Rejection—
Imagine . . . at my age,
fear lurks behind every hint of evaluation
of who I am, or what I do.

Success—
What is it anyway?
My perception of my work,
or someone else's?
Does satisfaction come from without
or within?

Failure—
That's an easy one:
choosing the path of least resistance . . .
taking the low road, the safe way, the crowded path . . .
No one would look at me, no one would scrutinize me,
no one would know me,
no one . . .
not even my mirror.

Pat McLean
Elementary School Administrator

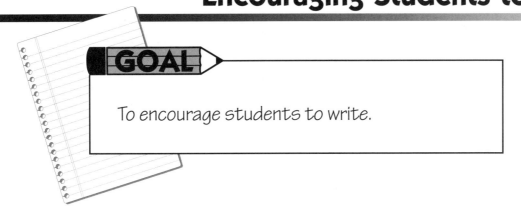

Encouraging Students to Write

GOAL

To encourage students to write.

2.2

Background

Words have power. They have the power to persuade, to soothe, to hurt, to encourage, and to make us laugh. Why, then, do so many students dread writing? Lucy Calkins (1994) suggests that many students fear writing because of the ways in which teachers teach writing in schools. Too frequently, teachers assign meaningless writing assignments, try to motivate students to complete the assignments, and then point out students' errors. It's no wonder many students don't like to write.

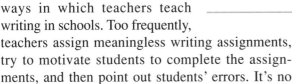

Words have power.

WRITING IS PERSONAL—ONE OF THE INTIMACIES OF LIFE. When you write, you share your heart, mind, and soul in fixed symbols with another person. Since writing is intrinsically personal, one of the most important things that teachers can do to encourage students to write is to learn about their students' interests. When teachers know their students' interests and their attitudes toward writing, teachers can provide motivating writing instruction that takes into account students' personal lives. Choice, challenge, and control are motivational factors that encourage student learning (Gambrell, 1996).

STUDENTS HAVE INDIVIDUAL TALENTS. Encouraging students to write should take many forms. Linda Rief (1999) suggests that teachers need to expand their no-

> ### 8 Intelligences
> - Bodily/Kinesthetic
> - Logical/Mathematical
> - Interpersonal
> - Intrapersonal
> - Musical/Rhythmical
> - Natural
> - Verbal/Linguistic
> - Visual/Spacial

tions of literacy and to take into account not only words but also the visual, the physical, the mathematical, and the sensual. As writers write, they use their many talents to put words on paper. Since students are individuals with unique talents, teachers can encourage writing by customizing some writing assignments to students' various talents. Gardner (1993) posits that eight intelligences define human talent. Teachers can encourage students to write by varying writing assignments using multiple intelligences as a guide.

WRITING IS FUN. Encouraging students to write by learning about their interests and tailoring assignments to individual strengths is one step toward promoting positive attitudes toward writing. Writing, however, is not only personal; writing can be fun for other reasons. Words have the power to make us laugh. Think about the jokes you know, the plays on words, the books in your class that use idioms in strange ways. Words that are used in unique ways are humorous. Word play is part of what can make writing fun, and helping students look for ways in which words make us laugh can also encourage students to write. (By the way, guess what I saw in Paris? Parasites.)

Writing instruction doesn't have to be a joyless affair:

- When teachers learn about their students and allow students choices in writing, teachers encourage writing.
- When teachers address the multiple intelligences of students in their classes, teachers encourage writing.
- When teachers help students see how much fun words can be, teachers encourage writing.

This section provides teaching strategies for encouraging students to write.

▶ Is this student having fun with writing?

TEACHING STRATEGY 1 ▶ ▶ ▶ ▶ ▶ ▶ ▶ ▶ ▶ ▶ ▶ ▶ Interest Charts

One of the primary ways to encourage students to write is to tailor writing assignments to students' interests. When students have writing projects that are of interest to them, they are more likely to have an intrinsic desire to write. You can use an Interest Chart to learn more about your students in order to tailor writing assignments to their interests. Certainly, you know many of your students' interests already. However, using an Interest Chart can provide you with many more insights about your students and their lives.

✛ Directions

1. Tell students that you want to learn more about their lives. Explain to students that you will be asking them to share their interests, feelings, and hobbies with you. Tell students that they should be honest; however, they should not include things that are overly private. Give students time to think about their interests, feelings, and hobbies.

2. Duplicate and distribute the Interest Chart that follows. Have students put their names and the date on the Interest Chart. Tell students to place one or more items in each of the sections of the chart. Give them at least 10 minutes to complete their Interest Charts. Provide students with extra charts if they write more than can fit in a section.

3. Collect the Interest Charts and read them carefully. Look for patterns of interest among the students. Where you see patterns of interest, adjust your instruction to take students' interests into account.

4. Return the Interest Charts to students. Have students place the Interest Charts in their writing folders to use as they select topics for writing.

5. Have students complete new Interest Charts every two or three months. Explain that many of their interests may change over time and that you want to stay current with their interests. Use the Interest Charts to plan your instruction and encourage students to use their Interest Charts to select topics for writing.

Name_____ Date_____

Interest Chart

My Hobbies	Sports I Like to Play	Other Interests I Have
My Likes	**My Dislikes**	**Books I Have Read**
Things I Love to Do	**Some Good Things about Me**	**Some Things about Me That Aren't So Good**

TEACHING STRATEGY 2 ▶ ▶ ▶ ▶ Writing Autobiographies

Students can share their writing histories and their opinions about writing instruction through a Writing Autobiography. As students think about their writing experiences and share those experiences in a Writing Autobiography, they provide teachers with information about their writing lives. When teachers read students' Writing Autobiographies, they learn about students in a personal way, which can help promote a positive attitude toward writing (Lenski, Wham, & Johns, 1999).

⟡ Directions

1. Introduce and discuss the idea of Writing Autobiographies. Tell students that an autobiography is an author's account of his or her life.

2. Tell students that you are interested in their writing histories and in their opinions about writing. Explain that you will use students' Writing Autobiographies as you develop writing assignments.

3. Duplicate and distribute the Writing Autobiography Thought Probes that follow. Read the thought probes with students. Remind students that writing in this case does not mean handwriting but writing sentences or stories. Tell students to consider these questions as they complete their Writing Autobiographies.

4. Provide students with ample time to complete their Writing Autobiographies. After students have finished, collect the papers and read them, looking for insights into students' writing histories. For example, if students complain about spending most of their writing time learning grammar, organize your writing instruction so that more time is devoted to teaching writing fluency.

5. Return the Writing Autobiographies to students. Ask students to share their Writing Autobiographies with their classmates either by reading them aloud or by displaying them on a bulletin board.

Writing Autobiography Thought Probes

1. Do you consider yourself to be a writer? Why or why not?

   _____

2. How did you learn to become the writer that you are?

   _____

3. What kind of writing do you like best?

   _____

4. What piece of writing are you most proud of? Why?

   _____

5. What do you like least about writing?

   _____

6. What is your favorite memory of writing?

   _____

7. What is your least favorite memory of writing?

   _____

8. What makes a person a writer?

   _____

9. How can your teacher make writing more enjoyable for you?

   _____

10. How can your teacher help you become a better writer?

    _____

TEACHING STRATEGY 3 ▶ ▶ ▶ ▶ ▶ ▶ Multiple Intelligences

Different students have different talents, identified by Gardner (1993) as eight aspects of intelligence, or multiple intelligences. Multiple Intelligences are an individual's learning strengths. Each student learns in preferred ways. Some students learn best through physical movement while others learn using shapes and colors. Some students may have obvious strengths in learning, such as the student who exhibits musical talent, but all students have capacities in all eight intelligences (Pike & Mumper, 1998). To encourage students to write, you should vary your writing assignments and expectations and tailor writing assignments to students' strengths.

⟲ Directions

1. Become aware of the various strengths students bring to writing situations by carefully reading the Multiple Intelligences and Writing Chart that follows. Try to match the talents of students in your classroom with the eight intelligences.

2. Tell students that each person learns in his or her own way. Tell students that generally there are eight ways that people learn. Explain that although these eight intelligences describe the most common ways people learn, students might identify their own unique learning strengths.

3. Have students write their learning strengths, along with their name, on a piece of paper. Read what students have described as their own learning strengths.

4. Because some students may be unaware of their own talents, guide students to understand what you perceive as additional areas of strength. Discuss students' learning strengths with them.

5. Celebrate multiple intelligences by congratulating students on their unique capabilities. Explain that all intelligences are valued in your classroom.

6. Vary your writing lessons based on the different aspects of intelligence. When you assign a writing project that is geared to the strength of only a few students, encourage other students to develop this area of learning.

7. Allow students as often as possible to choose writing projects that reflect their learning strengths.

8. Identify students who feel they have strengths in particular areas and who can be consulted as "experts" by other students.

Multiple Intelligences and Writing Chart

Bodily/Kinesthetic Intelligence (body smart)

Refers to the ability to use movement of the body to perform tasks and to solve problems.	• Help students enjoy the physical movements of writing and typing. • Let students choose where they write, such as sitting on a bean bag chair or lying on the carpet. • Encourage students to dramatize their writing and put physical movements in the scenes. • Help students connect writing to physical activities such as writing rules of games or writing letters to sports' heroes.

Logical/Mathematical Intelligence (number smart)

Refers to the ability to use numbers and logic. It also refers to the ability to recognize patterns, to categorize, to calculate, to classify, and to hypothesize.	• Help students recognize and use organizational patterns of writing, such as the main idea-detail paragraph pattern. • Emphasize writing genres such as fairy tales and folktales. • Teach students to use logical progression of ideas in writing. • Incorporate writing in mathematics lessons.

Interpersonal Intelligence (people smart)

Refers to the ability to understand personal relationships and to act on that knowledge. It also refers to the ability to be sensitive to the needs of others and to work with other people.	• Provide students the opportunity to write with other students. • Emphasize audiences in writing. Tell students to visualize their audiences as they write. • Encourage students to write about situations that involve other students and about personal conflicts in the classroom. • Teach students to observe others and to write dialogue.

Intrapersonal Intelligence (self smart)

Refers to knowledge about the self. It refers to the ability to engage in self-reflection about emotions and thinking and to understand behavior.	• Provide students with opportunities to write independently. • Encourage students to write about their feelings. • Let students complete longer writing projects at their own pace. • Provide students with the opportunity to write personal narratives.

(continued)

From Susan Davis Lenski and Jerry L. Johns, *Improving Writing: Resources, Strategies, and Assessments*. Copyright © 2000 by Kendall/Hunt Publishing Company (1-800-247-3458). May be reproduced for noncommercial educational purposes.

Musical/Rhythmical Intelligence (music smart)

Refers to the capacity to identify, express, and appreciate musical forms. It also refers to the ability to think in musical terms and to identify rhythms.

- Emphasize the rhythmic quality of language.
- Give students the opportunity to write poems and songs.
- Emphasize writing genres such as parody, satire, and caricature.
- Encourage students to write about musical patterns and themes.

Naturalistic Intelligence (nature smart)

Refers to a responsiveness to the environment and a love of the outdoors. It also refers to curiosity about and understanding of the natural sciences.

- Allow students to write outside, perhaps as an extension of outdoor recess or physical education class.
- Encourage students to write about environmental issues.
- Encourage students to make entries in writers' notebooks on field trips and on hikes.
- Provide students with opportunities to write to naturalists such as birders, forest rangers, and deep sea divers.

Verbal/Linguistic Intelligence (word smart)

Refers to the ability to use words in writing and speaking. It also refers to the ability to use language in creative ways.

- Emphasize unusual word forms and meanings such as puns, jokes, and etymologies.
- Encourage students to create word images and to write with descriptive language.
- Encourage students to recognize and experiment with creative writing styles.
- Provide students with the opportunity to edit class newspapers and books.

Visual/Spacial Intelligence (picture smart)

Refers to the ability to create mental images and to manipulate spacial configurations. It also refers to the ability to use shapes, forms, and space to create new ideas.

- Provide students with graphic organizers for planning their writing.
- Provide mind maps of writing genres such as narrative, persuasive, and expository writing.
- Provide students with the opportunity to create maps, graphs, and tables.
- Encourage students to read about illustrators and to illustrate their own writing.

TEACHING STRATEGY 4 ▶ ▶ ▶ ▶ ▶ ▶ ▶ ▶ ▶ ▶ ▶ ▶ ▶ Word Play

Humor is an important part of the social development of students (Tower, 1998). As students learn what is humorous in our culture, they learn how words can make people laugh. Young children often do not have a very sophisticated sense of humor. They tell knock-knock jokes that many adults think are absurd, and they aren't able to understand subtle forms of humor such as puns. But humor is important. Opening the door of humor by showing students examples of Word Play helps students learn how words can cause laughter, adds spice to their writing, and motivates students to have fun with writing. Word Play can also help students move beyond knock-knock jokes.

Directions

1. Tell students that words can be used in a number of ways. Tell them that words can make us laugh and cry. Also, tell students that words can be used in surprising ways.

2. Ask students to think of a joke that made them laugh. Identify the words that were used to cause the humor. Keep in mind that often there are cultural implications to humor that second language learners might find confusing.

3. Tell students that words can be used in ways that make us smile and laugh. Share a joke or a pun with students, such as "The first flea market was started from scratch." Identify the words in the pun that are funny: scratch makes you think of fleas, not a flea market. Be sure to provide the necessary explanation so students understand the joke or pun.

4. Tell students that some idioms in our language create humorous images. Share with students one of the books from the list that follows to show how words can be used to evoke humor.

5. Encourage students to think of a variety of ways to use words as they pursue their own writing.

Books That Use Word Play

Compiled by Jenny Bolander

Bayer, J. (1984)
A my name is Alice.
New York: Penguin.
(Grades 2–6)

Benson, H. (1995)
A moose is not a mouse.
Salt Lake City: Gibbs, Smith.
(Grades K–2)

Cox. J.A. (1980)
Put your foot in your mouth and other silly sayings.
New York: Random House.
(Grades 2–6)

Degen, B. (1985)
Jamberry.
New York: Harper and Row.
(Grades K–3)

Elting, M., & Folsom, M. (1980)
Q is for duck: An alphabet guessing game.
New York: Clarion.
(Grades 2–6)

Gwynne, F. (1980)
A chocolate moose for dinner.
New York: Aladdin.
(Grades K–3)

Gwynne, F. (1988)
A little pigeon toad.
New York: Aladdin.
(Grades 2–4)

Parish, P. (1999)
Amelia Bedelia.
New York: Harper Festival.
(Grades K–3)

Parish, P. (1999)
Bravo, Amelia Bedelia.
New York: Avon.
(Grades K–3)

Pilkey, D. (1994)
Dog breath: The horrible terrible trouble with Hally Tosis.
New York: Scholastic.
(Grades K–3)

Thaler, M. (1997)
Make your bed, Bananaheads.
New York: Troll.
(Grades K–2)

Walton, R. (1995)
Once there was a bull . . . frog.
Salt Lake City: Gibbs, Smith.
(Grades K–3)

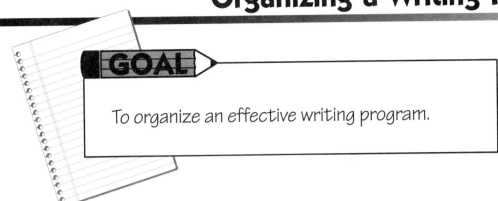

GOAL

To organize an effective writing program.

2.3

Background

Can writing be taught, or should teachers simply allow students the space and freedom to write? Maybe it's some of both. Students need the chance to write, the freedom to write, and an acceptance of their writing (Routman, 1994). They can learn how to become better writers through a comprehensive writing program that has been carefully designed by the teacher, a more knowledgeable person.

The teacher's role in a writing program should be similar to a mentor working with an apprentice (Dorn, French, & Jones, 1998). The teacher should:

- guide students' determination of goals and objectives,
- discover students' backgrounds and abilities, and
- scaffold lessons and projects so that students grow as writers.

Teachers can help students become better writers by organizing a writing program that is tailored to students' needs, rather than by following a textbook with a generic student in mind. In order to organize a writing program, teachers need to see themselves as writing mentors who will shape the environment in which students develop their own unique writing abilities.

Nancy Atwell (1987) suggests that teachers first consider their beliefs about writing before developing a writing program. Among those beliefs should be:

- a clear understanding of the components of good writing,
- how to organize a classroom environment so that students can write, and
- how to plan instruction that encourages students to grow as writers.

This section provides teaching strategies that you can use to organize an effective writing program.

TEACHING STRATEGY **1** ▶ ▶ ▶ ▶ ▶ ▶ **Defining Good Writing**

The first step in organizing an effective writing program is to define what good writing means to you. To some degree, defining good writing is subjective. The kinds of writing that one person likes might be unappealing to someone else. However, there are many components of writing that you and your students can agree upon as "good," or right for you. Once you and your students have an understanding of what constitutes good writing, you can organize a writing program that moves your writing and your students' writings toward that goal.

✛ Directions

1. Ask students to think about the meaning of "good" writing. Explain that not all writing is effective but that students should attempt to make each piece of their writing "good."

2. Read passages of books that you believe are examples of writings that express an idea and engage the reader. Tell students what you like about the book as in the following example.

   > I just read the book *If You're Not From the Prairie* by David Bouchard and Henry Ripplinger (1995). I love the book because of the poetic rhythm of the words, the pictures I visualize as I read, and the powerful emotions the book evokes within me.

3. Tell students that meaning grows out of experiences and ideas that the writer knows and cares about, that the writing is organized so that the reader can follow the ideas, and that the words engage the readers' interests.

4. Duplicate and distribute the student's story that follows or select a story appropriate for your grade level. Discuss with students why this story is an example of good writing for a fourth-grade student.

5. Divide the class into groups of three or four students. Distribute an index card to each group and ask students to describe three things that exemplify good writing.

6. Compile a list of the components of good writing. You can use some of the ideas from the following list of Components of Good Writing to help students understand what makes writing good.

7. Develop a class list called Components of Good Writing. Display the list in a prominent place in the classroom. Refer students to the list as they write.

GOOD WRITING: STUDENT EXAMPLE

The Lost Cell Phone

Hello, I'm Sally the cell phone. My owner dropped me when he was getting chicken. When he left, I nearly got stepped on. This nice man picked me up. Well, I thought he was a nice man. He just put me back on the floor, but in gum, ick! I wish my owner were here.

This kid picked me up, and didn't dial collect. He called everywhere, even China. I didn't know the Chinese could talk so fast! Then he threw me in the street. I wish I knew the number for 911! My poor antenna was broken.

People drove and walked past me, almost driving and walking over my poor little buttons. Days went by and nobody saw me or anything. Then a baby picked me up and took me to this house, and sucked on me. Boy, did he drool. Then he kept me in his crib, under his pillow.

One night when I was under the baby's pillow, I rang. The baby searched for me and when he found me he started to make funny noises. I lay in the baby's crib for two whole days and finally the baby took me with him in the car for a drive. Then he threw me out the car window. I hit the ground hard. My batteries fell out.

I was kind of woozy. I was not broken, but I was scared. I couldn't believe it. I was back at the chicken store! I wish my owner were here. He always treated me nice. He kept me warm and dry, he always pushed my buttons gently, and he talked softly into my ear.

Just when I was feeling sorry for myself, a person that works at the chicken place picked me up and took me inside. He put an ad in the paper to let my owner know that I was found. I hope my owner sees the ad and comes to get me and takes me home.

Tyler Botsford
Fourth Grade

COMPONENTS OF GOOD WRITING

- *Meaningful or interesting topic*

- *Ideas that are explained well enough so that others can understand them*

- *Words that make sense to the reader and arouse the reader's interest*

- *A limited, defined focus*

- *Enough information*

- *Visual details*

- *Clear, concise language*

- *An effective beginning*

- *An appropriate writing style*

- *A snappy ending*

TEACHING STRATEGY *2* ▶ ▶ ▶ **Creating a Literacy Center**

Writers need a place to write. While students certainly can write at their desks, having a special place in your classroom devoted to writing can go a long way in developing a community of writers. A Literacy Center can help students understand the importance of writing and provide students with a stimulating place to write (Morrow, 1997).

Directions

1. Tell students that you will be creating a Literacy Center in the classroom as a place for them to write.

2. Explain to students that the Literacy Center will be their writing place and that you would like their opinions about the kinds of things that should be placed in the Literacy Center.

3. Have students decide with you where to place the Literacy Center. If your room is small, the Literacy Center could be a desk pushed up against the wall. If you have a larger room, you could devote a larger table to the Literacy Center.

4. Duplicate and distribute the list of Literacy Center Materials that follows. Divide the class into groups of three or four students. Have students read the list, checking items that they would like in their Literacy Center. Then have them add other items to the list on the blank lines.

5. Use the lists from the groups of students to stock your Literacy Center. Encourage parent organizations or groups of parents to donate items on the list to the classroom.

6. Every four weeks have a student take an inventory of the materials at the Literacy Center to find out which materials need to be replaced. Ask students if there are materials that they would like to have added to the list. Keep the Literacy Center Materials as complete as possible.

7. Make sure students use the Literacy Center to write. Keep a list of students who have used the Literacy Center and encourage every student to use the Literacy Center as a place to write.

LITERACY CENTER MATERIALS

READING MATERIALS

_____ A book collection containing a variety of books including picture books, informational books, fiction, and easy-to-read books

_____ Books that span 3–5 grade levels and are changed every four weeks

_____ Magazines

_____ Newspapers

_____ Student-written books

_____ Read-aloud books

_____ _____

_____ _____

MANIPULATIVES

_____ Felt boards

_____ Storyboards

_____ White boards

_____ Alphabet stamps

_____ Stencils

_____ Stapler

_____ Hole punch

_____ Date stamp

_____ Brass paper fasteners

_____ Paper clips

_____ Tape

_____ Wikki sticks (waxy yarn)

_____ Binding machine

_____ Rulers

_____ Headsets and tape recorders

_____ Author's Chair

_____ _____

_____ _____

WRITING SUPPLIES

_____ Colored pencils

_____ Markers

_____ Crayons

_____ Small chalkboards

_____ Colored chalk

_____ Lined paper

_____ Unlined writing paper (various sizes)

_____ Envelopes

_____ Pencils

_____ Rulers

_____ Markers for boards

_____ _____

_____ _____

_____ _____

TEACHING STRATEGY 3 ▶▶▶▶▶▶▶▶▶ Planning Writing Instruction

All students should write at least four times a week for 35 to 40 minutes at a time (Graves, 1994). Many teachers wonder how to devote this much time for writing. When writing is a priority, however, teachers can find time in the day. The trick is to plan writing instruction so students don't waste time on things they already know and so students spend time on meaningful writing activities. Writing is content specific. Students can write in science class to reinforce new concepts; they can write newspapers in social studies; they can write in journals for themselves. Students also can write letters to inform or persuade, and they can write to entertain and/or reflect. Writing instruction should be organized so that all students can complete a variety of writing projects in a single year.

✛ Directions

1. Learn about your specific writing context by reflecting on the questions that follow.

   ? What are the students' writing abilities?
   What are the students' backgrounds in writing?
   What are the students' interests in writing?
   How willing are the students to learn?

2. State your instructional purposes for writing lessons by answering the questions that follow.

   ? What are my purposes for this lesson?
   What are my instructional goals?
   What could be my students' purposes for this writing?

3. Vary your topic choices by thinking about the following questions.

   ? What should be the topic of this piece of writing?
   Should this writing be student choice or teacher directed?
   Is this a single lesson or part of a larger unit?
   What is the place of this lesson in the curriculum?

4. Consider the class time you will be able to devote to this writing.

   ? Is this a piece of writing that can be completed in one day?
   Should this writing last over a longer period of time?
   Do school holidays interrupt the assignment?

5. Using the questions that follow, think about the audience for the assignment.

   ? Should students select an audience?
   Will I (as the teacher) be the only audience?
   Should we use the Author's Chair for this piece of writing?
   Is there a specific audience for this piece of writing?

6. Consider how this piece of writing should be published.

7. Think about the format for this piece of writing.

8. Identify the type of assessment that fits this piece of writing.

9. To complete the steps in planning writing instruction, you may want to duplicate and use the Writing Lesson Plan form that follows.

10. For additional writing lesson plans, access writing-specific web sites such as "Kathy Schrock's Guide for Educators."

Technology Tip

Kathy Schrock's Guide for Educators

The literature and language arts section of this web site includes links to sites on authors, genres, book talks, and lesson plans.

http://discoveryschool.com/schrockguide

Writing Lesson Plan

	Example		
Student Context	Students have written very few personal experience stories.		
Instructional Purposes	To teach students to value their own lives and to write with vivid language about themselves.		
Topic	Student choice		
Time	Three days 35 minutes each day		
Audience	Class book		
Format	Narrative		
Assessment	Story Structure Depth of emotions		

From Susan Davis Lenski and Jerry L. Johns, *Improving Writing: Resources, Strategies, and Assessments*. Copyright © 2000 by Kendall/Hunt Publishing Company (1-800-247-3458). May be reproduced for noncommercial educational purposes.

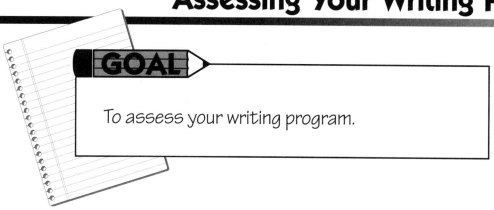

GOAL

To assess your writing program.

Background

From time to time it's a good idea to stop and take stock of your writing program. You need to determine whether you are a writing role model, whether your students have learned to think of themselves as writers, and whether your program is aligned with the writing goals of your curriculum. At least one checkpoint during the year is a good idea. If you assess your writing program during December or January, for example, you can make changes for the remaining portion of the school year. It's also a good idea to evaluate your writing program at the end of the year. What worked? What didn't work? What changes will you make next year?

To assess the growth of your writing program, think about three issues:

1. Think about how you, as the writing role model, have developed as a writer.

    • Have you begun writing for real reasons and real audiences?
    • Have you shared your writing joys and frustrations with your students?
    • Have you made progress in your own writing?

2. Think about how your students view themselves as they grow as writers.

    • Are your students enthusiastic writers?
    • Do your students write authentic pieces for real audiences?
    • Do your students have a positive self-concept about themselves as writers?

3. Assess the specifics of your writing program.

    • Have you organized instruction so that students can write?
    • Do you scaffold skill instruction?
    • Do you provide enough time for students to write?

Assessing these three areas can provide you with benchmarks as you continue to develop a more vibrant writing community. The strategies in this section should help you assess your writing program.

Written language helps people construct their social identities (Rubin, 1995). Therefore, writing is valuable for you as a person, not only as a teacher. As you grow as a writer, you will develop a deeper understanding of yourself and of how writing helps you grow as a person. Writing, therefore, should be both a personal goal and a professional goal. As you think about becoming a writer, it's a good idea to assess where you are at a given moment. Then you can record your own growth in becoming a writing role model. A *caveat*: be kind to yourself. Accept improvements in any area and celebrate your successes—just as you do with students.

 ## Directions

1. Read the Writing Role Model Survey items that follow to determine whether they fit your writing goals. Omit those items that you think do not fit your goals and substitute items that are more appropriate.

2. Record the date on the survey and on a calendar.

3. Duplicate the Writing Role Model Survey. Complete the Writing Record section of the Writing Role Model Survey. Record each piece of writing that you began during the past few months. An example follows. Then answer the survey questions.

Content	Form	Audience	Date	Status
Encouragement	letter	daughter	6/00	sent
Decision about house	diary	self	ongoing	in progress
Appreciation	poem	parent	begun 9/00	draft

4. Place the completed survey in your writing folder.

5. Make plans to take the Writing Role Model survey again in four months and to update your Writing Record. Write the date on your calendar.

6. After you have taken the survey two or three times, look for progress, no matter how small. Then celebrate!

Be kind to yourself.

Writing Role Model Survey

Writing Record

Content	Form	Audience	Date	Status
_____	_____	_____	_____	_____
_____	_____	_____	_____	_____
_____	_____	_____	_____	_____
_____	_____	_____	_____	_____
_____	_____	_____	_____	_____

1. I consider myself a writer, even in a small way.

   Yes   Not Sure   No

2. I write for real reasons and real purposes.

   Yes   Not Sure   No

3. I enjoy writing most of the time.

   Yes   Not Sure   No

4. I share my writing with friends, family, and/or students.

   Yes   Not Sure   No

5. I am becoming a better writer.

   Yes   Not Sure   No

ASSESS STUDENTS' WRITING ATTITUDES

Assessing your students' attitudes toward writing can be a valuable source of information. You can judge whether your writing program is helping students learn that they are indeed writers. If students exhibit a negative attitude toward writing, you may need to exhibit more enthusiasm yourself and give your writing program more time. If students still are negative, ask them why they don't like writing. Make adjustments as necessary. When you assess your students' writing attitudes, however, you need to be tolerant. Celebrate successes, no matter how small.

Directions

1. Read the Student Writing Survey items that follow to determine whether they fit your instructional goals. Omit those items that you think do not fit your goals and substitute items that are more appropriate.

2. Record the date on the survey and on a calendar.

3. Duplicate the survey. Tell students that you want to know what they have written in the past few months. Explain that recording writing projects is a way to acknowledge how much they have accomplished.

4. Write an example of two or three Writing Record entries on the chalkboard or on an overhead transparency. An example follows.

Content	Form	Audience	Date	Status
Request for new playground equipment	letter	school board	8/00	sent
New puppy	poem	family	begun 9/00	draft

5. After students have completed the Writing Record, have them answer the questions.

6. Collect the surveys and read them to determine whether students have a positive attitude toward writing.

7. Place the completed surveys in students' writing folders.

8. Make plans to give students the Student Writing Survey again in four months and have them update their Writing Records. Write the date on your calendar.

9. After you have given the survey two or three times, look for progress, no matter how small. Then celebrate!

Name _____ Date _____

Student Writing Survey

Writing Record

Content	Form	Audience	Date	Status
_____	_____	_____	_____	_____
_____	_____	_____	_____	_____
_____	_____	_____	_____	_____
_____	_____	_____	_____	_____
_____	_____	_____	_____	_____

1. I like to write.

    Yes   Not Sure   No

2. I like to publish my writing.

    Yes   Not Sure   No

3. I am a real author.

    Yes   Not Sure   No

4. I like to share my writing.

    Yes   Not Sure   No

5. My friends and family like my writing.

    Yes   Not Sure   No

ASSESSING YOUR WRITING PROGRAM

Writing programs should be evaluated based on the goals of the program (Tompkins, 1994). To assess your writing program, first be clear about your instructional goals. As you develop instructional goals, you might need to align what you know about instruction with state and local goals. If you don't have state or local goals and you are unsure about what goals to use, look at the goal statements inside the front cover of this book. The writing goals listed are a good place to start. Then customize your classroom goals with other ideas that are important to you.

Directions

1. Read the Writing Program Survey items that follow to determine whether they fit your instructional goals. Omit those items that you think do not fit your goals and substitute items that are more appropriate.

2. Record the date on the survey and on a calendar.

3. Duplicate and complete the survey.

4. Reflect on your evaluation of your program and, if necessary, make adjustments to your program. Congratulate yourself on the successful components of your program.

5. Place the completed survey in a file folder.

6. Make plans to take the survey again in four months. Write the date on your calendar.

7. After you have taken the survey two or three times, look for progress, no matter how small. Celebrate successes!

Writing Program Survey

1. Teacher is a writing role model.

   Often   Usually   Sometimes   Not yet

2. Teacher organizes a positive writing environment.

   Often   Usually   Sometimes   Not yet

3. Teacher encourages students to write.

   Often   Usually   Sometimes   Not yet

4. Teacher provides necessary instruction.

   Often   Usually   Sometimes   Not yet

5. Students learn and use the writing process.

   Often   Usually   Sometimes   Not yet

6. Students write frequently.

   Often   Usually   Sometimes   Not yet

7. Students consider the functions, forms, and audiences of writing.

   Often   Usually   Sometimes   Not yet

8. Students write from their experiences.

   Often   Usually   Sometimes   Not yet

9. Students write in order to learn.

   Often   Usually   Sometimes   Not yet

10. Writing assessment is designed to help students improve their writing.

    Often   Usually   Sometimes   Not yet

Chapter 3

Informal Writing: Building Fluency

"Just get it down on paper, and then we'll see what to do with it."—Maxwell Perkins

Overview

You may have heard the saying that good writing is 10% inspiration and 90% perspiration. That's because writing is both an art and a craft. Writing can be highly creative and, at the same time, it can be highly conventional (Cooper & Odell, 1999). When writers write, words can flow so quickly that each sentence is a surprise and the writing activity is thoroughly satisfying. Or writers can deliberate, mulling over thoughts and organizing ideas into carefully crafted groups of words. Often writers have moments of inspiration and moments of deliberation during the same writing event.

> Good writing is 10% inspiration and 90% perspiration.

Writing, therefore, is both a group of skills to be taught and an expression of ideas (Britton, *et al.*, 1975). In this book, we call the expressive form of writing "informal writing."

INFORMAL WRITING IS SIMILAR TO SPEECH. This is the kind of writing that can be termed "talk written down." As you know, when we talk, we use all sorts of verbal cues to express our meaning. We may gesture with our hands, use facial expressions, and use the tone of our voices to get our meanings across to our listeners. Since readers can-

▶ Do your students have confidence in their writing abilities?

not take advantage of verbal cues, writing is usually different from speech. Informal writing, however, is much closer to speech. Informal writing is the ability to let the mind wander through words. It is expressing what the mind is thinking without taking the time to conform that meaning to the conventions of language. It is the work of the mind that is important in informal writing, not the organization or correctness of the words.

INFORMAL WRITING ACTIVITIES ARE ESSENTIAL TO A BALANCED WRITING PROGRAM. Think for a moment about a skill you have learned or that you watched someone else learn. For example, think about learning to play the cello. Imagine for a moment taking the cello in your arms and lifting your bow to the strings. Then imagine a teacher explaining the fingerings for the notes, how to read music, and how to move the bow across the strings. After being taught each one of these skills, would you be ready for a cello performance? Of course not. You need to practice and practice and practice. The same principle holds true for writing. Students need to prac-

tice writing in order to build the kind of writing fluency that good writers need.

INFORMAL WRITING HELPS STUDENTS EXPLORE THEIR THOUGHTS AND IDEAS, MAKE TENTATIVE RESPONSES TO LITERATURE, AND INVESTIGATE THEIR LEARNING. When students write using informal writing activities, they use words and language to discover the meaning of their experiences and of their learning (Murray, 1982). In addition to giving students a deeper understanding when writing, informal writing activities also can help students learn the craft of writing. When students have the opportunity to experiment with language in risk-free environments, they build writing fluency.

There are three ways you can structure informal writing activities so that students can experience the range of possibilities in writing.

• One way to help students experience writing is to give them opportunities to write in journals. When students write in journals, they learn to reflect about themselves and their lives. They come to grips with their own thoughts and feelings. They discover who they are and what they think. They write to discover.

• A second type of informal writing activity is responding to literature. When students read, they construct meanings. By responding to literature in writing, students can deepen their construction of meaning and better understand what they are reading. In this type of informal writing activity, students write to give a personal response.

• The third type of informal writing activity is writing to learn. Through activities such as writing in response to content learning, students process, learn, and remember content material.

These three types of informal writing activities can help students deepen their thinking while they improve their writing fluency.

As students experience informal writing activities, they need to express themselves without fear of being judged for what they are writing. As in any type of learning, practice should not be evaluated. Therefore, when students engage in informal writing

Three Ways to Experience Writing

• Journals

• Response to Literature

• Writing to Learn

activities, your assessment of their writing should be encouraging yet minimal.

Your role as a teacher of writing is to encourage students to write, to reflect, and to learn in order to build their writing fluency (International Reading Association and National Council of Teachers of English, 1996). And, as students write, they will reap the benefits of developing the expressive side of writing as they discover their interpretations of events, clarify meanings of literature, and learn content materials through writing. This chapter contains resources, teaching strategies, ideas, and activities to help students develop the expressive side of writing so that writing can be inspiration as well as perspiration. Ideas for assessment also are included.

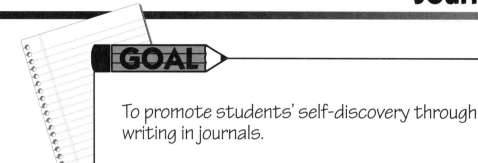

GOAL

To promote students' self-discovery through writing in journals.

Background

Writing is not merely a process of recording thoughts, experiences, and ideas—writing can be a process of discovery. When you write, you can relive experiences from a different time and perspective, you can let your imagination redefine reality, you can explore new worlds, and you can become more aware of your own personal beliefs. Writing can take you places your mind doesn't know.

Not all writing is this magical. When writers have the chance to write in a nonthreatening situation, however, their thoughts become clearer and they generate more ideas. Perhaps that's why many people keep journals (Mallon, 1984). A number of artists, scientists, engineers, dancers, and teachers write in journals to record events and to learn about their reactions to life. Journals are a spontaneous, unplanned means of understanding oneself (Craig, 1983).

Writing in journals helps clarify thoughts, but it also has another benefit for students learning to write. Journal writing helps writers develop fluency (Newman, 1983). When students put words on paper, they are experimenting with language and how

▶▶▶

Journal writing helps writers develop fluency.

◀◀◀

words fit together to make sentences. Each time students write in journals, they are practicing language. They are learning how to formulate ideas, how to put those ideas into words, how to make sentences readable, and how to string together sentences to make thoughts comprehensible. Journal writing, therefore, accomplishes two tasks:

• it helps students understand what they think, and
• it helps them learn ways to write those thoughts.

All students can increase their writing fluency when given the opportunity for journal writing—even students as young as those in kindergarten (Bouas, Thompson, & Farlow, 1997). They just need time and the opportunities to write. However, just telling students to write in journals may not work. Some students will ask, "What do I write?" Therefore, we have included a variety of teaching strategies, activities, and ideas for you to use as you help students understand the value of writing in journals and to give them the chance to become more fluent writers by journal writing.

TEACHING STRATEGY 1 ▶ ▶ ▶ ▶ ▶ ▶ ▶ ▶ ▶ **Personal Journals**

Personal Journals are journals where students can write what they think, see, or feel. These journals are notebooks where students can write whatever they want. Personal Journals are places where students can keep entries of ideas and thoughts that can eventually be used in other types of writing. Such journals are not graded, and students decide whether or not something in the journal will be shared with another person.

✛ **Directions**

1. Tell students that they will be writing in Personal Journals at least three times each week. Explain that Personal Journals are places to record thoughts, feelings, and ideas.

2. Provide students with blank notebooks or have them bring them from home. Tell students that these notebooks are their own personal places to write. Explain that, even though the Personal Journals will be students' own private possessions, you cannot guarantee that no one will read them. Tell students that they should not write anything that is so personal that it cannot be shared with their classmates.

3. Tell students to begin keeping lists of writing topics. Help students create lists by providing them with the list of Journal Topics that follows. Make copies of the list and distribute a copy to each student. Staple the list in the front of each student's Personal Journal.

4. Each week give students 10 minutes to create additional lists of writing topics. Divide the class into groups of three or four students. Have students brainstorm ideas for their Personal Journals. Encourage students to add to their lists at other times during the week.

5. Provide students with at least 15 minutes three times each week to write in their Personal Journals. During journal writing time, have students refer to their lists, decide on a topic, and write steadily for 15 minutes. Encourage students to write whatever comes to their minds.

6. Tell students that you will not be grading their Personal Journals but that you will read their journals occasionally. Explain that writing in Personal Journals is something students do for themselves, not for a grade. Tell students that journal writing is practice writing and an idea bank for other writing. Then read their journals when you have time. Do not feel you need to read each student's journal every week.

JOURNAL TOPICS

Things on my mind . . .

What I usually talk about . . .

What bothers me . . .

What pleases me . . .

How I spend my time . . .

What surprises me . . .

Books I have read . . .

People I admire . . .

My dreams . . .

Things I look forward to . . .

Things I enjoy . . .

Things that I dread . . .

What I have learned recently . . .

How I feel about my life and family . . .

Favorite places . . .

What I want to know . . .

What I would like to change . . .

My goals . . .

My biggest problems . . .

Dangerous things . . .

Valuable possessions . . .

Past experiences . . .

Places I'd like to go . . .

Things I wonder about . . .

TEACHING STRATEGY 2 ▶ ▶ ▶ ▶ ▶ ▶ ▶ ▶ ▶ ▶ ▶ ▶ ▶ **Class Diary**

A Class Diary is a record of events of the class written by different students. A Class Diary is an excellent way to introduce journal writing. It can take the form of a big book, a small notebook, or posters on the wall. A Class Diary is a type of informal writing similar to a graffiti wall or messages to friends. When writing a Class Diary, students record events and write reactions, but they will not spend time revising their writing or editing it. They will just write.

Directions

1. Explain to students that they will be writing a Class Diary and that it will be a record of events that take place in the class and will include students' reactions to those events. Tell students that they will be writing excerpts but that those excerpts will not be revised or graded.

2. Assign one or more students to be the day's recorder of events. Have students observe the class with an eye toward the things that happen, either planned or unplanned.

3. Provide students with several large sheets of paper. Have them list an event with a short description of the event at the top of the sheet. Place the sheets of paper on a large table at the end of the day. Tell students that on the following day they will be writing their reactions to the events.

4. On the next day, tell students that during free time they can write their reactions to the events on the paper. Explain that their writing should be school-appropriate writing since it will be read by you and by other students. Give students time during the day to write their responses.

5. Leave the Class Diary pages on a table or post them on the wall for several days so students can read what others have written. After several days, compile the pages into a class book with a front and back made of construction paper. Leave the Class Diary where students can read it.

TEACHING STRATEGY 3 ▶ ▶ ▶ ▶ ▶ ▶ Double-Entry Journals

Journals can be written in many forms. They can be lists of words or phrases, long paragraphs, or even charts. Double-Entry Journals are a type of chart. In them students record facts and their responses to those facts. Charting ideas with Double-Entry Journals can be a way to help students explore their feelings and write them down. The entries in Double-Entry Journals can be used for future writing assignments, for Personal Journals, or for process-writing papers.

 Directions

1. Duplicate the Double-Entry Journal page that follows and give each student a copy. Explain to students that they will be writing a different type of journal.

2. Tell students that in a Double-Entry Journal they will record facts and their responses to those facts. Provide an example similar to one that follows.

Fact	My Reaction
My dad asked me to mow the lawn.	I felt grown up and responsible.
I finished my report.	I felt relieved.
It rained.	I was disappointed because I couldn't play outside.

3. Ask students for other examples of facts and their reactions to those facts. As students volunteer ideas, write them on the chalkboard or on an overhead transparency. Collect several examples.

 4. Tell students to write several Double-Entry Journal entries on their papers. Give students at least 10 minutes to write.

5. Give students time to write in their Double-Entry Journals on a regular basis. Have students keep these journals in their writing folders to use as ideas for other pieces of writing.

Double-Entry Journal

Fact	My Reaction

TEACHING STRATEGY 4 ▶ ▶ ▶ ▶ ▶ ▶ ▶ **Interactive Journals**

The audience for most journals is the writer. Typically, only the person writing the journal will read it. However, some journals can be used as informal methods of communication between two or more writers as in Interactive Journals. Interactive Journals are written by more than one person. One writer begins an entry and then another writer responds. The second writer returns the journal to the first writer who reads it and replies. By writing in Interactive Journals, students can communicate with each other through the written word, increase their writing fluency, and have fun (Gambrell, 1985).

✦ Directions

1. Tell students that they will be creating a journal for an audience who is someone other than themselves. Ask students whether they would like to write to members of their class, members of another class, senior citizens, family members, or college students. Have students identify the audiences for their journals.

2. Assist students in locating someone belonging to the audience groups that they identified. Once the audiences are identified, have students write a letter to the recipients explaining the purposes of journal writing and the process you will use to exchange journals.

3. Have students write the first journal entry. For the first entry, have students write about something they think will be of interest to their audiences. For example, have students read their lists of journal topics and write about something they care about deeply.

4. Provide students at least 15 minutes to write in their journals.

5. Facilitate the journal exchanges. Sometimes a parent or an aide can coordinate the exchanges. Give the journal recipients several days to read and respond to the initial journal entries. Then facilitate the exchange of journals.

6. Encourage students to read their journal responses in a nonjudgmental manner. As students read, have them look for the thoughts and ideas of the writer. Then have students write a second entry, either responding to the writer or beginning a new topic. Continue the exchange for the period of time that you consider appropriate.

 **Ideas and Activities**

1. Have students keep a story journal. After reading a story to the class, ask students to write a short entry about the story and put the entries in a class story journal. Some students may want to illustrate their entries. When you have finished compiling the story journal, place it in the classroom library.

2. Have students survey family members about their use of journals or diaries. Many families have journals that were written several generations ago. Have students query family members to discover whether any family journals exist. To find family journals, have students develop a list of questions to use as they interview family members. Some examples of interview questions follow.

Have you ever written a diary or a journal?

If you have, why did you write in a diary or a journal?

Do you know of a relative who has written a diary or a journal?

3. At the end of each month, have students brainstorm things you have done in the classroom. Have students develop individual lists and then have them share their lists in small groups. Ask each of the small groups to compile a list of classroom events together. Have students copy their lists in their journals and use the lists as an idea bank for journal entries.

4. Obtain a selection of published diaries or journals from your local library or from the Internet. Bring the books to class and arrange them on a table. Tell students that these books are examples of informal writing. Read sections of the diaries out loud. Explain that the purpose of writing in diaries is to write for oneself rather than for a public audience, so the writing may not conform to the rules of Standard English. Have students listen for the conversational tone of the writing, the thought fragments, and the way the entries move from one subject to another. Tell students that journal writing can help writers discover their own feelings. Then have students read sections of the journals themselves. Ask them to try to identify components of diary writing that differ from other types of books. After students have read examples of diaries and journals, have them write in their own journals.

Technology Tip

Scholastic's Diary Maker

This multimedia tool uses the diaries of famous people to help teach students to write. It also provides historical and cultural lessons.

Macintosh and Windows
800-223-4011 (FAX)

5. Have students make two Idea Catchers to record ideas for journal entries. Make a ring book by cutting paper into halves and punching two holes in the top of the pages. Fasten the pages with metal rings. Have students write the title Idea Catcher on the cover and decorate it with an imaginative picture. Have students place one Idea Catcher in their book bags to take home and have them place one in their desks at school. Encourage students to think of writing topics at various times during the day and, when they do, have them record their ideas in their Idea Catchers. When students are asked to do journal writing, have them refer to their Idea Catchers for topics.

6. Have students write weekend family journal entries at home. Write a letter to their parents asking them to make a journal entry with their child to share with the rest of the class. Tell parents that the writing can be a story, a description, a video or a movie review, or a letter. Reassure parents that the writing will be shared, not graded. Collect the family journal pages and compile them into a class book. For those parents who decide not to contribute to the class book, have the child develop a page with another student, another teacher, or individually.

7. Encourage students who take vacations during the school year to write vacation journals. Explain that a vacation is a unique opportunity to observe new things and to engage in new experiences. Tell students to begin writing about their vacations during the planning stages. Explain that when students are planning vacations they are making decisions about what they want to do, and they are making predictions about what they will do and see. Have students write how their family is making decisions, what each person in the family wants to do, and what decisions are reached. Then encourage students to make predictions about how they will feel during the vacation. Tell students to continue to make journal entries twice a day, once in the morning and once in the evening. After students return from their vacations, have them share their vacation experiences by reading sections of the journals to the class.

8. Create a flip book for weekly writing in journals. To create a flip book, fold 3 sheets of 8½- by 11-inch paper so that one sheet has a 3-inch flap, one has a 4-inch flap, and one has a 5-inch flap. Line up the folds and use a long-arm stapler to fasten the pages. List the days of the week, one per page. Have students take their weekly journals with them at all times. Encourage students to write in their journals every day.

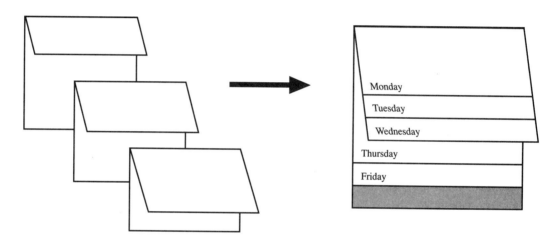

9. Identify a book in which one of the characters writes in diaries or journals. Read the book to the class. Ask students why the character decided to write in a journal, what the character wrote, and how the journal was used in the story. Explain that journal writing is a common activity that many people use to discover their thoughts and to record events. The next time students write a fictional story, encourage them to include a character who uses journals to write ideas and record events. You may want to use the following list as a resource for books that have characters who write in journals.

Books with Characters Who Write in Journals

Compiled by Jenny Bolander

Ada, A. (1997)
Dear Peter Rabbit.
New York: Aladdin.
(Grades K–2)

Anderson, J. (1987)
Joshua's westward journal.
New York: Morrow.
(Grades 3–6)

Bunting, E. (1992)
Our teacher's having a baby.
New York: Clarion.
(Grades K–2)

Coy, J. (1996)
Night driving.
New York: Henry Holt.
(Grades 2–3)

Craig, J. (1994)
A letter to Santa.
Mahwah, NJ: Troll.
(Grades K–2)

Denenberg, B. (1998)
Journal of William Thomas Emerson, a Revolutionary War soldier.
New York: Scholastic.
(Grades 4–6)

Hest, A. (1997)
The private notebook of Katie Roberts.
New York: Scholastic.
(Grades 3–6)

James, S. (1996)
Dear Mr. Blueberry.
New York: Aladdin.
(Grades 1–3)

Lasky, K. (1998)
Dreams in the golden country: The diary of Zipporah Feldman.
New York: Scholastic.
(Grades 4–6)

Murphy, J. (1998)
Journal of James Edmond Pease, a Civil War Union soldier.
New York: Scholastic.
(Grades 4–6)

Pfeffer, S. (1989)
Dear Dad/Love Laura.
New York: Scholastic.
(Grades 5–6)

Taylor, J. (1996)
The gold dust letters.
New York: Avon.
(Grades 3–6)

Woodruff, E. (1998)
Dear Levi: Letters from the Overland Trail.
New York: Scholastic.
(Grades 3–6)

Responding by Writing

GOAL

To help students expand meanings of literature by responding in writing.

3.2

Background

As students read, they reach provisional understandings of text and often choose to move through the text, resulting in what Mackey (1997) terms "good-enough" reading. "Good-enough" reading is sufficient for some reading tasks. One legitimate purpose for recreational reading, for example, might be merely to finish a book. In this case, the reader might be satisfied with minimal comprehension. Reading, therefore, can be viewed as an act of compromise between the need for a deep comprehension of text and the desire for momentum—to find out what happened (Mackey, 1997). For much of the reading required in schools, however, "good-enough" reading is not good enough. Responding in writing to literature can help students move beyond "good-enough" reading to focus on what the reader is seeing, feeling, and thinking (Rosenblatt, 1985).

▶▶▶

Responding in writing to literature can help students move beyond "good-enough" reading.

◀◀◀

When students write in response to stories or books that they have heard or read, they begin to listen to their hearts as they read. Stories have the power to reach our emotions, to help us understand life. As students read, they begin to comprehend the story by understanding the plot, setting, theme, and characters. Then, as students respond to the stories in writing, they can pay attention to their feelings. As they identify their thoughts and feelings, students can reach deeper levels of comprehension about the text. Writing in response to literature, therefore, can help students construct meanings of texts while it promotes writing fluency.

It's important that you give students a variety of response activities to pursue. When engaged in different response activities, students think in different ways (Ollmann, 1996). For example, if students write in Response Journals, they write primarily about their feelings. When students write a Two-Column Response, they identify a quotation from the book and use their background experiences to create meaning. Each strategy promotes student learning. Therefore, we encourage you to use a variety of the resources, teaching strategies, ideas, and activities presented in this section. If you do, your students will learn how to expand meanings of literature while writing, and they will become more fluent writers.

▶ Would writing about this story help the student understand the content more clearly?

TEACHING STRATEGY 1 ▶ ▶ ▶ ▶ ▶ ▶ ▶ ▶ ▶ **Response Journals**

Response Journals encourage students to express their feelings about and reactions to books they have read (Barone & Lovell, 1990). Response Journals are usually spiral notebooks that students can use to record their thoughts, feelings, and reactions to stories as they read them. As students write in Response Journals, they take the time to move beyond their initial comprehension of the text to a richer understanding of the story.

⟵⊹⟶ Directions

1. Introduce Response Journals by modeling your own response to literature. Tell students about a book you are reading. Tell students the name of the book and the author and then give them a brief summary of the book. Then complete one of the Response Ideas on the following page and model it for the class.

2. After you have shown students a response to your own reading, tell students that they will be writing in Response Journals. Explain that writing in Response Journals helps students think about what they have read, perhaps in a new way.

3. Tell students that after they have read a book or a story they will engage in response activities. Duplicate the list of Response Ideas on the following page and distribute copies to students.

4. Explain to students that after they have read a book they should choose one of the activities to complete. Tell students that the activities have been designed to help them think about the story.

5. Provide students with adequate time to complete Response Journals after reading a story or a book.

RESPONSE IDEAS

1. Write a letter to a friend about the book.

2. Write several endings to the book.

3. Write a play about the main character.

4. Rewrite the story using students from the class as characters.

5. Write a calendar of story events.

6. Design a classified ad for something in the book.

7. Create a glossary of words from the story.

8. Write a horoscope for a book character.

9. Identify phrases from the book that could be used as quotations for a display.

10. Pretend you're a story character and write a letter to someone in the class.

11. Compose a song about the plot of the book.

12. Write a picture book about the events in the story.

13. Write a news report about the plot.

14. Create a budget for travel to the setting of the story.

15. Develop a web site for the main character of the book.

16. Keep a journal from the point of view of one of the characters.

17. Write a newspaper article about one of the characters.

18. Write a fictional journal entry about a book character.

19. Create a political cartoon about a character in the book.

20. Write a radio show about the book.

TEACHING STRATEGY 2 ▶ ▶ ▶ ▶ ▶ ▶ ▶ ▶ ▶ ▶ ▶ ▶ Two-Column Response Charts

Two-Column Response Charts (Ollmann, 1991/1992) are designed for students to think more deeply about specific things authors write in stories. Authors often include pearls of wisdom embedded within texts. Of course, any quotation from a story may be meaningful for one person and not significant to another. Two-Column Response Charts offer students an avenue for identifying quotations that interest them and a chance to write their reactions to the quotations. This activity can lead to lively discussions about the literature.

⬩ Directions

1. Tell students that different readers will construct different meanings from the same text. Tell students that they can identify and respond to sentences from texts using Two-Column Response Charts.

2. Introduce the Two-Column Response Charts by showing students a completed chart similar to the example from *Children of the Wild West* (Freedman, 1983) that follows. Point out the sentences that were chosen and the responses. Tell students that a different person completing the chart could have entirely different responses.

Quotes	Responses
"The growth of photography and the opening of the American West took place at the same time" (p. 9).	I didn't realize that photography was invented at that time. I thought there were photographs before the 1840s.
"They called themselves 'emigrants' because, as they started their journey, they were actually leaving America" (p. 17).	The West was not part of the United States at that time. The United States is really a young nation.
"It took a full acre of sod to build a typical one-room sod house, which measured 16 by 20 feet and weighed about 90 tons" (p. 29).	Sod houses are fascinating. They seem small and dirty. The size of this house is about the same size as our living room. Thinking about an entire family living in such a small place is mind-boggling.

3. Give students a two-column chart or have them divide a piece of paper in half. On the top of the left side of the paper have students write the word "Quotes" and on the right side have them write "Responses" as in the Two-Column Response Chart that follows.

4. Tell students that as they read they should identify quotes that interest them and write the quotes and the responses on the chart.

5. After students have written at least three quotes and responses, divide the class into groups of three or four students and have students share their Two-Column Response Charts.

Name_____ Date_____

Two-Column Response Chart

Quotes	Responses

TEACHING STRATEGY 3 ▶ ▶ ▶ ▶ ▶ ▶ ▶ **Response Questions**

When students read on their own, they may miss important parts of the story and have minimal comprehension as a result. When students have to write responses as they read, they stop and reflect, thus increasing their understanding of the story (Berger, 1996). Students also should be encouraged to write responses to their self-selected reading. The following list of Response Questions can help guide students' comprehension as they read independently.

Directions

1. Provide students with a spiral notebook for their Response Questions. Tell students to use this notebook for their self-selected reading response notebook.

2. Duplicate and distribute copies of the Response Questions that follow. Tell students that they can use these questions to respond to their independent reading.

3. Ask students to write two or three times per week in response to their independent reading. Tell them to choose one of the questions from the list of Response Questions and answer it in their notebooks. Provide students with adequate time for writing.

RESPONSE QUESTIONS

AUTHOR

1. Why do you think the author wrote this book?
2. How does the author organize the book?
3. How does the author create suspense or humor?
4. Who do you think the author intended as the primary audience for this book?
5. What does the author have to know in order to write this book?
6. How does the author interest you in the book?
7. Why do you think the author wrote the ending this way?
8. How do you picture the author?
9. How does the author use setting in this book?
10. What would you ask the author if you could?

CHARACTERS

1. How would you describe the main characters?
2. Would you choose the main characters as friends? Why or why not?
3. How do the characters change in the story?
4. How does the author create an image of the main characters?
5. How does the author help the reader get to know the main characters?
6. How are some of the characters different from other characters?
7. How are the characters like your friends or family?
8. How are the characters like other characters in books you have read?
9. Which character was your favorite? Why?
10. How would you change one of the characters?

PLOT

1. What happened in the story?
2. What was the sequence of events?
3. What was the problem in the story?
4. How was the problem resolved?
5. What parts of the plot kept you interested in the story?
6. What part of the plot was the most exciting to you?
7. Did the ending surprise you? Why or why not?
8. Was the plot effective? Why or why not?
9. What other directions might the plot have taken?
10. What was the point of the story?

STYLE AND MOOD

1. How did you feel while you were reading this book?
2. What part of the book was your favorite?
3. Did you like the author's style of writing? Why or why not?
4. How did the mood of the story change during the book?
5. Why did the author select the mood of this story?
6. What picture has the author's writing left in your mind?
7. How is this book like something you have written?
8. How would you describe the author's style?
9. Did you like the first sentence of the book? Why or why not?
10. What sentences did you think were especially effective?

TEACHING STRATEGY 4 ▶▶▶▶▶▶▶▶▶ **Response Cards**

Response Cards are a strategy to encourage students to respond to literature in a variety of ways. Response Cards' questions can be organized in many ways. Questions can be organized by Bloom's Taxonomy, or they can be priorities that the teacher and students have established. The purpose of using Response Cards is to guide students' responses to literature in the areas that are important in the curriculum.

Directions

1. Duplicate and distribute the Response Card that follows or create one with categories that you feel are important.

2. Tell students that each category has different questions. Point out the names of the six categories on this card:

   - knowledge
   - comprehension
   - application
   - analysis
   - creative thinking
   - critical thinking

   If necessary, discuss and explain the categories.

3. Have students read the questions under each category. Tell students that they can answer any of the questions when their category is selected.

4. When you want students to write responses to literature, select a category. Have students write a response to any question in that category on that day. Provide ample time for students to write.

5. After students have learned how to use the Response Cards, allow students to select their own categories during writing time. Tell students that they need to alternate categories each time they write.

6. Create new Response Cards periodically. Have students suggest categories and questions for the new cards.

Response Card

Knowledge	Comprehension
1. Who are the main characters?	1. Retell the story in your own words.
2. What is the story about?	2. Describe the main characters.
3. List the sequence of events.	3. Explain the problem and resolution.

Application	Analysis
1. What does the author do to "paint a picture" of the setting?	1. What happened at the beginning, middle, and end of the story?
2. Choose a new title for the section you have just read.	2. How did the author draw you into the story?
3. If you could interview a character from the book, what questions would you ask?	3. What are some of your favorite words, phrases, or sentences from the story?

Creative Thinking	Critical Thinking
1. If you could change a character in the story, who would it be?	1. What character would make a good friend?
2. What would happen if the story took place in a different time?	2. Would you recommend this book to someone else? Why or why not?
3. How would the story change if it were written from a different point of view?	3. What is the most memorable part of this book? Why?

From Susan Davis Lenski and Jerry L. Johns, *Improving Writing: Resources, Strategies, and Assessments.* Copyright © 2000 by Kendall/Hunt Publishing Company (1-800-247-3458). May be reproduced for noncommercial educational purposes.

 # Ideas and Activities

1. Have students identify an interesting character in a book they have read so they can write a literary letter (Atwell, 1987). A literary letter is a letter students write to a character in a book. Tell students that they should use information from the story to write things that they think will interest the character, to introduce themselves to the character, and to ask the character questions.

2. Most students are familiar with talk shows on television where a host invites people to "talk" with the host. Tell students that you will be creating a talk show with one of the characters in a story as the main guest. Ask one student to volunteer to play the character's role. Have the rest of the students write interview questions for the story character. Ask students playing the character to read the interview questions and respond to some of them in writing. Then have students dramatize the talk show with one student as host and another as the story character guest.

3. Many students are interested in writing to authors. After students read a book by a living author, have them research the author's life and write a letter posing questions about authoring decisions (Ollmann, 1992). You may want to send the letter to the author's publisher, find the author's home page on the Internet, or have students directly write to the author using the "Ask the Author" web site that follows.

 **Technology Tip**

Ask the Author

Web site for students to ask authors questions and read answers from them.

http://ipl.org.youth/AskAuthor

4. Before students have read a story, write a letter to an Advice Column from a character in the story discussing the main problem in the story. Have small groups of students read the letters. Then ask students to write a return letter to the character and offer a solution to the problem presented in the letter to the Advice Column. After students have read the story, ask them to revise their original letters.

 5. Have students write in Book Buddy Journals (Gillespie, 1993). Ask groups of two students to choose the same book to read. After they have read part of the book, direct each student to write three entries in a journal beginning with the sentence starters, "I predict . . .," "I notice . . .," and "I conclude. . . ." After each student has written three entries, have students trade journals and read their buddy's journal entries. Tell students to respond to at least one of their buddy's entries. Repeat the procedure after students have finished reading the book.

6. Explain to students that authors develop characters in stories to have specific personalities. Tell students that they can analyze characters' personalities by creating a Personality Plot (Wham & Lenski, 1996). To create a Personality Plot, have students write a list of descriptive personality traits across the top of a chart and a list of the story's characters down the side of the chart. Then have students discuss which characteristics they believe describe each character and place an X on the chart to indicate their choices, similar to the example from *The Three Little Hawaiian Pigs and the Magic Shark* (Laird, 1990) that follows. Finally, have students write a brief description of one of the characters.

PERSONALITY PLOT			
Characters	Cautious	Fun-loving	Hungry
First Pig		X	X
Second Pig		X	X
Third Pig	X		
Shark			X

7. After students have read a story or a book, have them respond using a Hexagonal Essay (Carroll & Wilson, 1993). A Hexagonal Essay includes the six areas of Bloom's Taxonomy (i.e., knowledge, comprehension, etc.). Tell students to begin by writing a plot summary and to follow it with a personal association. Then have students discuss the themes of the book. At the analysis level, have students analyze literary devices and, for synthesis, have them compare and contrast the story with other stories. Finally, have students evaluate the literature. Use the hexagonal essays to explain the various levels at which students can respond to stories as they read them.

8. Locate and read books to the class that have been written in diary or journal form as in the following list. Have students respond to the diary or journal entries as if they were a character in the book. Encourage students to imagine being in the same time period as the author of the book and to use the same writing style as the author. The following resource is a list of books that have characters who write in diary or journal form.

Books Written in Diary or Journal Form

Compiled by Jenny Bolander

Ahlberg, J. (1986)
The jolly postman.
Boston: Little, Brown.
(Grades K–2)

Ahlberg, J. (1991)
The jolly Christmas postman.
London: Heinemann.
(Grades K–2)

Ahlberg, J. (1995)
The jolly pocket postman.
London: Heinemann.
(Grades K–2)

Alcott, L. (1993)
Louisa May Alcott: Her girlhood diary.
Mahwah, NJ: Bridgewater.
(Grades 4–6)

Blos, J. (1997)
A gathering of days.
Livonia, MN: Seedlings.
(Grades 5–6)

Cleary, B. (1991)
Strider.
New York: Morrow Junior Books.
(Grades 4–6)

Cleary, B. (1998)
Dear Mr. Henshaw.
New York: Scholastic.
(Grades 3–6)

Columbus, C. (1990)
I, Columbus: My journal, 1492–3.
New York: Walker.
(Grades 4–6)

Denenberg, B. (1997)
So far from home: The diary of Mary Driscoll, an Irish mill girl.
New York: Scholastic.
(Grades 4–8)

Filipovic, Z. (1994)
Zlata's diary: A child's life in Sarajevo.
New York: Viking.
(Grades 4–8)

Books Written in Diary or Journal Form

Continued

Gregory, K. (1996)
Winter of red snow: The Revolutionary War diary.
New York: Scholastic.
(Grades 4–6)

Hopkinson, D. (1997)
Birdie's lighthouse.
New York: Atheneum.
(Grades 4–6)

Laminack, L. (1998)
The sunsets of Ms. Olivia Wiggin.
Atlanta, GA: Peachtree.
(Grades 3–6)

Lasky, K. (1998)
Journey to the New World.
Livonia, MN: Seedlings.
(Grades 4–6)

Lowry, L. (1998)
Looking back, a book of memories.
Boston: Houghton Mifflin.
(Grades 4–6)

Smith, R. (1987)
Mostly Michael.
New York: Delacorte.
(Grades 4–6)

GOAL

To help students learn content material through writing activities.

3.3

Background

There are a number of ways that students can process information in order to learn. One of them is through writing (Elbow, 1981). When students engage in a writing activity about a specific topic, they need to think about the topic and form ideas and opinions. As they form ideas and opinions, students make decisions about what they believe, and they make a commitment to those decisions. Students form their ideas in language, that is, words and sentences. As they choose words to express ideas, they revise and clarify their thinking. Students learn content material through the mental processes they experience as they write.

No student is too young or too old to use writing as a learning tool.

Asking students to record what they have learned helps them understand what they know (Fulwiler, 1987). For this reason, having students write in order to learn is a powerful learning tool, both in content area learning and for writing instruction. When students write in order to learn, they wrestle with new terms and concepts and learn how to write them in sentences. Students learn to become fluent not only by writing but in the contexts for their writing. Therefore, writing in order to learn is not merely a language arts strategy; it also is a way to help students process information.

Students of all ages should engage in writing to learn strategies. No student is too young or too old to use writing as a learning tool. Sometimes we think that young students cannot participate in writing to learn. However, a number of strategies are especially appropriate for young students. For example, young students can "write the room," or write about the displays and bulletin boards in the classroom. They can write sentences about the classroom and about content subjects while building their writing fluency. Older students can engage in a number of writing to learn activities such as RAFT, Learning Logs, and Writing Format Fiesta. These strategies are a fun way to encourage students to learn and to help them build writing fluency.

The resources, teaching strategies, ideas, and activities in this section are designed to help students use writing as a learning tool. Each strategy should be adapted for your grade level and the content you want to teach. All of the strategies have been tried in classrooms and have been effective in helping students learn content material through writing.

▶ Could this student be "writing the room"?

Teaching Strategy 1 ▶ ▶ ▶ ▶ ▶ ▶ ▶ ▶ ▶ ▶ ▶ ▶ ▶ ▶ ▶ ▶ ▶ ▶ ▶ **RAFT**

RAFT is a writing strategy that can be adapted for writing to learn in content areas (Santa, Havens, & Harrison, 1989). RAFT is an acronym for **R**ole, **A**udience, **F**ormat, and **T**opic, all of the major components of writing. RAFT also can be used to design creative writing lessons in content areas.

 **Directions**

> **RAFT**
>
> Role—refers to the perspective of the writer
>
> Audience—refers to the reader's perspective
>
> Format—form of the writing product
>
> Topic—specific content of the writing

1. Tell students that they will be writing in content areas using the RAFT technique. Explain that RAFT stands for **R**ole, **A**udience, **F**ormat, and **T**opic.

2. Provide students with models of RAFT writing frameworks such as the ones listed below. Write the examples on a chalkboard or on an overhead transparency. Tell students that these examples of RAFT writing frameworks are your own examples and that they should use ideas that are different from the ones you have illustrated.

Science
Role: A planet
Audience: Readers of personal
   advertisements
Format: Personal advertisement
Topic: Description of self

Geography
Role: A landform (e.g., canyon)
Audience: A star
Format: A journal entry
Topic: How landforms are created
   and change

Physical Education
Role: A piece of sports equipment
Audience: An alien from space
Format: Rules of the game
Topic: Your role in the game

Mathematics
Role: A unit of measurement
Audience: An ant
Format: A poem
Topic: The uses of a specific unit of
   measurement

3. Have students select a content area subject to use as a writing springboard such as science, social studies, physical education, geography, mathematics, health, art, or music. Ask students to write the name of the content area on a piece of paper.

4. Tell students to write down the word "Role" under the content area term. Explain that the role of the writer is the perspective the writer takes. Tell students to think of a role, or writer's perspective. Give students several minutes to think of the writer's role and to write it on their papers.

5. Explain to students that all writing has at least one audience and that a writer can determine who that audience is. Tell students to think of audiences for their stories. Give them a few minutes to think about their audiences and then to write them down.

6. Tell students that writing can take a variety of formats. There are many different types of writing other than books and magazines. Provide students with some ideas about formats for writing by duplicating and distributing the list that follows. Have students choose one of the writing formats or think of a different format for their writing and include that on their RAFT papers next to Format.

7. Finally, explain that an integral part of writing is the topic of the writing. Tell students that the topic of writing should be consistent with their role, audience, and format. Give students a few minutes to think about their writing topics and to write them on their RAFT frameworks.

8. After students have completed their RAFT frameworks, tell them to write one or more stories using the **R**ole, **A**udience, **F**ormat, and **T**opic that they selected. Students may need more than one day to write RAFT stories. After several students have written their RAFT stories, have them share the stories with the class.

9. See Appendix D for 549 Writing Formats.

Writing Formats

Advertisements
Advice columns
Allegories
Alphabet books
Anecdotes
Announcements
Apologies
Applications
Appointment books
Autobiographies
Autograph books

Ballots
Banners
Beauty tips
Billboards
Book jackets
Brochures
Bulletins
Bumper stickers

Captions
Cartoons
Catalogs
Certificates
Character sketches
Charts
Comics
Commentaries
Commercials
Computer programs
Contracts
Coupons

Debates
Definitions
Deposit slips
Diagrams
Diaries
Dictionaries
Directories

Editorials
Envelopes
Essays

Fables
Flyers
Folktales
Fortune cookies

Graphs
Greeting cards
Guidebooks

Horoscopes

Indexes
Interviews
Invitations
Itineraries

Jingles
Jokes
Jump rope rhymes
Junk mail

Lab reports
Letters
Lists
Lyrics

Maps
Memoirs
Memos
Menus
Messages
Minutes of meetings
Myths

Newsletters
Notes

Opinions

Paragraphs
Petitions
Plays
Postcards
Posters
Prescriptions
Puzzles

Questionnaires

Recipes
Record albums
Requests
Reviews
Riddles
Rules

Scripts
Signs
Slogans
Songs
Speeches
Summaries
Surveys

Tables
Telegraphs
Telephone directories
Tickets
Tongue twisters
Travelogues

Valentines

Want ads
Weather reports

Yearbooks
You Are There stories

TEACHING STRATEGY 2 ▶▶▶▶▶▶▶▶▶▶▶▶ Learning Logs

Learning Logs are journals that emphasize writing as a tool for learning. There are three major purposes for having students write in Learning Logs (Martin, 1992):

1. Learning Logs give students the opportunity to process and reinforce concepts learned in school.
2. Learning Logs provide students and teachers with documentation of students' learning.
3. Learning Logs give students the opportunity to review content information before they are tested.

Learning Logs are a powerful strategy for students to learn through writing.

⬦ Directions

1. Tell students that they will be writing in journals about content area subjects. Explain that writing can be a tool to learn more about any content subject.

2. Provide students with spiral notebooks to use as Learning Logs. Tell students that periodically you will be giving them writing assignments to complete in their Learning Logs. Explain that these pieces of writing will be assessed only for completion, not for their content. Emphasize that writing in Learning Logs is a tool for students to learn rather than an evaluation of learning.

3. Think of a variety of Learning Log assignments such as the Learning Log Ideas that follow. Make the assignment specific for the content that students should be learning.

4. Give students at least 10 minutes to write their responses in their Learning Logs.

Learning Log Ideas

Business

- Write a letter of application for a job.
- Write a newspaper want ad for a position.
- Develop a safety report on a new product.
- Write a profile of a new business.
- Write interview questions for a local entrepreneur.

Fine Arts

- Write a reaction to a favorite piece of art or music.
- Write an explanation of a work of art created by a student.
- Write a report on a visit to a museum, art gallery, or concert.
- Write a letter to an artist or musician.
- Write a comparison between different types of art or music.

Health

- Write about types of health careers.
- Write a response to an article on a health issue.
- Describe the health clubs in your community.
- Monitor your physical activity. Write a reaction.
- Create a play to emphasize healthy living.

Mathematics

- Describe a pattern you noticed during math class.
- Describe the exact steps you took to solve a problem.
- Describe your feelings about math.
- Describe the strategy you used to solve a problem.
- Describe a mathematician.

Science

- Describe the changes in the weather in your area of the country.
- Write sample journal entries of an award-winning scientist.
- Describe a day in the life of an insect.
- Describe your favorite biome.
- Observe the sky at various times of the day and night. Write about what you see.

Social Studies

- Write a monologue of a famous historical person's thoughts.
- Name a political figure you admire. Explain your choice.
- Write a daily log of the activities of a castle dog (or other animal).
- Pick a country to visit. Write what you know about that country.
- Choose any historical period that interests you. Write why you would or would not want to live in that time period.

TEACHING STRATEGY 3 ▶ ▶ ▶ ▶ ▶ ▶ **Writing Format Fiesta**

Students rarely pay attention to all of the types of writing that they use in their daily lives until you draw their attention to them. The Writing Format Fiesta strategy helps students notice the writing in their lives and helps them connect that writing to learning in content areas. Writing Format Fiesta is an explosion of writing formats that typically are not found in a particular area of learning. You can use this strategy to have students create new Writing Format Fiesta ideas or write using the ideas that are presented in the strategy.

⟷ Directions

1. Tell students that they will be using writing in new ways using the strategy Writing Format Fiesta. Explain to students that there are hundreds of writing formats that can be fun to use when writing. (See the chart that follows for examples.) Tell students that Writing Format Fiesta is a new way to think about writing to learn.

2. Explain to students that all pieces of writing have a format. That format can be books, magazine articles, newspaper articles, poems, and essays. Tell students that there are many other formats they could use when writing to learn. Provide students with the list of formats found in Teaching Strategy 1 or help students develop their own lists of formats. (Additional formats for writing can be found in Appendix D.)

3. Print the list of writing formats on posters and hang them around the room for students to use for inspiration.

4. Model an example of ways to connect writing formats with content learning by writing an example on the chalkboard or on an overhead transparency. For example, tell students that an agreement is a writing format. For students who have been studying the cutting of old growth forests, tell them that the following statement would be an example of a writing assignment that merges the format "agreement" and the content that is being learned in science class.

Writing Format Fiesta Assignment

Craft an agreement between loggers and environmentalists about how much timber to cut in a given year.

5. Divide the class into groups of three or four students. In the groups, have students create writing ideas that fit the formats using all of the content areas that you teach in your grade. Tell students that if they are unsure of the meanings of some of the writing format terms to look for the definitions of the terms in a dictionary.

6. After students have developed a list of ideas, have them choose three of them to write about within the next week. Provide adequate time for students to write in class.

WRITING FORMAT FIESTA EXAMPLES

Abridgment: Write an abridgment of a story you have read recently.
Address: Provide the address for the vertex angle in an isosceles triangle.
Advice column: Write an advice column for a new athlete in your sport.
Analogy: Write an analogy to describe the differences between WWI and WWII.
Anecdote: Write an anecdote about a molecule.
Announcement: Create an announcement for a musical event featuring a favorite band.
Anthem: Create words for an anthem about eating healthy foods.
Bedtime story: Write a bedtime story beginning: Once upon a time there was a square.
Biographical sketch: Write a biographical sketch about a political leader.
Boast: Write a boast about your knowledge about science.
Bumper sticker: Write a bumper sticker about an event in history.
Calendar quip: Make up a health saying, or quip, for every day in one month.
Catalog description: Create a catalog description for sports equipment.
Complaint: Write a letter of complaint about pollution to a member of Congress.
Diet: Develop a diet for a sumo wrestler.
Epilogue: Write the epilogue for your career as a geographer.
Explanation: Explain the associative property of addition.
Habit: Describe your reading habits.
Hagiography: Create a patron saint of algebra.
Hyperbole: Describe an athletic event using hyperbole.
Index: Create an index for the historical events of the past decade.
Insult: Create an insult for a character in a book you are reading.
Interview: Write interview questions for a biologist.
Justification: Write a justification for your favorite subject.
Letter: Write a letter to your favorite person in history.
Lie: Write a mathematical lie.
List: List famous paintings for sale at an auction.
Memory: Write your memory of learning to read.
Myth: List the misconceptions, or myths, you had about musicians.
Palindrome: Write a mathematical palindrome.
Pedigree: Write the pedigree for your favorite bird.
Poster: Make a poster of the highest mountain peak on each continent.
Prescription: Write a prescription for becoming a successful scientist.
Rules of etiquette: Create a list of rules of etiquette for zoo animals.
Sale notice: Design a sale notice for a clipper ship.
Self-description: Describe yourself in terms of the colors of the spectrum.
Speech: Write a speech for a group of astronauts before they leave for space.
Survival guide: Write a survival guide for living under the sea.
T-shirt: Create a T-shirt slogan about the earth.
Wanted poster: Develop a wanted poster about a war criminal.
Wise saying: Collect wise sayings about economics.
Wish: Write your wishes for the next generation.
Yearbook inscription: Write a yearbook inscription to you from a character in a book.
Yellow pages ad: Create a yellow pages ad for a new business.

Based on McIntosh, M. (1997). 500 writing formats. *Mathematics Teaching in the Middle School, 2,* 354–357.

Ideas and Activities

1. Tell students that they are constantly making observations and that these observations can be a rich source of writing topics. Have students list the classroom activities in which they are participating. For example, perhaps your class is observing the growth of plants under different growing conditions. List plant growth as one of the classroom activities. After students have listed classroom activities, have them choose an activity that interests them and create an Observational Notebook for the activity. Have them record their observations several times during the day.

2. Students can learn from the displays in the classroom by Writing the Room. Provide students with clipboards or stenographer's notebooks. Tell them to walk around the classroom writing what they see and what they have learned as evidenced by various displays around the room. After students have participated in Writing the Room, have them share their writing with a friend and compare their learning.

3. When introducing a new topic, have students participate in New Topic Preview. Write the name of the new topic on the chalkboard or on an overhead transparency. Tell students that they will be learning about the new topic. Under the name of the topic, list several terms or concepts associated with the topic. Have students read the terms. Then ask students to write what they know about the topic. Place the writing in their writing notebooks. After you have finished teaching the topic, have students read their New Topic Preview and think about how much they have learned.

4. The Internet has many web sites that provide ideas for students' writing. Tell students that when they are reading a web site they should think about what they have learned. Explain that writing can help students process information. To model writing after reading a web site, have students access the Internet Public Library and click on a site that interests them. Tell them to read an interesting section and to write their observations and ideas.

Technology Tip

Internet Public Library Youth Division

Web site for students to do experiments with Doctor Internet, tour a museum, read about books other students are reading, talk to authors, and find resources for science projects.

KIDPROJ
http://www.kidlink.org:80/kidproj/

5. Identify a topic in an instructional unit that students are in the process of learning. Write the name of the topic on the chalkboard or on an overhead transparency. Explain to students that they have learned about the topic but that you want them to process what they have learned by participating in Focused Free Writing. Tell students that in Focused Free Writing they can write whatever they want about the topic but that they need to write for the entire time allotted for the activity. Give students 5 to 10 minutes to write. After students have finished writing, collect the papers to determine what students know about the topic.

6. Many of the subjects students study involve instructions or directions. For example, when students play a game such as baseball, there are numerous rules that the participants must follow. Often these rules are not written. Tell students that they will be writing instructions or directions for their favorite game. Have them choose a game they like, think about the rules of the game, and write the instructions or directions in their journals. After students have finished writing, you may want to help students revise their writings and post the instructions or directions in the classroom.

7. Most students are not as familiar as adults are with taking minutes. Introduce the concept of minutes by explaining to students that minutes are an official record of a meeting. Show students an example of minutes of a meeting you attended. Tell students at the beginning of a class that you will be asking them to take minutes of the class. As students proceed through the class, have them write what they did and the amount of time it took. At the end of the day, divide the class into groups of three or four students. Have students compare copies of the class minutes that they wrote.

8. Copy the sheet of Exit Cards that follows, cut the sheet into individual cards, and give one to each student. On days when you want students to remember something specific that they learned, have them write an Exit Card at the end of the day. Tell students that before they can leave for the day they need to give you a completed Exit Card. Explain to students that they need to think about the things that they learned during the day. Then tell them to write what they learned, what they had trouble learning, and what they want to learn on the Exit Card and to give it to you when completed. Use the Exit Cards to assess what students learned and what you need to teach.

Exit Card

Name: _____ Date: _____

Today I learned:

Today I had trouble with:

Tomorrow I want to learn more about:

Exit Card

Name: _____ Date: _____

Today I learned:

Today I had trouble with:

Tomorrow I want to learn more about:

Exit Card

Name: _____ Date: _____

Today I learned:

Today I had trouble with:

Tomorrow I want to learn more about:

GOAL

To assess students' informal writing
assignments.

Background

Informal writing is a different kind of writing; it is practice with language so that students can build writing fluency. When you think about assessing informal writing, you need to define the purpose of the writing and the purpose of the assessment (Spandel & Stiggins, 1997). The purpose of informal writing is to have students become fluent writers by promoting self-discovery, by constructing meaning through responding, and by learning content material through writing. The assessments used for informal writing should reflect these goals.

Frank Smith (1988) wrote that assessment is the greatest danger in education. Nowhere is

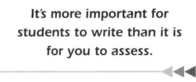

It's more important for students to write than it is for you to assess.

this more true than in the assessment of informal writing. If the purpose of informal writing is to encourage fluency, risk-taking, and creative language, then checking to see if students remembered to capitalize proper nouns is counterproductive to the purpose of the assignment. However, many teachers are uncomfortable leaving writings ungraded. Therefore, we have provided two ways to assess informal writing for you to use or adapt. When assessing students' informal writings, however, remember that it's more important for students to write than it is for you to assess. Save the rigorous assessment for other types of writing.

▶ Is it difficult for you to leave a paper ungraded?

INFORMAL WRITING SCALE

You can develop an Informal Writing Scale to fit your writing purposes. If you use this type of assessment, you will need to collect students' writing periodically and apply the assessment to their work. Some teachers find that occasionally using an Informal Writing Scale keeps students on their toes.

Directions

1. Duplicate and distribute the Informal Writing Scale that follows. Tell students that occasionally you will be assessing their informal writing with that scale.

2. Collect students' informal writing once every two weeks and assess it using the Informal Writing Scale.

Informal Writing Scale

1. Student has written the required amount.

3	2	1
Definitely	Partially	Minimally

2. Student has written about the topic.

3	2	1
Definitely	Partially	Minimally

3. Student has used acceptable conventions of language for the assignment.

3	2	1
Definitely	Partially	Minimally

4. Student has used interesting language.

3	2	1
Definitely	Partially	Minimally

5. Student was personally engaged in the writing.

3	2	1
Definitely	Partially	Minimally

INFORMAL WRITING RUBRIC

You can assess informal writing assignments using an Informal Writing Rubric (Beach, 1999). You can develop your own rubric to reflect your own teaching priorities. To use the Informal Writing Rubric that follows, have students complete a week's worth of informal writing assignments. Then apply the rubric to students' work.

Directions

1.   Duplicate and distribute the Informal Writing Rubric that follows. Tell students that you occasionally will be assessing their informal writing with this rubric.

2.   Collect students' informal writing once every two or three weeks and evaluate it using the Informal Writing Rubric.

Informal Writing Rubric

4	3	2	1
• Writes original, thoughtful papers • All assignments completed on time • Highly engaged in writing activities	• Writes interesting papers • Most assignments completed on time • Usually engaged in writing activities	• Writes solid papers • Some assignments completed on time • Sometimes engaged in writing activities	• Writes papers that exhibit little thought • Assignments rarely completed on time • Rarely engaged in writing activities
Date	Date	Date	Date
Date	Date	Date	Date
Date	Date	Date	Date
Date	Date	Date	Date
Date	Date	Date	Date
Date	Date	Date	Date

Chapter 4

Writing Content: Identifying Thoughts

"I know what I know and I write it."—Octavio Paz

Overview

"Writers don't improve their craft unless they have a real purpose, a real audience, and a real investment in their writing" (Fox, 1990, p. 47). Writing is, after all, a way for writers to express their thoughts and ideas. These thoughts and ideas are the content of writing. The content of writing depends on the writer's reasons for writing, the topic of the piece, and the audience for whom the piece is written.

When writers sit down at a desk with pen and paper or at a computer keyboard, they have decisions to make. Some of the first decisions writers make involve a writing plan. The process of planning has two steps:

1. The writer must understand the writing task. This task includes the outcome of the writing.
2. The writer must carry out the task by making decisions about topics, purposes, and audiences.

The time needed for each of these steps varies from writer to writer. Writers, therefore, first think about what they want to do and then try different ideas to make it happen (Hayes & Nash, 1996).

An example of a writer making decisions is a veterinarian's technician preparing a report on the status of the health of a dog. The outcome is the report, and the technician then needs to address the following questions:

Why am I writing this (purpose)?
What shall I write (topic)?
What do I know? What do I need to find out (ideas)?
Who will read this (audience)?

In the example of a technician reporting on the health of a dog, the technician is writing about the dog's health—with information coming from the dog's file, to be read by the veterinarian and the dog's owners—with the purpose of writing to inform. Similar decisions are made by all writers.

Students need to have opportunities to make writing decisions and develop personal responsibility for their writing. When asked, students responded that they would rather make writing decisions than have teachers make all of their decisions for them (Zaragoza & Vaughn, 1995). Students said that they liked to choose their own topics, decide on their audiences, and sign up to conference with their teachers. Students who are given ownership over writing decisions feel in control of their writing. These students are more motivated to write and they learn to act like writers.

When students have the chance to write for their own purposes about topics they choose for se-

"Writers don't improve their craft unless they have a real purpose, a real audience, and a real investment in their writing."

lected audiences, they perform at their best (Beaver, 1998). It is the teacher's role to provide students with instruction on ways to generate topics, discover purposes, and identify audiences. This chapter provides resources, teaching strategies, ideas, and activities to help teachers instruct students on how to make decisions about the content of their writing. Some ways to assess content also are included.

▶ Do you think this student has considered the audience for whom he is writing?

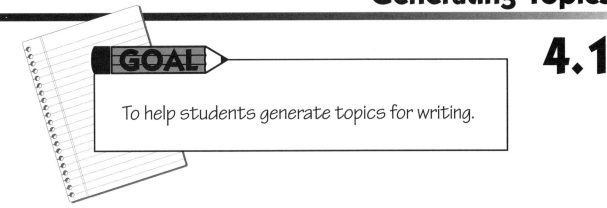

Generating Topics

GOAL

4.1

To help students generate topics for writing.

Background

"I don't know what to write about." This statement, echoed by many students, actually emphasizes a very important point. Content is the essence of writing. Every other part of writing—the organization, the mechanics, the style—takes a distant second place compared with the meat of writing, the content. Helping students generate topics for writing, therefore, is one of the key parts of writing instruction.

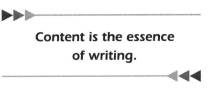

Content is the essence of writing.

There are three areas from which students can choose topics for writing: personal experiences, imagination, and outside knowledge.

PERSONAL EXPERIENCES. Some writing educators suggest that students should write primarily from their personal experiences (Graves, 1994). When writing from personal experiences, students are encouraged to look at their lives from a writer's point of view. What have they done? What do they want? What do they think? Students writing about personal experiences "read their worlds" (Freire & Macedo, 1987). They take situations, events, memories, and opinions and form them into stories and essays.

IMAGINATION. Writers can find topics in their imaginations. Where creative ideas originate is still somewhat of a mystery (Sharples, 1996). Some

people are able to take their background experiences and knowledge and organize them in unique ways.

Having students imagine topics, therefore, is not an easy instructional goal to achieve. However, students need to let their imaginations take them to new places. They need to dream new dreams. They need to invent new ideas. Students also need the freedom to find topics in their imaginations.

OUTSIDE KNOWLEDGE. Writers need to write about topics outside of themselves in addition to writing about their personal experiences and from their imaginations (Stotsky, 1995). To gather information for writing topics, students can read, write, listen, and learn about new subjects. They can question other people, interview them, and discuss new things. In short, students can learn new information. Then students can write about topics using this new knowledge.

In schools, teachers frequently assign topics for writing. However, best practice suggests that teachers should allow students to choose their own topics from time to time (Bromley, 1999). This section provides resources, teaching strategies, ideas, and activities you can use to help students think of their own writing topics and you can use to assign students topics to write about.

91

Teaching Strategy 1 ▶ ▶ ▶ ▶ ▶ **Examine the Possibilities**

There is a wealth of topics that students can write about. Some of these topics can be found in students' own personal experiences. Others will be part of students' imaginations or learning. Sometimes students should have the chance to write whatever they want. To select a topic, however, students need to Examine the Possibilities.

Directions

1. Tell students that they will be writing about any topic they choose. Remind them that writers often choose their own writing topics.

2. Before students select a topic, have them examine the possible topics in their lives by using the strategy Examine the Possibilities.

3. Duplicate and distribute the list that follows. Tell students that in order to think of topics for writing they should try some of the items from the list. Inform students that they will have three days to think of topics for writing. Remind students each day to try one or two of the items on the list. Give students class time if necessary.

4. After three days, ask students to write down their topics for writing. Then discuss the ways they generated their topics. If students used another activity to think of a topic, add that activity to the list.

Examine the Possibilities: Ways to Think of Writing Topics

- ▲ Read journals
- ▲ Talk with others
- ▲ Interview others
- ▲ Visualize stories and events
- ▲ Think about experiences
- ▲ Read books or magazines
- ▲ Free write
- ▲ Write five or more beginning sentences
- ▲ Doodle
- ▲ Outline
- ▲ Create lists
- ▲ Record dreams
- ▲ Attend plays
- ▲ Watch movies or television
- ▲ Look at pictures
- ▲ Explore the Internet

TEACHING STRATEGY 2 ▶ ▶ ▶ Let Me Tell You About . . .

Sometimes writers find their own writing topics by talking with others. Writers often have stories in their lives that they could tell, if they had someone to listen to them. Students can generate topics by talking with classmates. The strategy Let Me Tell You About . . . gives students the opportunity to talk about topics of interest. Through discussion, students can explore and expand topics for writing.

✛ Directions

1. Tell students that they will be writing about topics of their own choosing. Ask students if they have topics that they would like to write about. For those students who already have topics, ask them to begin writing. Those students who need to generate topics can participate in Let Me Tell You About . . . .

2. Duplicate and distribute the list that follows. Ask students to check three items on the list. Explain that they will be discussing their checked items with their classmates as one way to explore ideas for writing.

3. Divide the class into groups of two or three students. Ask students to bring their Let Me Tell You About . . . lists to the group.

4. Ask one student to volunteer to begin sharing. Tell the student volunteer to give the list to the other members of the group. Direct the members of the group to choose an item on the list. Give the student volunteer time to talk about the subject or to tell a story. Have the group members discuss whether there is a topic for writing in that discussion. After the first student has found a topic, provide time for the other group members to discuss their lists.

Name_____ Date_____

Let Me Tell You About . . .

Please ask me about one of these ideas that I've checked:

_____ my family

_____ my pet

_____ something I like to do

_____ a special friend

_____ an exciting event

_____ a fun party

_____ things I don't like

_____ a TV show

_____ being lost

_____ my neighborhood

_____ my lessons

_____ a hero

_____ things I like a lot

_____ my town

_____ things I collect

_____ a time I was afraid

_____ a good story

_____ my favorite food

_____ a special place

_____ a vacation or trip

_____ a time I helped someone

_____ ways I've changed

_____ when I was little

_____ places I've lived

_____ my favorite sport

_____ a computer game

_____ a favorite book

_____ a special toy or game

TEACHING STRATEGY 3 ▶ ▶ ▶ ▶ ▶ ▶ Parent Recommended Topics

Parents are a natural source of ideas for their children's writings. After all, most parents have known their children from birth. Parents have observed their children doing funny things, having adventures, learning, and growing. When asked, parents may be able to share many ideas for students' writings.

Directions

1. Tell students that you will be sending a letter to their parents asking them for some of their favorite memories to use as writing topics. Ask students to alert their parents in advance that a letter will be sent home.

2. Duplicate or adapt the following letter and send it home with students. Give parents at least three days to think of topics before returning the letter to school. After three or four days, ask students to place their parents' letters in students' writing folders.

3. For parents who cannot read English or do not want to complete the letter tell students they can give the letter to a friend or to a relative. Or students may be able to translate the letter for their parents. Tell students that a third option is to complete the list of topics themselves.

4. When students are asked to select topics for writing, have them refer to their Parent Recommended Topics list.

PARENT RECOMMENDED TOPICS

Dear Parent,

   In school, students often have the opportunity to choose their own topics for writing. Because you have more knowledge about your child than just about anyone else, I would like you to list ten possible writing topics for your child. To identify writing topics, think for a moment about your child. Think of a funny story, a trip, or a learning experience your child will remember. Or think of the times your child got into trouble. Any of these ideas could make good topics for writing. You will love the stories your child will write about these topics.

   Please list ten writing topics and return this letter to school with your child in three days. If you have any questions, don't hesitate to ask your child or to call me at school.

Sincerely,

Potential Writing Topics

1. _____

2. _____

3. _____

4. _____

5. _____

6. _____

7. _____

8. _____

9. _____

10. _____

 # Ideas and Activities

1. Stock a backpack or a briefcase with writing tools such as markers, colored pencils, crayons, scissors, glue, a stapler, various sizes of colored paper, lined paper, unlined paper, and blank books of various sizes. Send the backpack or briefcase home with students on a rotating basis. Have students use the writing tools to take notes of experiences and events outside of school. Allow students to have the backpack or briefcase for two or three days. After two or three days, have students return the backpack or briefcase with their notes. Have students share their writing ideas with the class. Then have students place their writing notes in their writing folders.

2. Tell students that some of the best writing topics can surface while they are sleeping. These nighttime topics are the result of the mind remembering stories and events subconsciously. Create a note on an index card that says "I remember. . . ." Give a copy of the note card to each student. Have students place the note cards by their beds. Ask students to read the note cards before going to sleep. Tell students to have a pencil or pen next to the cards. Tell students that if they think of an idea when they wake up they should write it on the note cards. Have students return the note cards to school the next day. Invite students to share the ideas they generated as they slept.

3. Save old greeting cards and place them in a box. Cover the inside message with lined paper. Tell students that they can think of ideas for writing from looking at the cover of the greeting card. Have students choose a greeting card, look at the cover, and imagine a story. Then have young students write the story inside the card. Older students should write a summary of their story inside the card and the entire story on additional paper.

4. The Internet has a wealth of ideas for writing topics. Have students explore the Internet to learn about new things and to write about them. The CD-ROM "Around the Web in 80 Minutes" teaches students how to use the Internet.

➤ Technology Tip

 ### Around the Web in 80 Minutes

A multimedia CD-ROM instructional tool for teaching both novices and experts how to use the Internet. A key function of the software is to dynamically assess users' skills and adjust instruction to their needs.

Intelligent Systems, Inc.
http://www.gkis.com
1-888-581-9307

5. Another fertile area for writing topics is "First Day" topics. Have students create a list with the title "First Day." Tell students about your first day teaching or your first day on a summer vacation. Explain to students that often first days are memorable and that they can make good topics for writing. Divide the class into groups of three or four students and have students brainstorm First Days in their lives. After groups of students have thought of ideas, have students share their ideas with the entire class. Create a First Day list and display it in the classroom. Tell students that when thinking of writing topics they can use the list as a source for ideas. A list of "Last Day" topics could also be developed.

 6. Create several new proverbs for students or use the list that follows. Write the proverbs on the chalkboard or on an overhead transparency. Read the proverbs with the students. Explain that a proverb is a wise saying. Divide the class into groups of three or four students. Have students create their own proverbs. After students have thought of several proverbs, share them with the class. Have students select one or more proverbs to use as the topic for a story.

- There's no place like www.home.com.
- Oh, what a tangled web site we weave when first we practice.
- Give a man a fish and you feed him for a day; teach him to use the Net and he will be busy for weeks.
- Computer users and their leisure time are soon parted.

7. Have students write to music. Select a common topic on which students will focus. Stimulate students' minds with pictures and trade books. Select a piece of music that you think resembles the topic at hand. Play the music and have students list thoughts and ideas. These ideas then can be turned into writing topics.

8. Keys are ubiquitous in our society. Bring a key to class. Show students the key. Ask students to imagine what the key will unlock, who will use it, and where it will be used. Have students list as many ideas as they can. Tell them to place the lists in their writing folders to use as story starters.

9. Tell students that one of the ways they can think of topics is to read books. Some books have plots that return where they started. These circular plots are easy to replicate in new ways. Read a book with a circular plot or choose one from the list that follows. Point out the ways in which the plot returns to its starting place. Have students write stories that use this technique. Some books with circular plots are on the list that follows.

Books with Circular Plots

Compiled by Jenny Bolander

Arnold, T. (1988)
Ollie forgot.
New York: Dial.
(Grades K–2)

Brett, J. (1989)
The mitten.
New York: Putnam.
(Grades K–3)

Duquennoy, J. (1994)
The ghost's dinner.
Racine, WI: Artists & Writers Guild.
(Grades K–2)

Hutchins, P. (1968)
Rosie's walk.
New York: Macmillan.
(Grades K–2)

Kellogg, S. (1972)
Won't somebody play with me?
New York: Dial.
(Grades 1–3)

Morgan, A. (1994)
Sadie and the snowman.
Toronto: Kids Can Press.
(Grades K–2)

Neitzle, S. (1995)
The dress I'll wear to the party.
New York: Mulberry.
(Grades K–2)

Numeroff, L. (1996)
If you give a mouse a cookie.
New York: HarperCollins.
(Grades K–2)

Numeroff, L. (1998)
If you give a pig a pancake.
New York: Laura Geringer.
(Grades K–2)

Skorpen, L. (1998)
We were tired of living in a house.
New York: Putnam.
(Grades K–2)

Titherington, J. (1982)
Pumpkin, pumpkin.
New York: Scholastic.
(Grades K–2)

VanAllsburg, C. (1981)
Jumanji.
Boston: Houghton Mifflin.
(Grades 3–6)

VanLaan, N. (1995)
The big fat worm.
New York: Knopf.
(Grades K–2)

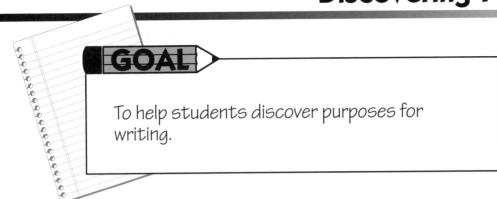

GOAL

To help students discover purposes for writing.

Background

Why do people write? They write for as many different reasons as there are pieces of writing. Writers usually begin composing texts by having one or more purposes for writing. Their purpose may be to inform a relative about a wedding shower, to explain to the public the reasons why a school bond needs to be passed, or to entertain readers with a story. Writers' purposes should be a guideline that helps writers know what to say and to keep them on target (Prain, 1995).

The nature of writing, however, resists attempts to clarify purposes (Smith, 1990). Writers can set out intending to write with the primary purpose of informing and have their writing change in midstream to that of explaining. The process of writing creates its own realities as writers use initial purposes to direct the stream of words. As writers compose words, purposes may change.

All writing activities, however, should begin with some sort of real purpose, even if that purpose

changes during writing. Writers need to have some reason to write, as fuzzy as it is, before they can proceed with the process of writing. In schools, however, the purposes for writing often do not go beyond completing an assigned task (Bright, 1995). Writing for an assignment rarely promotes the kinds of purposes writers should bring to writing situations.

Students in schools should have the opportunity to write for their own purposes. When writing for individual reasons, students can learn how real writers discover and refine their purposes while writing. That doesn't mean that teachers should never assign writing projects. However, when teachers assign writing projects, they should help students understand the purposes for the project. This section provides resources, teaching strategies, ideas, and activities to help students discover purposes for writing.

TEACHING STRATEGY 1 ▶ ▶ ▶ ▶ ▶ Finding Reasons to Write

There are a multitude of writing purposes and reasons to write. We live immersed in so much print that we often take for granted the amount of writing that is in our environment. We live in a world that is filled with writing. Each piece of writing was created for a specific purpose. The strategy Finding Reasons to Write can help students become more aware of the writing in their worlds and the purposes behind that writing.

⟐ Directions

1. Tell students that there are many reasons to write. Explain to students that when they begin using Finding Reasons to Write they can discover many purposes for writing.

2. Duplicate and distribute the Finding Reasons to Write list that follows. Fold or cut the list in half so that students see only the left-hand side. Give a copy of the list to each student.

3. Read the Finding Reasons to Write list with students. For each reason to write, have students generate ideas about the types of writings that match the purposes. After students have shared a number of ideas, copy the Types of Writings on the chalkboard or on an overhead transparency and have students read the types of writing suggested on the right-hand side of the list. Tell students this list contains examples of types of writing. Explain to students that there are many more types of writing. Have students add additional ideas to the list.

4. Tell students to keep their own lists of Finding Reasons to Write and place them in their writing folders. Remind students to read their lists when they are searching for purposes to write.

FINDING REASONS TO WRITE*

Purposes	Types of Writings	Purposes	Types of Writings
To record events	Lists Diaries Autobiographies Commentaries Letters Minutes of meetings Family histories	To entertain or amuse	Quizzes Jokes Bumper stickers
To explain	Charts Recipes Brochures Invitations Textbooks Rules	To narrate	Fables Stories Myths
		To invent	Plays Poems Song lyrics Slogans
To analyze	Theories Arguments Essays	To inform	Announcements Book jackets News broadcasts Labels Catalogues Weather reports
To persuade	Applications Instructions Advertisements Signs Warnings CD covers	To find out	Surveys Interviews Questionnaires
To invite a response	Complaints Invitations Notices Notes	To invite reflection	Questions Quizzes Quotations
		To summarize	Postcards Verdicts Signs
To predict	Graphs Forecasts Timetables	To give an opinion	Editorials Viewpoints Graffiti
To command or request	Directions Rules Warnings	To express gratitude	Thank you notes

*Adapted from Learning Media. (1992). *Dancing with the pen: The learner as writer*. Wellington, New Zealand: Ministry of Education.

TEACHING STRATEGY 2 ▶ ▶ ▶ ▶ ▶ ▶ ▶ ▶ **Authors' Intentions**

Authors often reveal their purposes when they write about themselves (Prain, 1995). To discover Authors' Intentions, students can read autobiographies or personal experience stories and try to identify the authors' purposes. As students learn about the various purposes authors have for writing, they can adapt the authors' purposes to use in their own writings.

 ## Directions

1. Have students bring to class a short autobiography or have them write their own personal experience stories.

2. Tell students that when they read stories about authors' lives they can predict Authors' Intentions. Explain that learning about the intentions and purposes authors have for writing can help students add to their repertoires new reasons to write.

 3. Divide the class into groups of three or four students. Give each student a short autobiography or a personal experience story written by a classmate. Have students read the stories silently. After they have read the stories, have students summarize the stories to the members of their group.

4. After students have summarized the stories, have them predict the intentions of the authors. To provide students with some ideas about Authors' Intentions, duplicate and distribute the list that follows. Explain to students that the list contains some, but not all, of the purposes for which authors write.

 5. Have students add more Authors' Intentions to the list using the list as a trigger for ideas. Have each member of the group share ideas with the class. Display the completed list so students can use the ideas as they think of purposes for writing.

Authors' Intentions*	
to boast	to justify self
to confess mistakes	to make a joke of past experiences
to discover aspects of self	to make an accurate record of past events
to exact revenge	to make excuses
to express anger	to rewrite the past
to give advice	to set the record straight
to inspire	to tell a good yarn
to invent a new identity	

*Adapted from Prain, V. (1995). Helping students identify how writers signal purpose in autobiographical writing. *Journal of Reading, 38*, 476–481.

TEACHING STRATEGY 3 ▶▶▶▶▶▶▶▶ Matching Purpose to Format

The purposes for writing will influence the format writers use. The format, in turn, influences the writers' purposes. For example, when a cook writes a recipe, the purpose for the writing is to list the ingredients and directions to make something to eat. Most recipes follow a certain writing format. When a cook writes a recipe, the format will guide the way the cook writes. The recipe will not contain a critique of the cookies. A different writing format would accomplish that purpose. When students learn how to match their writing purposes to the format for writing, they can make their own writing purposes more clear.

✛ Directions

1. Tell students that their writing purposes should match the format they choose for writing.

2. Divide the class into groups of three or four students. Duplicate and distribute Appendix D, 549 Writing Formats. Provide each group with a copy of the Appendix and a dictionary of literary terms. You also may wish to use only a portion of Appendix D.

3. Have students select 10 different writing formats. Tell students that if they aren't familiar with the format to look up its definition in a literary dictionary or an unabridged dictionary.

▶ If a recipe is not written clearly, would cookies still be tasty?

4. Have students write their lists in alphabetical order on the left-hand side of a piece of paper. Then have students brainstorm writing purposes for each of the writing formats. Have students list the purposes for writing on the right-hand side of the page as in the following example

Formats	Purposes	Formats	Purposes
1. advertisement	to inform	6. guarantee	to promise
2. baby book	to remember	7. junk mail	to persuade
3. caption	to clarify	8. magic spell	to change
4. commentary	to comment	9. plea	to ask
5. euphemism	to improve	10. wager	to predict

5. After the groups have finished listing writing formats and purposes, have members of each group share their lists with the class. Display the lists on a poster. Remind students to match their writing purposes and writing formats.

 **Ideas and Activities**

1. Invite young students to write a class letter to Mickey Mouse for his November 18, 1928, birthday. Ask students to discuss purposes for writing to Mickey. Provide examples of purposes, such as to tell Mickey they like his ears or to wish him a happy birthday. Then compose a class letter using the purposes the students suggested. Send letters to the address that follows.

    Mickey Mouse
    1313 Harbor Blvd.
    Box 3232
    Anaheim, CA 92803

2. Tell students that writers need to have an identified purpose for writing. Divide the class into groups of three or four students. Have students develop several purpose statements that would be considered too vague. Model examples for students such as "to write a story" or "to finish an assignment." Have students generate other purpose statements that are vague. After students have created lists of purpose statements, have them share the statements with the class. Model ways in which the purpose statements could be refined so that they are more specific, such as "to write a story about my brother's stay in the hospital." Remind students that authors may not have exact purposes for writing before beginning writing; nevertheless, their purposes should not remain vague.

3. Have students write for a variety of purposes. Tell students that their writing can be published in a variety of sources; one such source is the Internet. Divide the class into groups of three or four students. Have groups choose different purposes for writing, such as to tell a story about a class event, to write a poem about a class experience, to draw a picture about a class pet, or to review books read in class. Discuss the purposes for writing. Have students complete their writing projects and submit them to the "Looking Glass Gazette" web site.

Technology Tip

Looking Glass Gazette

Web site that publishes stories, poems, artwork, book reviews, and creative work of students up to age 13.

www.cowboy.net/~mharper/LGG.html

---

4. Tell students that some of the purposes for writing can be to capture the moment, to share feelings, to develop a sense of wonder, to savor life, to share experiences, and to be heard (Dakos, 1989). Write these writing purposes on the chalkboard or on an overhead transparency. Have students choose one writing purpose. Divide the class into groups based on writing purposes. Have students generate a list of topics that fit their writing purposes. Ask members of the group to share their lists with the class. Display the lists so students can use them during writing time.

5. Tell students that different professions have different purposes for writing. Provide a number of examples, such as: attorneys write legal briefs, restaurant managers write flyers or menus, and factory workers write production ideas. Divide the class into groups of three or four students. Have groups of students generate lists of professions. Share the lists. As a class, brainstorm purposes for writing for the professions mentioned.

6. Discuss authors' biographies with students so they can begin to understand how authors' life experiences have an impact on their writing purposes (Johns & Lenski, 1997). Many authors' biographies also discuss how other writers influenced the authors and their desire to write. Brief biographical sketches of many popular children's authors are included in the books that follow.

   Hill, S. (1994). *Books alive!* Winnipeg, Manitoba: Peguis.

   Kovacs, D. (1995). *Meet the authors.* New York: Scholastic.

   Silvey, A. (1995). *Children's books and their creators.* Boston: Houghton Mifflin.

7. Tell students that some stories and plays have a problem that the characters will resolve. This problem can be a situation or a conflict. It can be subtle or clear. Explain to students that the problem of a story can be developed in four ways: the conflict between a character and nature, the conflict between a character and society, the conflict between characters, and the conflict within a character. Tell students that the purposes that authors have for writing stories will influence the types of problems they select. Read a story from the following lists that illustrates each of the four ways of structuring problems in fiction. Ask students to identify the problem in the story and to discuss the author's purposes for writing a story with that problem. Remind students when they write their own stories to create problems or situations that reflect their authoring purposes.

Conflict between a Character and Nature

Compiled by Jenny Bolander

Babbitt, N. (1995)
Tuck everlasting.
O'Fallon, MO: Book Lures.
(Grades 3–6)

Byars, B. (1996)
Midnight fox.
New York: Puffin.
(Grades 3–6)

Byars, B. (1996)
Summer of the swans.
New York: Puffin.
(Grades 3–6)

Cottonwood, J. (1995)
Quake: A novel.
New York: Scholastic.
(Grades 3–6)

Davis, D. (1989)
The secret of the seal.
New York: Random House.
(Grades 4–6)

George, J. (1991)
My side of the mountain.
New York: Puffin.
(Grades 3–6)

Paulsen, G. (1996)
Hatchet.
New York: Aladdin.
(Grades 4–6)

Taylor, T. (1995)
The cay.
New York: Camelot.
(Grades 4–6)

Taylor, T. (1995).
Timothy of the cay.
New York: Avon.
(Grades 4–6)

Conflict between a Character and Society

Compiled by Jenny Bolander

Creech, S. (1996)
Walk two moons.
New York: Harper Trophy.
(Grades 3–6)

Cushman, K. (1996)
Midwife's apprentice.
New York: Harper Trophy.
(Grades 4–6)

Fleischman, S. (1994)
The whipping boy.
Orlando: Harcourt Brace.
(Grades 4–6)

Kellogg, S. (1973)
The island of the skog.
New York: Puffin.
(Grades 2–4)

Konigsburg, E.L. (1998)
The view from Saturday.
New York: Scholastic.
(Grades 3–6)

Lowry, L. (1990)
Number the stars.
New York: Yearling Books.
(Grades 4–6)

Lowry, L. (1993)
The giver.
Boston: Houghton Mifflin.
(Grades 4–6)

Naylor, P. (1992)
Shiloh.
New York: Dell.
(Grades 3–6)

Spinnelli, J. (1990)
Maniac Magee.
New York: Little Brown.
(Grades 4–6)

Conflict between Characters

Compiled by Jenny Bolander

Estes, E. (1990)
A hundred dresses.
New York: Scholastic.
(Grades K–3)

Griffith, H. (1997)
Alex and the cat.
New York: Greenwillow.
(Grades K–2)

Hoban, R. (1970)
A bargain for Francis.
New York: Scholastic.
(Grades K–2)

Kline, S. (1992)
Mary Maroney.
New York: Bantam, Doubleday.
(Grades 2–4)

Marshall, J. (1997)
George and Martha:
The complete story of two
best friends.
Boston: Houghton Mifflin.
(Grades K–3)

Marthis, S. (1996)
The hundred penny box.
Boston: Houghton Mifflin.
(Grades 4–6)

Paterson, K. (1994)
The flip-flop girl.
New York: Dutton.
(Grades 3–6)

Smith, R. (1984)
The war with Grandpa.
New York: Dell.
(Grades 3–6)

White, E.B. (1995)
Charlotte's web.
New York: Harper Trophy.
(Grades 2–4)

Yolen, J. (1995)
The ballad of the pirate queens.
San Diego: Harcourt Brace.
(Grades 4–6)

Conflict within a Character

Compiled by Jenny Bolander

Blume, J. (1991)
Tales of a fourth grade nothing.
New York: Dell.
(Grades 2–4)

Gwynne, F. (1990)
Pondlarker.
New York: Simon & Schuster.
(Grades K–3)

Haddad, C. (1998)
Meet Calliope Day.
New York: Delacorte.
(Grades 3–6)

Hendry, D. (1993)
Back soon.
Mahwah, NJ: Troll.
(Grades K–3)

Laskay, K. (1996)
Lunch bunnies.
Boston: Little Brown.
(Grades K–2)

McManus, P. (1996)
Never cry "Arp!"
New York: Henry Holt.
(Grades 3–6)

Numeroff, L. (1996)
Why a disguise.
New York: Simon & Schuster.
(Grades K–2)

Rylant, C. (1991)
Henry and Midge and the bedtime thumps.
New York: Simon & Schuster.
(Grades 1–3)

Spinelli, J. (1998)
Wringer.
New York: HarperCollins.
(Grades 4–6)

Waber, B. (1988)
Ira says goodbye.
Boston: Houghton Mifflin.
(Grades K–2)

> To help students identify appropriate audiences for their writing.

Background

If you want to give the best possible gift to a writer, give an audience (Elbow, 1981). An audience is any person who reads a writer's work. Audiences can be small and private, or they can be large and public. Students can write for a pen pal—a known audience of one. They also can write for publication on the Internet—an unknown audience of many. Audiences vary with the purposes that a writer has for a piece of writing. The important thing about audiences, however, is that they exist.

Writing is primarily a social act. The main purpose of writing is to be read by another person. Students need to have a variety of real audiences for their writing because it is the audience that shapes a piece of writing. As writers visualize their audiences, they decide what to include in a piece of writing, what to omit, and whether their writing needs to be scholarly or conversational. It is the awareness of audiences that drives many writing decisions (Dahl & Farnan, 1998).

Unfortunately, most students in schools write for one audience, the teacher. In a large study Britton *et al.* (1975) identified four main audiences for students' writings:

- themselves
- the teacher
- a known audience (such as other students)
- an unknown audience (such as for publication).

Of the 2,000 pieces of writing these scholars read, over 95% of them were written for the teacher as the audience.

Britton and his colleagues also distinguished between the roles a teacher could take as an audience. The teacher could be a real audience, someone interested in reading the piece of writing, or the teacher could be a pseudo-audience, someone who reads the writing as an examiner. Over half of all of the pieces of writing in the study were written for the teacher in the role of teacher-as-examiner rather than for a real audience.

▶ Is this student writing for an audience of one—the teacher?

Students understand that when a teacher reads their writings in the role of teacher-as-examiner, the teacher is not a real audience. When students consistently write for the teacher as their audience, they have difficulty developing a sense of *audience awareness*. Audience awareness is when writers think about their audiences while writing (Rubin, 1998). Writers who think about their audi-

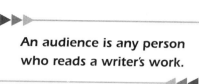

An audience is any person who reads a writer's work.

ences care about their writing, because they know that their writing is a vehicle for communicating thoughts and ideas to someone else. It is because of readers that writers write. This section, therefore, contains resources, teaching strategies, ideas, and activities to help students identify appropriate audiences when they write.

TEACHING STRATEGY 1 ▶ ▶ ▶ ▶ ▶ ▶ Targeting an Audience

When students write for a real audience, they are more deeply motivated to write (Hubbard, 1985). To target an audience is a challenge for students because they frequently write only for their teachers. Therefore, students need to brainstorm a list of audiences for their writing before they can target appropriate audiences for their work. Helping students find audiences for their writing reinforces the real reason for writing—to communicate thoughts and ideas to readers.

Directions

1. Tell students that when they write they should write with the intention that someone else will read their work. Explain that, before students decide exactly what to write, they need to target an audience to read their writing.

2. Duplicate the list of Audiences for Students' Writings that follows and distribute it to students. Tell students that this is a partial list of people for whom they can write.

3. Read the list together in class. Think carefully about the possibilities of the audiences and about whether students could write to a particular audience. List these topics for writing after the appropriate audience.

4. Tell students that this list is not complete, that there are other ideas for audiences for students' writing. Divide the class into groups of three or four students. Have students generate additional audiences to add to the list.

5. Display the amended list in a prominent place in the classroom. Tell students that as they think of additional audiences they should add them to the list.

6. As students begin a piece of writing, have them refer to the list of audiences and choose an audience that fits the topic of their writing.

Audiences for Students' Writings

1. Students in your class
2. Students in other classes in the school
3. Students in other local schools
4. Students in classes in other states
5. Students in other countries
6. Students identified via the Internet
7. Administrators in the school
8. Support staff in the school (cooks, crossing guards, secretaries)
9. School board members
10. Classroom or hall displays
11. Family
12. Relatives or friends
13. Community newspapers
14. Community members
15. City officials
16. State or federal representatives
17. TV stations
18. Governmental officials
19. Local businesses
20. Local organizations
21. Travel bureaus
22. Chambers of commerce
23. Foreign embassies
24. Classroom publications
25. Literary journals
26. Waiting rooms in dentists' or doctors' offices
27. Public libraries
28. Writing contests
29. Authors of books
30. Heroes
31. Pen pals
32. Local radio stations

From Susan Davis Lenski and Jerry L. Johns, *Improving Writing: Resources, Strategies, and Assessments*. Copyright © 2000 by Kendall/Hunt Publishing Company (1-800-247-3458). May be reproduced for noncommercial educational purposes.

Teaching Strategy 2 ▶ ▶ ▶ ▶ ▶ ▶ ▶ ▶ ▶ ▶ ▶ Writing Letters to Public Figures

Most students are intrigued by public figures such as sports heroes, movie stars, singers, and authors. Often, students would like to write to their heroes to tell them about their lives, to ask them questions, and to proclaim their adoration. Public figures, therefore, can be a truly authentic audience for students' writing. We can encourage students to write to real audiences, such as public figures, by helping students find ways to contact them. While students are pouring out their hearts to their heroes, many of our writing goals are accomplished: students are writing for real purposes, expressing themselves in written language, and writing to real audiences.

 Directions

1. Tell students that they can write letters to their heroes, that writing letters is an excellent form of communication, and that public figures are authentic audiences.

2. Have students identify public figures to whom they would like to write. Assist students in finding addresses for their heroes. You can find addresses by searching the Internet or by contacting a publisher or agent. Tell students who are interested in writing to a basketball player that you have addresses for the major basketball teams. For students interested in writing to basketball players, duplicate Appendix C, Basketball Teams' Addresses, and distribute it to them.

3. After students have identified a public figure to whom they would like to write, have them tell the class the name of their audience. If more than one student wants to write to the same person, ask those students to work together.

4. Tell students to think about their audiences and to list questions that they have for them. Have a student identify a public figure, such as Steve Kerr, a basketball player. Write the name of the public figure on the chalkboard or on an overhead transparency. Have the class volunteer questions for the public figure such as the ones that follow.

Questions for Steve Kerr
1. How do you like the team you're playing on now?
2. How does this team compare to the Chicago Bulls?
3. What was it like to play with Michael Jordan?
4. How did you learn to shoot those three-point shots?
5. What is it like to be on another championship team?

5. After students have contributed questions for one public figure, have them develop questions for their own writing. Give students several minutes to think of questions.

6. Have students write letters to their heroes, beginning with an introduction of themselves and then moving to the questions they have for their heroes. End the letters with a kind or funny remark and the students' home or school addresses.

7. Send the letters and wait for replies. Encourage students to share replies to their letters with their classmates. You may want to display the replies on a bulletin board.

TEACHING STRATEGY 3 ▶ ▶ ▶ ▶ ▶ Publishing in Magazines

An acceptance letter! Hooray! Having a piece of writing accepted for publication in a magazine or journal can be a real thrill. Seeing your name in print and knowing that your work has passed muster is an authentic writing boost. Publishing in a magazine or journal means that your writing is being read by a public audience, an audience much wider than your own circle of friends. This excitement can become a regular part of your classroom when you encourage students to send their writing to magazines and journals for publication. Knowing the ground rules for getting student writing published helps. But beware. Sending a piece of writing to a journal can also result in a rejection letter. The assistant editor of *Highlights* receives nearly 2,000 drawings and 500 poems each month, but they publish only 12 drawings and 12 poems in each issue (Kellaher, 1999). It's a good idea to have a back-up plan.

⟷ Directions

1. Tell students that there are many magazines and journals that publish students' writing. Explain to students that some of the authors of the writing in the magazines and journals are young people just like themselves.

2. Discuss the roles of the authors and their audiences. Explain that when students are reading magazines and journals they are the audience. Tell students that they can also be the author of a published piece of writing for others to read.

3. Duplicate copies of Appendix B, Audiences for Student Writing, and distribute copies to students. Tell students that the magazines and journals on this list have published students' writing in the past and could be an appropriate audience for some of their work.

4. Ask students if they are familiar with any of the publications on the list from Appendix B. Encourage students to discuss what they know about the publications. Have students bring copies of publications to class.

5. Ask students if any other publications on the list from Appendix B could be potential outlets for their own writing. Tell students that they need to read the specifications carefully before they choose an outlet for their writing.

6. Have a student choose a publication for the class to examine. Write the name and specifications of the publication on the chalkboard or on an overhead transparency as in the following example. Ask students to identify the age range, the focus of the magazine, and the types of writing that are published.

Cobblestone (ages 8–15)
Editorial & Ordering Address:
Cobblestone Publishing, Inc.
7 School Street
Peterborough, NH 03458
603-924-7209
Fax: 603-924-7380
E-mail: http://www.cobblestonepub.com
(stories, poems)

7. Ask students to select several possible publications from the list in Appendix B. Make arrangements to order sample copies of those publications for your classroom or school library. After receiving the publications, have students carefully read them to determine whether they would be good outlets for their writing.

8. Have students select a list of three publications that would be appropriate for a piece of writing. Ask students to rank the publications in the order of appropriateness. Then have students copy submission information for each of the publications.

9. Encourage students to send in a piece of writing to the first publication on their lists. Monitor students' submissions to make sure they have included all of the information the editor requested, such as a self-addressed stamped envelope (SASE). Tell students that they can submit their writing to only one publication at a time.

10. Wait for the responses from the editors. While waiting, reassure students that, if their writing is not accepted, they can submit it to other publications. When you receive letters from editors, stay calm. If a student's writing is accepted, celebrate. If a piece of writing is rejected, help students learn to take it in stride and try again with another publication. Remind students that submitting writing for publication is a risky venture.

 # Ideas and Activities

1. Tell students that you will be incorporating an Author's Chair (Graves & Hansen, 1983) as a way to share writings with members of the class. Set up a chair or stool in a prominent place in the classroom. Provide students with a small microphone so that their audience will hear their reading. At a prescribed time, such as 10 minutes before lunch, ask students to volunteer to read in the Author's Chair. Tell students that they can read an entire piece of writing or a section of their writing. Before students read in the Author's Chair, have them think about their audience, other students in the class. Tell students that they need to be sensitive to what their audience will want to hear and that, by reading overly long passages, they may lose the interest of their audience. Remind students that the Author's Chair is a way for them to share their writing with a known audience.

2. Invite students to share parts of their writing through the activity Read into the Circle. Gather students together into a circle. Tell students to bring their most recent pieces of writing. Explain that sharing parts of writing with an audience and gauging its reactions is valuable feedback to writers. Tell students to choose a stellar sentence from their writing to share with other students. Have one student volunteer to read a sentence to the class. Wait at least 30 seconds before moving to the next reader. During the wait time, ask the reader to look at the faces of the audience and think about whether the sentence produced the desired results. Then have another student Read into the Circle.

3. Remind students that their families are important audiences for their writing. Explain that many homes have a message board or a writing pad next to the telephone or on the refrigerator. Tell students that messages are writings that have an immediate audience. Bring an erasable message board to class. Write a message to the students on the board, such as "Take out your social studies book." Have them read the message and follow the directions. Then ask students if they have message boards at home. If students do not have an identifiable message board, encourage students and families to create a message board to communicate with each other through writing (Laster & Conte, 1998/1999).

4. Tell students that they will be writing for an audience in their school. Pair younger students with older students, such as students in first grade with students in fifth grade. Have the younger students dictate stories to the older students, who transcribe the stories using the language of the storytellers. Then have the older students write the stories in book form with a title page and illustrations. Arrange a time for the older students to share their stories with the younger students as the audience. Reinforce the idea that sharing writing with students in different grades is a way for students to participate in being writers, readers, and audiences (Bajtelsmit & Naab, 1994).

5. Once a week have students write a letter to you. Give students a packet of paper appropriate for letter writing with enough paper for four letters each month. You might want to give young students a few words to begin their letter, such as "Summer was fun because. . . ." Respond briefly to each of the letters. Save the letters in file folders. At the end of the school year, return each student's letters. Give students time to read through their letters and to note the writing progress they made during the year.

6.   Tell students that as they write they need to visualize their audiences. Explain that they need to try to picture their audiences in their minds. If students are writing for a known audience, such as relatives, tell them to picture those people reading their writing. Tell students that if they are writing for an unknown audience, such as readers of hall displays, they need to picture an audience in their minds. Explain that as they invent audiences they should try to predict what will make their readers interested in their writing. Give students time to visualize their audiences. Then have students discuss who their audiences will be and what they will look for in a piece of writing.

7.   Tell students that they can be the audience for their own writing. Explain that "yourself-as-audience" means that the writing will be written primarily for themselves. Tell students that, even though they are the same person as writer and as reader, the writer "you" is different from the reader "you" (Rubin, 1998). Have signs or T-shirts printed with the words "reader" on one side and "writer" on the other side. Tell students to place the signs on their desks or put on the T-shirts with the word "writer" showing when they write for themselves as the author. Then have them reverse the signs or T-shirts when they read their finished pieces. Discuss how they felt in the different roles.

8.   Tell students that when they have written for an audience their work is "published." Then have a Publication Celebration. Have students make a list of the audiences for whom they have written in the past month. Display the list in a prominent place in the classroom. Have students read the list. Discuss the variety of audiences that have read the writings of students in the class. Celebrate by having a special treat for the class and a Publication Celebration.

9.   Tell students that the Internet is another place for them to find an audience for their writing. There are several web sites that publish students' writing, or students can publish their work on their family's web site. Explain that the audience for Internet publishing is often wider than publishing in a print journal; one never knows who will access a web site and for what reason. Consequently, on-line publishing can be a viable publishing alternative to traditional modes of publishing. The Internet site "KidPub" is one of the many that publish students' writing. Access the site and read the kinds of writing that are published on this site. If it would be a good audience for your students' writing, encourage students to submit writing to this site.

➔ Technology Tip

KidPub

Web site that publishes work submitted by students.

KidPub
www.kidpub.org/kidpub/

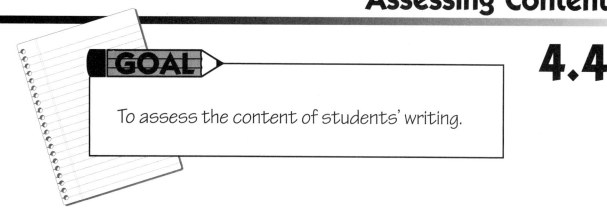

Assessing Content

GOAL

To assess the content of students' writing.

4.4

Background

If writers aren't careful, they can fall into a rut. Teachers see this happen a lot. A student writer begins the year writing adventure stories starring a popular super hero as the main character. By spring, students are writing stories with the same characters and the same plot. Some students tend to write the same thing over and over unless they are urged to vary their writing topics, purposes, and audiences. Because students need a variety of writing experiences to grow as writers, teachers should assess the content of students' writings.

Teachers can assess students' writing content in three different ways:

1. Teachers can compare their students' writings with writings of previous students.

2. Teachers can evaluate how effective students have been in matching topics with authors' purposes and audiences.

3. Teachers can evaluate ways in which students have written a variety of topics, for a variety of purposes and audiences.

Good assessment should influence instruction. Therefore, students should be part of the assessment picture by monitoring their own writing content. Teachers also should have regular input into students' writings by making positive comments on students' papers (Straub, 1997). Additional types of assessment strategies that teachers can use to evaluate students' writing content are presented in this section.

▶▶▶ —————————————

Good assessment should influence instruction.

————————————— ◀◀◀

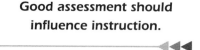

PAPER SORTS

ASSESSMENT STRATEGY **1**

The Paper Sorts strategy is similar to a word sort. Students sort papers into various groupings with different categories. For example, in Topic Paper Sorts students sort writings by various topics. Purpose Paper Sorts classify papers by purpose, and Audience Paper Sorts divide papers by audience. When students have the opportunity to sort their own writings, they make critical decisions about the kinds of topics, purposes, and audiences they have identified in their papers.

Directions

1. Have students place on their desks the writings they have done over a period of time. Tell students that they will be sorting their papers by topics, purposes, and audiences.

2. Remind students of the various types of topics, purposes, and audiences you have emphasized during the year. Tell students that you expect them to have written about several topics, for several different purposes, and to several different audiences.

3. Have students first sort their papers by topics. Walk around the class and assist students as necessary. After students have sorted their papers, ask them to list the different topics that were the subjects of their writings. Discuss your expectations with the class. For example, if you expected students to have written about seven different topics, tell them. Repeat the Paper Sorts by purposes and audiences.

4. Ask students to reflect on their success in varying writing content. Then have them create content writing goals for the remainder of the school year.

MATCHING TOPICS, PURPOSES, AND AUDIENCES

ASSESSMENT STRATEGY 2

Students need to assess their effectiveness in matching topics, purposes, and audiences. Through discussions about their own writings, younger students can learn how writers think of topics that match their purposes and audiences. Older students can assess their successes in matching topics, purposes, and audiences independently. When students learn how to assess their successes in matching topics, purposes, and audiences, they learn how to act like writers.

Directions

1. Tell students that they should reflect on their effectiveness in writing about topics that fit their purposes for a specific audience. Reassure students that this is a difficult activity and that all answers they give will be valued.

2. Duplicate and distribute copies of the Matching Topics, Purposes, and Audiences survey that follows.

3. If you teach young students, discuss the items together in small groups. If you teach older students, have the students complete the survey independently.

4. After students have completed discussing or answering the survey questions, ask them to write content goals in their writing notebooks.

Matching Topics, Purposes, and Audiences

Title _____

1. The topics of this paper were _____

   _____.

2. My purposes for writing this paper were _____

   _____

   _____.

3. The audiences for this paper were _____

   _____

   _____.

4. The reasons why this was a good topic for my audiences were ___

   _____

   _____.

5. The topics fit my purposes because _____

   _____

   _____.

6. I think this paper was effective because _____

   _____

   _____.

WRITING CONTENT RECORDS

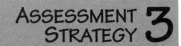

Students should keep track of the content of their papers. As they write, students can deliberately vary their topics, purposes, and audiences if they know what they have written in the past. Writing Content Records can also be a part of a teacher's assessment of writing content. Teachers can use Writing Content Records to note how effective students have been in varying topics, purposes, and audiences.

Directions

1. Tell students that they should keep Writing Content Records for each piece of writing they complete. Explain that students can use their Writing Content Records to vary topics, purposes, and audiences in future writings. Tell students that you will evaluate their writing content from time to time by using their Writing Content Records.

2. Duplicate and distribute the Writing Content Records sheet that follows. Give students a copy to place in their writing folders.

3. After students have finished a piece of writing, have them complete a line in their Writing Content Records.

4. Periodically, review students' Writing Content Records to determine whether students are varying topics, purposes, and audiences.

Name _____ Date _____

WRITING CONTENT RECORDS
Writing Title
Topic
Purpose
Audience
Writing Title
Topic
Purpose
Audience
Writing Title
Topic
Purpose
Audience
Writing Title
Topic
Purpose
Audience

Chapter 5

Writing Structures: Understanding Organizational Patterns

"The art of writing cannot be learned all at once."—Jean Jacques Rousseau

Overview

When we read, we often have seemingly intuitive knowledge about what will happen next in a story. For example, when reading a murder mystery, such as Agatha Christie's *Murder on the Orient Express*, we know that some type of crisis will occur that sets the stage for a murder, that a murder will take place, that characters will be developed who could turn into suspects, that red herrings will be introduced, and that the murderer will be found by a clever private eye. When we read, the content of the text may hold surprises, but the text's organization will be fairly predictable.

The reason why we have this knowledge about the text's organization is through many, many experiences with texts. Texts are written in organizational patterns that have been developed in our society over several centuries (Williams, 1996). Writers have refined different organizational patterns over time so that when we read we are aware of the directions in which the text will guide our thinking. Some of the organizational patterns that have been fairly stable over time are personal experience stories, works of fiction, exposition, and persuasion.

We become aware of the patterns of texts primarily through reading and writing. As we read, we subconsciously look for texts to move in predictable directions. Writing, however, is another matter. Writers generally need to be taught the organizational structures of texts. Inexperienced writers sometimes think that writing is simply talk written down (Wray & Lewis, 1997). It's not. Writing follows accepted organizational rules so that readers can comprehend content while following the train of thought presented in the text.

Students need to become aware of the patterns of texts. Students who have had many experiences hearing stories will learn the pattern of fictional works easily and apply those organizational features of fiction to their writings (Lancia, 1997). They will easily understand that the story takes place in a particular setting with main characters who are involved in a plot and that the story may have a theme. Fiction is the easiest type of pattern to teach students because of their many experiences with that type of text. Students are usually less familiar with personal experience stories, exposition, and persuasion. Therefore, students need explicit instruction in the ways texts are organized, and they need practice with these types of writings (Downing, 1995).

Students will probably discover some aspects of text organization on their own while participating in writing activities. For most students, however, the experience of writing will not help them become effective writers of informational texts (Stotsky, 1995). Students who participate in writing workshops for the bulk of their writing instruction still need teachers to help them co-construct strategies for writing (Collins, 1998). For example, students who want to persuade their parents to give them a

> **Students need to become aware of the patterns of texts.**

larger allowance may need the teacher to help them organize their thoughts so that their arguments are reasonable, logical, and persuasive. Teachers, then, need to develop lessons to help students learn how texts are organized. This chapter provides resources, teaching strategies, ideas, and activities to help you teach students the specific organizational patterns of writing. Ideas for assessment also are included.

▶ Can this teacher help students by sharing his own writing experiences?

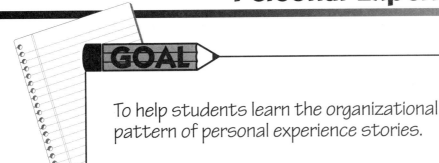

GOAL

To help students learn the organizational pattern of personal experience stories.

Background

"Guess what happened to me?" Students burst into classrooms on a regular basis brimming with stories about their lives. That's because students' lives are filled with events and experiences that they want to share. Students love to tell stories about their lives. They tell stories about themselves to their teachers, to their friends, and even to strangers. Students' lives are filled with stories that they are more than willing to tell others.

Personal experience stories are a natural extension of storytelling. They are the written form of stories of an author's experiences. When students write personal experience stories in schools, they bring their private lives into the classroom. Students' lives and families converge with the public setting of schools through the sharing of personal experience stories, which leads to a stronger sense of community (Madigan & Koivu-Rybicki, 1997). When students share their lives with their teachers and classmates, they reveal new sides of themselves.

The organizational pattern of personal experience stories is known to most students through stories they have heard or read. Personal experience stories can be written about any topic, but the story must be a true event or experience of the author. The topic for all personal experience stories, therefore, is the self. Since authors of personal experience stories write about themselves, the stories are written in the first person using the personal pronoun "I." The purpose of personal experience stories is to share the author's feelings about an event or experience. Personal experience stories are organized by a be-

ginning-middle-end structure. All stories have a beginning that introduces the experiences and the author's reactions to them, a middle that describes the events in a sequence, and an ending that summarizes the events and the author's feelings.

Students will find that personal experience stories are among the easiest types of stories to write. However, many students need instruction in the organizational pattern of personal experience stories. This section presents resources, teaching strategies, ideas, and activities to help students learn the organizational pattern of personal experience stories.

▶ Might this student have an interesting story to share?

TEACHING STRATEGY 1 ▶ ▶ ▶ ▶ ▶ ▶ Organizational Pattern

Personal experience stories have a specific organizational pattern: beginning, middle, and end. This pattern can be taught to students who may have a vague notion of the way stories are written or told. There are two basic steps to teach story structure:

1. Tell students explicitly the organizational pattern of personal experience stories.
2. Show them an example of a personal experience story that was written by a student at their grade level.

Students can identify patterns in stories that were written at their own developmental level easier than they can in stories that were written by professional authors. Writings that are too complex can discourage students and keep them from learning how to organize their own stories.

 **Directions**

1. Tell students that the stories they hear from others are often personal experience stories. Explain that personal experience stories are stories about the author's own experiences. Tell students that personal experience stories have a beginning, middle, and end.

2. Duplicate and distribute the Organizational Pattern Outline that follows. Tell students that in most cases personal experience stories follow the outline.

 3. Divide the class into groups of three or four students. Have students read the Organizational Pattern Outline or read it with them. Discuss the components of a personal experience story. Explain the outline as needed.

4. Tell students that you will show them an example of a personal experience story. Locate a personal experience story that was written by a student at your grade level or, if appropriate, use the Student Example that follows.

5. Make a transparency of the Student Example of a personal experience story. Identify the features that make the piece of writing a personal experience story rather than a different organizational pattern.

6. Locate additional pieces of writing that could be classified as personal experience stories. Have small groups of students read the stories and look for organizational features.

7. Later, have students write their own personal experience stories. Provide time for sharing.

ORGANIZATIONAL PATTERN OUTLINE
PERSONAL EXPERIENCE STORIES

Beginning

✓ Has descriptive title

✓ Introduces the event or experience

✓ States author's feelings, reactions,
   or learning

Middle

✓ Provides events in sequence

✓ Gives details

✓ Includes author's feelings, reactions,
   or learning

End

✓ Summarizes event or experience

✓ Restates author's feelings, reactions,
   or learning

PERSONAL EXPERIENCE STORY: STUDENT EXAMPLE

The Blizzard of '99

The first week of the new year brought a big winter snowstorm. It snowed over 18 inches in one night. The snow was really deep and very cold. We all felt stranded because we couldn't get our car out of the drive.

Introduces experience

Shares feelings

My sister and I started scooping the snow from our driveway. It was very hard work, and we felt like we were getting nowhere. Next, our neighbors saw that we were struggling and they came over to help. Samantha, Elena, Rachel, and I all took turns using shovels and brooms to move the snow. It was exhausting work! Finally, with everyone working together we were able to clear our drive. We were really thankful and happy to have such good neighbors. We could now get out of our drive.

Events in sequence

Incorporates feelings

The big winter snowstorm helped us learn to work together as a team in order to accomplish a certain goal. In conclusion, it's good to have friends who are willing to lend a helping hand.

Summarizes

Rebecca Mondron
Third Grade

TEACHING STRATEGY 2 ▶ ▶ ▶ ▶ ▶ ▶ ▶ ▶ ▶ ▶ ▶ **Memory Writing**

For students to be able to write personal experience stories, they need to search their memories to find topics. Personal experience stories are not made up; they are true accounts of an author's experiences. In order to write personal experience stories, students need to think about their experiences, reactions, or feelings and write about them in the organizational pattern that is commonly used for personal experience stories. Memory Writing is a strategy to help students think of topics for their stories.

⟷ **Directions**

1. Tell students that all of their memories are valuable and that many can be turned into stories.

2. Give students a key word or phrase, such as a good time with a friend. Ask students to recall ideas and mental pictures related to the topic. Wait several minutes for students to think.

3. After students have thought about the topic, tell them to write what comes to mind. Give them five minutes to write.

4. Divide the class into groups of three or four students. Invite students to share their memories with their groups.

5. Have students place their free writings in their writing folders. Tell students that these pieces of free writing could be developed into personal experience stories.

6. Duplicate and distribute the Memory Prompts that follow. Tell students to use the list of Memory Prompts when they need to think of a topic for a personal experience story. Remind students to think, free write, and share before they write their stories. The Memory Prompts also could be used for additional lessons related to Memory Writing.

▶ Could skipping stones with a brother prompt many memories to share?

MEMORY PROMPTS

I remember a time when . . .

- I made something.

- I played a game.

- I had the hiccups.

- I lost something.

- I learned something new.

- I met someone.

- I performed in front of an audience.

- I saw a great movie.

- I said good-bye to someone.

- I solved a problem.

- I started a hobby.

- I visited a relative.

- I had something on my mind.

- I told a story.

- I was upset.

- I was thrilled.

- I took a vacation.

- I was surprised.

- I had a dream.

- I was afraid.

- I set a goal.

- I changed something.

TEACHING STRATEGY 3 ▶▶▶▶▶▶▶▶▶▶▶ Writing Frame

Personal experience stories have a distinct organizational structure. After students have thought of an idea for a topic, they need to develop the idea in the typical story pattern. Students can organize their ideas in many ways. Young students generally are more successful when they organize their ideas with a Writing Frame. Writing Frames provide students with important background knowledge about ways different pieces of writing can be organized. A Writing Frame gives students experience writing with a specific organizational pattern without having to know how to write the transitions.

⟷ Directions

1. Tell students that once they have ideas for stories they need to organize their ideas using the organizational pattern of personal experience stories. Remind students that personal experience stories have a beginning, middle, and end.

2. Young students and students who have little background with personal experience stories should begin organizing their ideas with a Writing Frame. Duplicate and distribute the Writing Frame that follows. Tell students that they will be writing their ideas on the Writing Frame.

3. Provide students with a model of a Writing Frame as in the example that follows. Develop your own story or use the example. Make a transparency of the example, show it to students, and explain how the story was developed from the Writing Frame.

4. Have students write their own stories using a Writing Frame.

Writing Frame Personal Experience Story Example
One day I went fishing in the lake. **First**, my brother rowed us into a small cove where we threw in our fishing lines complete with wriggling worms on the hooks. **Then**, we waited for a fish to bite. **Finally**, we went home with no fish. **It was** a disappointing day for me. **I felt** frustrated **because** we didn't catch any fish. **I learned that** you won't catch fish every time you go fishing. Bummer!

Writing Frame
Personal Experience Stories

One day I_____

_____.

First,_____

_____.

Then,_____

_____.

Finally,_____

_____.

It was_____.

I felt_____ **because**_____

_____.

I learned that_____.

TEACHING STRATEGY 4 ▶▶▶▶▶▶▶ **Graphic Organizer**

Graphic Organizers are another way to organize information before writing. Graphic Organizers are similar to outlines, but they form a visual representation of the writing's organization. Graphic Organizers can be used before, during, and after writing. Before writing, students can plot their ideas on a Graphic Organizer and refer to it when they write. Students also can use Graphic Organizers during writing. As writers complete sections of writing, they can refer to the Graphic Organizer to remind themselves of the pattern of their writing. After writing, students can map out the ideas from their writing on a Graphic Organizer to verify that they have all of the components of the writing pattern. Older students especially will find Graphic Organizers useful for learning the organizational patterns of different writing structures.

⟡ Directions

1. Remind students that personal experience stories have a specific organizational pattern. Tell students that a Graphic Organizer is a visual representation of the writing pattern.

2. Students who are independent writers can organize their ideas on Graphic Organizers. Once students have thought of an idea for a personal experience story, duplicate and distribute the Graphic Organizer that follows. Give each student a copy.

3. Have students map out their ideas for their stories on Graphic Organizers. Provide guidance as necessary. Tell students that organizing their ideas before they write will help them organize their writing.

4. Allow students time to plot their ideas on Graphic Organizers. If students have not generated enough ideas before writing, have them partially complete their Graphic Organizers and begin writing.

▶ Could this student use a Graphic Organizer to assist her in writing about learning to ride a bike?

5. Tell students that they also can assess their writing organization by using Graphic Organizers after writing. Have students place several copies of the Graphic Organizer in their writing folders. After students have written personal experience stories, have them use their Graphic Organizers to determine whether they organized their writing according to the writing pattern.

Name_____ Date_____

Graphic Organizer
Personal Experience Stories

Event or Experience

Feelings, Thoughts, Reactions

What happened?

1. _____

2. _____

3. _____

4. _____

5. _____

Summary

What I learned

TEACHING STRATEGY 5 ▶▶▶▶▶▶ Revealing Emotions

A personal experience story is pretty dull if it doesn't include the author's feelings, reactions, and learning. Often, students have difficulty putting their feelings into words. Many times their vocabularies of feeling words are limited to sad, happy, and mad. To help students add depth to their stories, teach them some of the words that describe the emotional states that everyone experiences. Adding emotions to stories can make the difference between a mediocre story and an interesting one.

◆ Directions

1. Tell students that an element of personal experience stories is the use of the author's feelings, reactions, and learning. Explain that students can improve their stories by adding words that express emotions.

2. Duplicate and distribute the list of Emotions that follows. Have students read the list or read it with them.

3. Have each student select one word from the list of Emotions. Ask students to think of a time when they felt that way. (If students are unsure of the meaning of a word, tell them what the word means.) Have students visualize themselves feeling what the word describes.

4. Select a word yourself, such as downcast. Make your face look downcast. Ask students to guess the word that you are pantomiming. If students have difficulty guessing the word, tell them the letter with which the word begins.

5. Invite students to pantomime the words they chose. Ask other students to guess the words their fellow students are pantomiming.

▶ What words could this girl be using to describe her emotions?

6. Have students look through magazines and newspapers for pictures that have people experiencing the emotions described by the words that they chose. Have students create an Emotions Booklet with pictures next to words describing emotions.

7. When students have a topic for writing a personal experience story, have them use their list of Emotions to find a descriptive word that expresses their feelings, reactions, and learning. Encourage students to use words from the list in their writings.

Emotions

alone
awful

bashful
blue
brave
bright

cheerful
clumsy
confident
courageous

daring
delighted
depressed
despised
downcast
downhearted
dreadful

fantastic
foolish
friendly
furious

glad
gloomy
good
grand
great

happy
hated

important

joyful

mysterious

nervous

overjoyed

pleased
powerful
proud

relaxed

sad
scared
sharp
shy
silly
small
starved
strange
stressed
strong
superb

terrific
thrilled
timid
tough

uneasy

warm
weak
wise
wonderful

 **Ideas and Activities**

1. Have students ask friends and relatives to tell them stories. Tell students that grandparents are particularly good at telling stories about their lives. Remind students to listen carefully as they hear their relatives' stories. Ask them to listen for the beginning, middle, and end of the stories. Tell students to ask the storytellers how they felt after their experiences. When students hear stories outside of school, have them write the topics of the stories and the names of the storytellers on a list in their writing folders or on a class poster.

2. Have students create a time line about their lives or parts of their lives. Give each student a piece of paper that has a horizontal line drawn on it with hash marks at equal intervals. On the left side of the line write the year that the oldest student in the class was born. Write successive years to the right. Ask students to write on the time line the events that occurred in their lives. Encourage students to be specific.

3. When students are thinking of topics for personal experience stories, encourage them to participate in free writing loops. Have them respond to the following phrases with free writing. Explain that authors often think of topics when free writing. Three sentence starters that inspire personal thoughts follow.

   - I think . . .
   - I wonder . . .
   - I believe . . .

4. Many web sites publish personal experience stories. Encourage students to identify web sites, such as "MidLink Magazine," to publish their stories.

Technology Tip

MidLink Magazine

 Web site that contains an electronic magazine for students where they can write articles and poetry, participate in projects, exchange art and writing, and view projects of other students in grades 4–8.

http://longwood.cs.usf.edu/~MidLink/

5. Family members are a terrific resource for events in students' lives. Have students ask parents and family members to talk about family events in which the students have participated. Tell students to listen to their families' stories and remember that the stories are told from other perspectives. Encourage students to write a list of these experiences to place in their writing folders for future reference.

6. Most students are fascinated by their names. Have students research the meanings of their names. Then have them write personal experience stories that describe ways in which they acted like the meanings of their names.

7. Invite a professional storyteller to the school or to your class to tell stories. Remind students that not every story will be a personal experience story. Have students listen carefully for the organizational patterns of the stories that the storyteller relates.

8. Tell students that many books are written as personal experience stories. Read one or more books to students or place a number of books on a shelf for students to read. Remind students to notice that the book is written in the first person; that the story has a beginning, middle, and end; and that the author reveals emotions. Explain to students that, although it seems as if the story were actually happening to the author, frequently books written in the first person are fiction and the events did not really happen. A list of books written in the first person follows.

Books Written in the First Person

Compiled by Jenny Bolander

Blume, J. (1986)
Superfudge.
Livonia, MN: Seedlings.
(Grades 2–4)

Cameron, A. (1996)
The stories Julian tells.
Orlando: Harcourt Brace.
(Grades 2–4)

Cameron, A. (1997)
More stories Julian tells.
New York: Knopf.
(Grades 2–4)

Cleary, B. (1998)
Dear Mr. Henshaw.
New York: Scholastic.
(Grades 3–6)

Greene, B. (1975)
Philip Hall likes me. I reckon maybe.
New York: Dell.
(Grades 4–6)

Howard, E. (1991)
Aunt Flossie's hats.
New York: Scholastic.
(Grades 3–6)

Howe, D. & Howe, J. (1997)
Bunnicula.
New York: Scholastic.
(Grades 3–6)

MacLachlan, P. (1991)
Journey.
New York: Yearling Books.
(Grades 3–6)

MacLachlan, P. (1993)
Baby.
New York: Delacorte.
(Grades 3–6)

MacLachlan, P. (1994)
Skylark.
New York: HarperCollins.
(Grades 3–6)

Peck, R. (1998)
Strays like us.
New York: Dial.
(Grades 4–6)

Polacco, P. (1994)
Pink and Say.
New York: Scholastic.
(Grades 4–6)

Viorst, J. (1987)
Alexander and the terrible, horrible, no good, very bad day.
New York: Aladdin.
(Grades 3–6)

Viorst, J. (1988)
The tenth good thing about Barney.
New York: Aladdin.
(Grades 3–6)

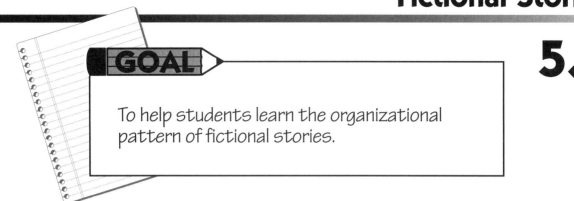
GOAL

To help students learn the organizational pattern of fictional stories.

Background

Fictional stories have a unique structure that is similar to personal experience stories but different from expository and persuasive writing. Unlike other types of writing, fictional stories are not true. They are figments of writers' imaginations. Writers can shape and develop their stories in any way they want, letting their imaginations take them to distant places. Fictional stories, therefore, will vary widely. However, all fictional stories have roughly the same type of organizational pattern.

The structure of fictional stories is well-known to most children and adults in our society. Not only do students read and hear fictional stories, but they also view them on television and at movies. Television stories and movies have the same elements as do print materials. Both books and movies have characters, a plot, a setting, a theme, and a point of view.

The *characters* of fictional stories are the people or personified animals who are the focus of the story. These characters have qualities which are revealed through their thoughts, actions, appearances, and sayings. Stories can have a single character or many characters. The characters of fictional stories are involved in some sort of plot. The *plot* is the action that takes place in the story, usually in a series of events that begins with a problem to be resolved and that ends with a resolution. The problem may be as simple as deciding where to find a kitten to buy or as complex as surviving an Arctic storm. Every fictional story, however, has some sort of problem to be resolved. The characters and the plot take place in a setting. The *setting* of a fictional story is the time and place of the story. Through the character, plot, and setting, the author of a fictional story frequently introduces a thought or idea. This

▶ Some students have very vivid imaginations.

thought or idea is called the *theme* of the story. Themes also can range from simple to complex. Finally, all stories are written from a *point of view*.

Most fictional stories are written in the third person with the author relating the story using the characters' names and the pronouns "he," "she," "they," etc. Some fictional stories are written in the first person. These stories are written as if the author is telling the story as in *Sarah, Plain and Tall*

(MacLachlan, 1985). First-person fictional stories seem to be true, but they're not.

Fictional stories have a distinct organizational structure. By teaching students how to write stories with characters, plots, settings, themes, and from a point of view, students can write more vivid stories. This section includes resources, teaching strategies, ideas, and activities to help teach students to learn the organizational structure of fictional stories.

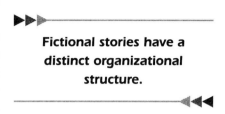

Fictional stories have a distinct organizational structure.

TEACHING STRATEGY 1 ▶ ▶ ▶ ▶ ▶ ▶ Organizational Pattern

Even though students are familiar with the organizational pattern of fictional stories from reading and hearing books, they should be taught the organizational pattern of fictional writing. Many students know some of the aspects of fictional stories from their background knowledge. However, learning the basics of writing fiction can help students develop plots more completely so that they can write interesting stories.

⟵✛⟶ Directions

1. Tell students that fiction is the type of writing they most frequently have read in books. Explain that fictional stories are not true, that they have characters in them, and that they have a plot. Remind students that fictional writing can take the form of stories other people tell, television plots, or movies.

2. Duplicate and distribute the Organizational Pattern Outline for fictional stories that follows. Tell students that fictional stories follow the outline in most cases.

 3. Divide the class into groups of three or four students. Have students read the Organizational Pattern Outline or read it with them. Discuss the components of fictional writing with students.

4. Tell students that you will show them an example of fictional writing. Locate an example of fictional writing written by a student at your grade level or, if appropriate, use the Student Example that follows.

5. Make a transparency of the Student Example. Identify the features that make the piece of writing fictional rather than a different organizational pattern.

 6. Locate additional pieces of writing that could be classified as fictional. Have small groups of students read the stories and look for their organizational features.

ORGANIZATIONAL PATTERN OUTLINE
FICTIONAL STORIES

Introduction

☐ Introduces the main character and the setting

☐ Introduces the main problem that will be resolved

☐ Introduces the theme

Interior Paragraph (may be more than 1)

☐ Develops the plot by giving events in sequence

☐ Uses the setting to provide details

☐ Develops the problem through events

☐ Develops characters through events

☐ Develops the theme through characters' actions

Conclusion

☐ Resolves the characters' problem

☐ Restates the theme in a subtle or explicit way

FICTIONAL STORY: STUDENT EXAMPLE

The Picnic

Yesterday Tanya got to play with Alissa. How did Tanya get to

play with her? Tanya spotted a familiar bike. It was Alissa's! Tanya

was on her bike. She was fast. She knew where Alissa's house was.

But Alissa was in the house. She came back out and Tanya and Alissa

had a little picnic. They got the food and put the food in a wagon.

Then they went to a shady place to eat. They saw a butterfly and

squirted their drink in the air. They had a fun picnic.

Erin Bohlin
First Grade

Introduces main characters

Introduces problem

Resolves problem

Conclusion

TEACHING STRATEGY 2 ▶ ▶ ▶ ▶ ▶ **Plot Relationships Chart**

The plot of fictional stories can be distilled into one sentence using the strategy Plot Relationships Chart (Schmidt & Buckley, 1991). A Plot Relationships Chart is a good strategy to teach students the organizational pattern of fictional writing because the plot is described in a single sentence. Writing the entire plot in a single sentence forces students to create a clear, focused plot. Students of all ages can create Plot Relationships Charts.

⟷ Directions

1. Tell students that they will be creating a single-sentence plot using a Plot Relationships Chart. Remind students that a plot needs to have a main character who is faced with some type of problem to resolve. Tell students that the entire plot can be expressed with the following sentence: Somebody . . . wanted . . . but . . . so. . . . Write "Somebody wanted but so" on the chalkboard or on an overhead transparency with spaces to fill in the blanks. Use the following example as a guide.

    _____ wanted _____,
    (Somebody)

    but _____, so _____.

2. Read a book to your students. Have students identify the main character. Write the name of the main character on the first line. Then ask students to identify the goal of the character. Write the goal of the character on the second line. In most stories, the character faces a problem. Write the problem on the third line. In fictional writing, problems are resolved in some way. Write the resolution for the problem on the last line. An example using the story *The Paperboy* (Pilkey, 1996) follows.

    The paperboy **wanted** to stay in bed, **but** he had to deliver his papers, **so** he went out into the cold thinking of other things.

3. Have students think of plots for fictional writings and have them write their plots on Plot Relationships Charts. Before students begin writing, have them share their Plot Relationships Charts with their writing partner for feedback. Remind students to have a clear idea of their plots before writing fictional stories.

TEACHING STRATEGY 3 ▶▶▶▶▶▶▶▶▶▶ **Writing Frame**

Fictional stories have a distinct organizational structure. One of the challenges of writing fictional stories is to organize ideas so that the story is told clearly. After students have thought of the key elements of a plot, they need to develop the idea in the typical fictional organizational pattern. Students can organize their ideas in many ways. Young students generally are more successful when they organize their ideas with a Writing Frame. Writing Frames provide students with important background knowledge about ways different pieces of writing can be organized. A Writing Frame gives students experience writing with a specific organizational pattern without having to know how to write the transitions.

⊕ **Directions**

1. Tell students that once they have ideas for their stories they need to organize their ideas using the organizational pattern of fictional stories. Remind students that fictional stories have a plot that is developed through the use of characters and a setting.

2. Young students and students who have little background with fictional stories should begin organizing their ideas with a Writing Frame. Duplicate and distribute the Writing Frame that follows. Tell students that they will be writing their ideas on the Writing Frame.

3. Provide students with a model of a Writing Frame as in the example that follows. Develop your own story or use the example. Make a transparency of the example, show it to students, and explain how the story was developed from the Writing Frame.

4. Have students write their own fictional stories using a Writing Frame.

Writing Frame
Fictional Story Example
Jeremy **lived in** a crowded neighborhood in a large city. Jeremy **wanted to** learn how to play soccer. **That was a problem because** there was very little room to run and play in his neighborhood. Jeremy **solved the problem by** asking his neighbors to help him clear the trash from a vacant lot. Jeremy and his neighbors cleared enough space to construct a half-sized soccer field.

Writing Frame
Fictional Stories

_____ **lived in** _____
Character

_____.
Setting

_____ **wanted to** _____
Character

_____.

That was a problem because _____

_____.

_____ **solved the problem by**
Character

_____.

_____.
Ending Sentence

TEACHING STRATEGY 4 ▶ ▶ ▶ ▶ ▶ ▶ ▶ ▶ **Graphic Organizer**

Graphic Organizers are another way to organize information before writing. Graphic Organizers are similar to outlines, but they form a visual representation of the writing's organization. Graphic Organizers can be used before, during, and after writing. Before writing, students can plot their ideas on Graphic Organizers and refer to them when they write. Students also can use Graphic Organizers during writing. As writers complete sections of writing, they can refer to their Graphic Organizers to remind themselves of the pattern of their writing. After writing, students can map out the ideas from their writing on Graphic Organizers to verify that they have all of the components of the writing pattern. Older students especially will find Graphic Organizers useful for learning the organizational patterns of different writing structures.

✛ Directions

1. Remind students that fictional stories have a specific organizational pattern. Tell students that a Graphic Organizer is a visual representation of the writing pattern.

2. Students who are independent writers can organize their ideas on Graphic Organizers. Once students have thought of an idea for a fictional story, duplicate and distribute the Graphic Organizer that follows.

3. Have students map out their ideas for their stories on Graphic Organizers. Provide guidance as necessary. Tell students that organizing their ideas before they write will help them organize their writing.

4. Allow students time to plot their ideas on Graphic Organizers. If students have not generated enough ideas before writing, have them partially complete their Graphic Organizers and begin writing.

5. Tell students that they also can assess their writing organization by using Graphic Organizers after writing. Have students place several copies of the Graphic Organizer in their writing folders. After students have written their stories, have them use their Graphic Organizers to determine whether they organized their writing according to the writing pattern.

Name _____ Date _____

Graphic Organizer
Fictional Stories

_____
Title

Setting
_____
Time   Place

Characters

Major   Minor

_____ _____

_____ _____

_____ _____

Problem
_____

Events

1. _____

2. _____

3. _____

4. _____

_____
Resolution

TEACHING STRATEGY 5 ▶▶▶▶▶▶▶▶▶▶ Character Webs

Tell students that fictional stories employ characters who have the same qualities as real people. Characters in stories should be described by their actions, their feelings, their appearances, and the things that they say. Help students develop characters in fictional stories by using Character Webs.

⟨✛⟩ Directions

1. Explain to students that characters in fictional stories should be described by their actions, their feelings, their appearances, and the things that they say. Tell students that using Character Webs can help them develop their characters.

2. Duplicate and distribute the Character Web that follows. Give a copy to each student. Point out the sections for characters' acts, feelings, appearances, and sayings.

3. Have students refer to stories they are writing. Ask students to highlight on their drafts the actions of their characters. Then have them list the actions on the Character Webs. Repeat the process for the characters' feelings, appearances, and sayings.

4. After the Character Webs are completed, have students analyze the balance of information they have given about their characters. If students have not described how their characters look, have them write ideas on their Character Webs. Give students 5 to 10 minutes to complete their Character Webs.

5. Tell students that Character Webs can help them as they revise their stories. Remind students to supply enough information about their characters so that the characters live in the minds of readers.

6. Provide extra copies of Character Webs to students as they develop additional stories. Tell students that they can use the Character Webs before writing or after they have finished a draft of a story.

Character Web
Fictional Stories

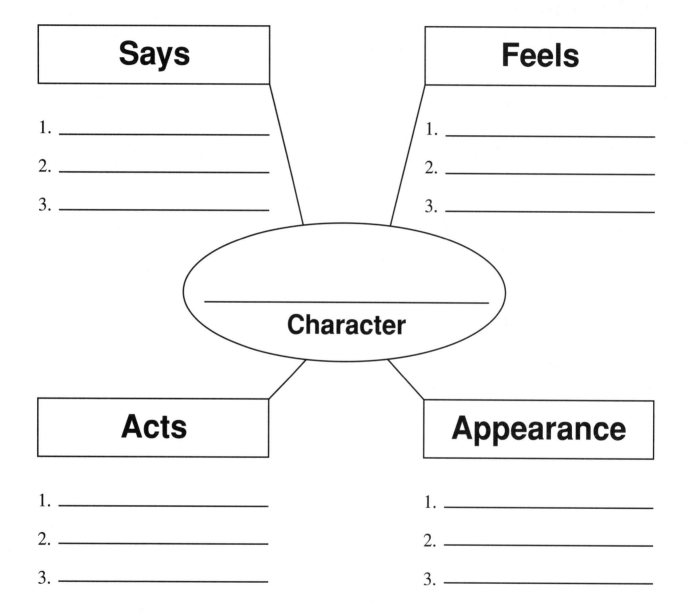

Says

1. _____
2. _____
3. _____

Feels

1. _____
2. _____
3. _____

Character

Acts

1. _____
2. _____
3. _____

Appearance

1. _____
2. _____
3. _____

 **Ideas and Activities**

1. Remind young students that stories have a beginning, middle, and end. Help them expand their knowledge by telling them that stories often introduce a character in the beginning, something happens in the middle, and the end is usually happy. To illustrate how fictional writing is organized, have students make a Story Tower. A Story Tower is a large piece of construction paper folded so that the beginning of the story is at the bottom, the middle is in the middle, and the end is at the top. Story Towers help students learn the basic organization of fictional writing. Read a short book that has an identifiable beginning, middle, and end. Tell students to listen and identify the beginning with the main character, the middle with the plot, and the end with the happy ending. Then have students make Story Towers with the directions that follow.

Directions:
Fold a 1-inch tab at the end of a 12" x 18" sheet of paper. Fold the remaining paper into thirds. Label the sections with Beginning, Middle, and End. Have students draw a picture in each section. Fold the paper into a triangular shape and glue tab.

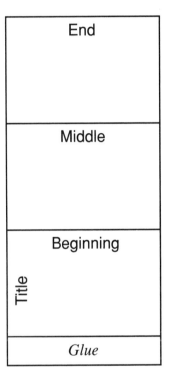

2. Tell students that writers often pattern characters after people they know. Tell students that they will be writing group stories that use students in the class as the characters of the stories. Give students pieces of mural paper that match their heights. Trace the outlines of students' bodies on the paper. Have students cut out their outlines and draw themselves on the paper. Hang the paper people in the classroom or in the hallway. Have students write positive characteristics under the paper people. Then divide the class into groups of three or four students. Randomly assign each group several paper people. Have the groups create stories using the paper people as main characters. Then have students write their group stories. Share the stories with the other members of the class.

3. Distribute to students sports pages from a newspaper to be used as the basis for fictional writing (Rogers, 1997). Tell students that photographs are a construction of reality; they do not record reality. Point out to students the features of the pictures such as the size, position, direction, camera angle, and focus. Ask students also to notice features of the photographs such as clothing, gestures, actions, and facial expressions. Divide the class into groups of three or four students. Give each group one photograph. Ask students to discuss the photograph in terms of what might have happened just before the photograph was taken, what might be happening outside of the frame, and what they think the subject of the photograph is thinking. Then have students create group stories using any of the ideas that they generated. After groups have created stories, have them share their stories with the class and then write their own stories. Remind students that the main character of a story is a critical part of fictional writing.

4. Tell students that they will be writing a group story. Put a blue, red, or yellow colored dot on each student's hand. Distribute the colors as evenly as possible. Have students form groups of three students, each with a student with one blue dot, a student with one red dot, and a student with one yellow dot. Explain to students that the blue dot represents the setting, the red dot represents the character, and the yellow dot represents the problem. Instruct students to think of an item that fits their color category. Once each group member has thought of a word, have them share their words with their group. Have each group create a short story using the ideas they generated. Give students five minutes to think of a story. Invite students to share their stories with the class. After students have generated one or more stories, give students writing paper with three colored dots on the top. Remind students that the dots stand for the settings, characters, and problems. Tell students to write fictional stories using the three elements that they practiced.

5. Tell students that the Internet is a good source for fictional writings by other students. Access "The Quill Society" web site that follows. Have students read some of the fictional stories. Then encourage students to submit their own fictional stories for publication.

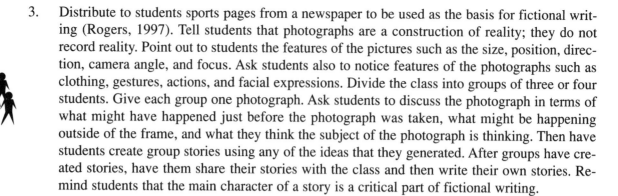

Technology Tip

The Quill Society

Web site that contains activities for students to explore their imaginations through writing advertisements, fantasy, mystery, science fiction, and poetry. Students receive comments from the "Board of Critics" and can discuss topics on a Bulletin Board.

www.quill.net

6. Tell students that most books have an identifiable plot structure. Read a story to the class that none of the students has heard. Read until the problem has been told. Have students predict the ways in which the character will resolve the problem. Tell students that writers make decisions about plots, characters, settings, and themes as they write and that a story can take many different directions.

7. Tell students that you will be writing a story using the game Relay Writing. Divide the class into four or five teams. Write the same number of columns on the chalkboard as the number of teams. Write a sentence to begin a story. Have students in each team form a line. Tell students that, when you tell them to begin, the first person in each line should walk to the chalkboard and write a sentence that will continue the story. Tell students that after the first student in each line writes a sentence, they should return to the end of the line. When the first student returns to the line, the next person in the line walks to the chalkboard to continue the story. After the teams are finished, read the stories. Point out the features of fictional writing such as characters, plots, settings, and themes.

8. Tell students that when writing fictional stories they need to describe the settings so that their readers can visualize their stories. Explain to students that writers need to picture the settings as they write. To practice creating descriptive settings, divide the class into groups of three or four students and give students pictures or photographs of landscapes. Ask students to brainstorm events that might have happened in those settings. Then have students write their fictional stories and place them in their writing files. Provide students with several opportunities to write stories with descriptive settings. After students have completed drafts of several fictional stories, ask them to choose a story to revise. Ask students to draw or paint pictures of the settings of their stories. After the drawings or paintings are completed, ask students to list the events of the plots of their stories in sequential order and to number them. Then ask students to record the numbers of the events of the plots onto their pictures of the settings, placing the numbers in the spots of the settings where the events occurred. For students who have most of the events clustered in one spot, ask them whether they would like to revise their plots to move the actions around the settings. Then remind students that when writing fictional stories they should picture the setting.

9. Tell students that the setting of a story will influence how the characters behave, what happens in the story, and how the characters resolve their problems. Remind students of a shared experience that they have had that took place outside of the classroom. For example, have students think about a field trip to a museum in which they participated. Ask students to complete the sentence, "_____ at the museum." Model an answer such as "We saw a dinosaur skeleton at the museum." Invite students to share their sentences. Point out ways in which the content of students' sentences depended on the setting of the museum. Read several short books to students that have settings as an integral part of the plots. The book list that follows has several examples of stories that have plots with integral settings. After reading a book, have students imagine the setting. Remind students that when they write fictional stories they should describe the settings as completely as possible.

Books with Settings Essential for the Story

Compiled by Jenny Bolander

Andrews, J. (1998)
Very first last time.
New York: Aladdin.
(Grades 2–3)

Creech, S. (1997)
Pleasing the ghost.
New York: Harper Trophy.
(Grades K–2)

DeFelice, C. (1996)
Apprenticeship of Lucas Whitaker.
New York: Farrar, Straus, and Giroux.
(Grades 4–6)

Fox, M. (1996)
Feathers and fools.
San Diego: Harcourt Brace.
(Grades 2–4)

Fritz, J. (1984)
Homesick: My own story.
New York: Yearling.
(Grades 3–6)

Henkes, K. (1997)
Sun and spoon.
New York: Greenwillow.
(Grades 3–6)

Lasky, K. (1990)
Dinosaur dig.
New York: Morrow.
(Grades 3–6)

London, J. (1993)
The eyes of Gray Wolf.
San Francisco: Chronicle Books.
(Grades 2–4)

Morimoto, J. (1992)
My Hiroshima.
New York: Puffin.
(Grades 3–6)

Paterson, K. (1999)
The king's equal.
New York: Harper Trophy.
(Grades 3–6)

Taylor, M. (1995)
The well.
New York: Dial.
(Grades 4–6)

Van Allsburgh, C. (1998)
Polar express.
Boston: Houghton Mifflin.
(Grades K–4)

Weisner, D. (1991)
Tuesday.
New York: Clarion.
(Grades 2–4)

Wild, M. (1993)
Going home.
New York: Scholastic.
(Grades 2–4)

To help students learn the organizational patterns of expository writing.

Background

Expository writing is the kind of writing that gives directions, explains a situation or event, or tells how a process happens. Expository writing has a specific organizational structure:

▶▶▶

Expository writing is a big part of our lives.

◀◀◀

- The main point is usually clearly stated or implied,
- The main point is then developed and supported by facts,
- The facts are presented in an orderly way, and
- The writing is directed toward a specific audience (Wray & Lewis, 1997).

All types of expository writing have these characteristics, but there are a variety of organizational patterns that are typically considered to be expository writing. Among the most common expository writing patterns are simple explanation, steps-in-a-process, compare and contrast, and cause and effect. Each of these types of expository writing has a slightly different organizational pattern, but all are nonfiction with main ideas and details.

There has been an increasing interest in teaching expository writing in schools because so much of the print we read in life is one kind of expository writing or another. Examples of expository writing with which all of us are

familiar include directions for income taxes, computer manuals, and labels on cans. Letters can also be expository when they describe or explain a situation or event. Expository writing, therefore, is a big part of our lives.

Students in schools should learn the various organizational patterns of expository writing, both to help them construct meaning from text and so that they can become writers of this common type of written communication (Ryder, 1994). Before students can write expository text effectively, however, they need to have knowledge about a specific subject. Expository writing entails knowledge that is organized and shared. For example, if students are writing a paper comparing the African animal population today with the animal population of the early twentieth century, they would have to know some information about that topic. That information may be part of students' background knowledge. If students have to find information from other sources, they engage in research (Harvey, 1998). Then they can organize information in any of the accepted patterns of expository writing. This section provides information to help students learn the organizational patterns of expository writing through various resources, teaching strategies, ideas, and activities.

Expository Writing Patterns

- Simple Explanation
- Steps-in-a-Process
- Compare and Contrast
- Cause and Effect

TEACHING STRATEGY 1 ▶▶▶▶▶▶▶▶▶▶▶▶ Explanation/ Definition Writing

Explanation/Definition Writing is one of the kinds of expository writing with which students are probably familiar. Many trade books and textbooks have sections that are organized by simple explanation. That means the writing begins with a main idea, details are given to support the main idea, and examples are given to illustrate the details. Although the main idea of any paragraph can be anywhere in the paragraph, or not even directly stated, most explanation writing that students will read or hear has the main idea stated in the first sentence. Explanation/Definition Writing is one of the easiest types of expository writing to teach students.

 ## Directions

1. Tell students that you will be introducing Explanation/Definition Writing. Tell students that writers choose the explanation/definition organizational pattern of writing when they want to explain a point or define a concept. Remind students that writers decide on writing patterns based on their topics, purposes, and audiences.

2. Describe Explanation/Definition Writing by using the Organizational Pattern Outline that follows. Make an overhead transparency of the example and point out the various components of the pattern. Remind students that Explanation/Definition Writing will follow the outline in many respects but that writing can deviate from the outline.

3. Tell students that you will show them an example of Explanation/Definition Writing. Locate an example of Explanation/Definition Writing written by a student at your grade level or, if appropriate, use the Student Example that follows.

4. Make a transparency of the Student Example. Identify the features that make the piece of writing Explanation/Definition rather than a different organizational pattern.

 5. Locate additional pieces of writing that could be classified as Explanation/Definition Writing. Have small groups of students read their writings and look for organizational features.

6. After students have seen how Explanation/Definition Writing is organized, help them develop a topic for writing that can be organized in a Writing Frame or on a Graphic Organizer. Young students and students who have little background with expository writing should begin organizing their ideas with a Writing Frame.

7. Provide students with a model of a Writing Frame by developing your own piece of writing or by using the example that follows. Make a transparency of the example, share it with students, and explain how the example was developed from the Writing Frame. Duplicate and distribute the blank Writing Frame that follows. Tell students that they will be writing their ideas on the Writing Frame.

Good habits are an important part of leading a healthy life. Getting regular exercise, eating nutritious foods, and getting plenty of sleep all are important components of a healthy life. **First**, most people need to have regular exercise to feel good and to stay healthy. **Another** part of staying healthy is eating nutritious foods. Eating plenty of fruits and vegetables is an essential part of good nutrition. **Finally**, sleeping is important. Getting seven or eight hours of sleep every night is part of healthy habits. **Habits such as regular exercise, eating nutritious foods, and getting plenty of sleep make up a healthy lifestyle.**

8. Students who are more independent writers can organize their ideas on Graphic Organizers. Once students have thought of ideas for writing, duplicate and distribute the Graphic Organizer that follows.

9. Have students map their ideas for their stories on the Graphic Organizers. Tell students that organizing their ideas before they write will improve their writing.

10. Before students write their Explanation/Definition papers, tell them that certain transition words help connect their sentences. Write the list of Explanation/Definition Transition Words on the chalkboard or on an overhead transparency. Introduce one transition word at a time by writing it in a sentence. Encourage students to try to use transition words in their writing. Remember, though, that students will misuse words frequently. Encourage many attempts and help students learn from their mistakes.

Explanation/Definition Writing Transition Words

also	first, next, then, finally
and	for example
another kind	for instance
another way	here's how
are made up of	in addition
as an example	is
consists of	it means
described as	like

ORGANIZATIONAL PATTERN OUTLINE EXPLANATION/DEFINITION WRITING

Introduction

▶ States the main idea and purposes for writing

▶ Gives three details that support the main idea

Interior Paragraph #1

▶ Restates the *first* detail

▶ Gives examples that illustrate this detail

Interior Paragraph #2

▶ Restates the *second* detail

▶ Gives examples that illustrate this detail

Interior Paragraph #3

▶ Restates the *third* detail

▶ Gives examples that illustrate this detail

Conclusion

▶ Restates the main idea

▶ Restates how the details support the main point

EXPLANATION/DEFINITION WRITING: STUDENT EXAMPLE

Living in a city would be fun. There would be more places to ride my bike, more places to go, I would have more friends, and there would be more shopping. One of the reasons I would like living in a city is that I could ride bikes around the city. The city has

sidewalks and bike paths to ride on. Another reason I would like the city is that my family could go to more places in a city. Big cities have museums, parks, and baseball games. I would also have more friends to play with because there are so many more people living in a city. Finally, there would be more stores to buy things in. Cities have shopping malls and really big stores. I would find living in a

city fun because all of these things are relaxing for me.

Josh Liming
Third Grade

From Susan Davis Lenski and Jerry L. Johns, *Improving Writing: Resources, Strategies, and Assessments.* Copyright © 2000 by Kendall/Hunt Publishing Company (1-800-247-3458). May be reproduced for noncommercial educational purposes.

Writing Frame
Explanation/Definition Writing

Main idea sentence

_____ .

Sentence giving three details

_____ .

First, _____

_____ .

Another, _____

_____ .

Finally, _____

_____ .

Concluding sentence repeating three details

_____ .

Name_____ Date_____

Graphic Organizer
Explanation/Definition Writing

_____
Topic

Detail #1 _____
Examples _____
_____
_____

Detail #2 _____
Examples _____
_____
_____

Detail #3 _____
Examples _____
_____
_____

_____
Conclusion

TEACHING STRATEGY 2 ▶ ▶ ▶ **Steps-in-a-Process Writing**

The type of expository writing that is organized as Steps-in-a-Process Writing is familiar to many teachers. Teachers frequently have students give step-by-step directions, such as directions to make a sandwich or directions to make a paper airplane. All of these writings are Steps-in-a-Process Writing. The important part of Steps-in-a-Process Writing is to give clear, concise directions that are sequential. It's fun to watch students follow each other's directions for making cookies when the directions start with placing the pan in the oven, but when you are writing directions for real, being accurate is important. Students can easily learn how to write accurate directions using Steps-in-a-Process Writing.

Directions

▶ Could a student this young complete a "Steps-in-a-Process" assignment?

1. Tell students that you will be introducing Steps-in-a-Process Writing. Tell students that writers can choose this type of organizational pattern when they want to state clear directions. Remind students that writers decide on writing patterns depending on their topics, purposes, and audiences.

2. Describe the Steps-in-a-Process Writing by using the Organizational Pattern Outline that follows. Make an overhead transparency of the example and point out the various components of the pattern. Remind students that Steps-in-a-Process Writing will follow the outline in many respects but that writing can deviate from the outline.

3. Tell students that you will show them an example of Steps-in-a-Process Writing. Locate an example written by a student at your grade level or, if appropriate, use the Student Example that follows.

4. Make a transparency of the Student Example. Identify the features that make the writing a Steps-in-a-Process piece of writing rather than a different organizational pattern.

5. Locate additional pieces of writing that could be classified as Steps-in-a-Process Writing. Have small groups of students read their writings and look for organizational features.

6. After students have seen how Steps-in-a-Process Writing is organized, help them develop topics for writing that can be organized in a Writing Frame or on a Graphic Organizer. Young students and students who have little background with expository writing should begin organizing their ideas with a Writing Frame.

7. Provide students with a model of a Writing Frame by developing your own piece of writing or by using the example that follows. Make a transparency of the example, share it with students, and explain how the example was developed from the Writing Frame. Duplicate and distribute the blank Writing Frame that follows. Tell students that they will be writing their ideas on the Writing Frame.

Writing Frame
Steps-in-a-Process Example

Here is how a chocolate cake **is made. First**, you gather all of the ingredients exactly, such as flour, sugar, chocolate, and shortening. **Next**, you mix them up until they form a smooth batter. **Then**, you pour the batter into cake pans and bake it in the oven for 35 minutes. **Finally**, you eat your chocolate cake with lots of ice cream.

8. Students who are more independent writers can organize their ideas on Graphic Organizers. Once students have thought of ideas for writing, duplicate and distribute the Graphic Organizer that follows.

9. Have students map their ideas for their stories on the Graphic Organizers. Tell students that organizing their ideas before they write will improve their writing.

10. Before students write their Steps-in-a-Process papers, tell them that certain transition words help connect their sentences. Write the list of Steps-in-a-Process Transition Words on the chalkboard or on an overhead transparency. Introduce one transition word at a time by writing it in a sentence. Encourage students to try to use transition words in their writing. Remember, though, that students will misuse words frequently. Encourage many attempts and help students learn from their mistakes.

Steps-in-a-Process Writing
Transition Words

after
as
before
finally
first, second, next, then, last
not long after
now
when

ORGANIZATIONAL PATTERN OUTLINE
STEPS-IN-A-PROCESS WRITING

Introduction

- States the topic and purposes for writing

Interior Paragraph #1

- Describes the *first* part of the process
- Gives examples that illustrate this part

Interior Paragraph #2

- Describes the *second* part of the process
- Gives examples that illustrate this part

Interior Paragraph #3

- Describes the *third* part of the process
- Gives examples that illustrate this part

Conclusion

- Restates the topic

STEPS-IN-A-PROCESS WRITING: STUDENT EXAMPLE

How to Make a Cookie Burger

If you want to make a cookie burger, you need to follow these steps. The first step is to get some chocolate frosting. You can make your own or buy the kind in a can. Next you need to get some vanilla wafers. You'll need lots of them because you might want to eat some as you work. After that you need to make sure you have an even number of wafers for the cookie burgers. You can eat any leftovers. Next you need a knife to put on the frosting. Then you place the cookies flat side up.

Before you begin frosting the cookies, make sure you have placed them in groups of two. Then you put the frosting on each and every cookie, flat side up. The very last thing you do is put each pair of cookies together to make the frosting sides touch. Then you have cookie burgers to enjoy!

Justin Stickney
Sixth Grade

States topic

Steps with examples

Conclusion

Writing Frame
Steps-in-a-Process Writing

Here is how a _____

is made. First, _____

_____

_____ .

Next, _____

_____

_____ .

Then, _____

_____

_____ .

Finally, _____

_____ .

Name_____ Date_____

Graphic Organizer
Steps-in-a-Process Writing

_____

Name of process

Steps in the process

1. _____

2. _____

3. _____

4. _____

5. _____

6. _____

_____

Conclusion

TEACHING STRATEGY 3 ▶ ▶ ▶ ▶ ▶ ▶ ▶ ▶ ▶ ▶ Compare and Contrast Writing

The Compare and Contrast Writing pattern is another type of expository writing that students frequently see. We compare and contrast things all of the time. We may compare and contrast prices in stores, models of cars, or even breeds of dogs. Because our society compares and contrasts things often, students may be familiar with the thinking process that is needed for Compare and Contrast Writing. They will, however, need instruction in this type of writing so that they can express their thoughts more clearly.

⟵⟶ Directions

1. Tell students that you will be introducing a type of writing called Compare and Contrast Writing. Tell students that writers choose this type of organizational pattern when they want to compare and contrast two or more things. Remind students that writers decide on writing patterns depending on their topics, purposes, and audiences.

2. Describe Compare and Contrast Writing by using the Organizational Pattern Outline that follows. Make an overhead transparency of the example and point out the various components of the pattern. Remind students that Compare and Contrast Writing will follow the outline in many respects but that writing can deviate from the outline.

3. Tell students that you will show them an example of Compare and Contrast Writing. Locate an example written by a student at your grade level or, if appropriate, use the Student Example that follows.

4. Make a transparency of the Student Example. Identify the features that make the piece of writing a compare and contrast pattern rather than a different organizational pattern.

5. Locate additional pieces of writing that could be classified as Compare and Contrast Writing. Have small groups of students read their writings and look for organizational features.

6. After students have seen how Compare and Contrast Writing is organized, help them develop topics for writing that can be organized in a Writing Frame or on a Graphic Organizer. Young students and students who have little background with expository writing should begin organizing their ideas with a Writing Frame.

7. Provide students with a model of a Writing Frame by developing your own piece of writing or by using the example. Make a transparency of the example, show it to students, and explain how the example was developed from the Writing Frame. Duplicate and distribute the blank Writing Frame that follows. Tell students that they will be writing their ideas on the Writing Frame.

Writing Frame
Compare and Contrast Example

Fairy tales **and** tall tales **are alike in several ways. Both** fairy tales **and** tall tales **are alike because** they aren't true. **They are also alike because** they have talking animals. Fairy tales **and** tall tales **are also different. They are different because they** have different settings. **They are also different because** they make different uses of exaggeration. Fairy tales **and** tall tales **are similar and different.**

8. Students who are more independent writers can organize their ideas on Graphic Organizers. Once students have thought of ideas for writing, duplicate and distribute the Graphic Organizer that follows.

9. Have students map their ideas for their stories on the Graphic Organizers. Tell students that organizing their ideas before they write will improve their writing.

10. Before students write Compare and Contrast papers, tell them that certain transition words help connect their sentences. Write the list of Compare and Contrast Transition Words on the chalkboard or on an overhead transparency. Introduce one transition word at a time by writing it in a sentence. Encourage students to try to use transition words in their writing. Remember, though, that students will misuse words frequently. Encourage many attempts and help students learn from their mistakes.

Compare and Contrast Writing
Transition Words

alike	however
also	in comparison
as well as	in the same way
both	instead
but	on the other hand
different	same
either . . . or	similar
have in common	unlike

ORGANIZATIONAL PATTERN OUTLINE
COMPARE AND CONTRAST WRITING

Introduction

- States the things being compared
- States how they are alike and how they are different

Interior Paragraph #1

- States one or more of the similarities
- Provides examples that illustrate the similarities

Interior Paragraph #2

- States one or more of the differences
- Provides examples that illustrate the differences

Conclusion

- Restates the things being compared
- States whether they are mainly alike or mainly different

COMPARISON AND CONTRAST WRITING: STUDENT EXAMPLE

Two Tribes

The Plains Indians and the Anasazi Indians were alike in some ways and

different in other ways. I learned that both of the tribes made their own clothes.

They also were careful about using the environment. For example, the Plains

Indians didn't just kill buffalo when they didn't need them, and the Anasazi

used water carefully. The tribes were also different. The Plains Indians lived on

flat grassy land. The Anasazi lived in the southwest in the desert. The Plains

Indians lived in teepees, and the Anasazi Indians lived in the cliffs of Mesa

Verde. The Plains Indians killed their food like buffalo, and the Anasazi had to

grow their food like corn, beans, and squash. The two tribes, the Plains Indians

and the Anasazi Indians, were alike in some ways but different.

Lauren Board
Third Grade

Name _____ Date _____

Writing Frame
Compare and Contrast Writing

_____ and _____

are alike in several ways. Both _____

and _____ are alike because _____

_____ .

They are also alike because _____

_____ .

_____ and _____

are also different. They are different because they _____

_____ .

They are also different because _____

_____ .

_____ and _____

are similar and different.

Name _____ Date _____

Graphic Organizer
Compare and Contrast Writing

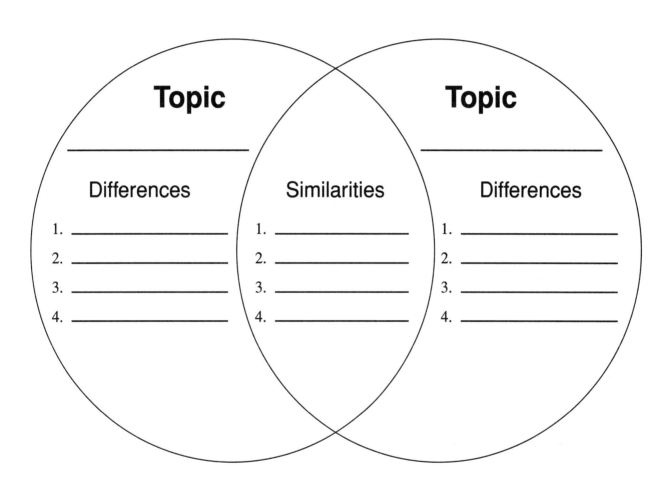

TEACHING STRATEGY 4 ▶ ▶ ▶ ▶ Cause and Effect Writing

Cause and Effect Writing is a bit more subtle than the other types of expository writing. In this type of writing, a cause is stated with its effect. Students typically have more difficulty with this type of writing. Cause and Effect Writing, however, is an important organizational tool for students to learn. Throughout their lives, students have learned that there are consequences for actions. In Cause and Effect Writing, students can learn the thinking and writing processes behind actions and consequences. With instruction, even young students can learn how to compose Cause and Effect Writing.

⊕ Directions

1. Tell students that you will be introducing Cause and Effect Writing. Help students understand cause and effect by using a concrete example, such as when they go out in the rain, they will get wet. Tell students that writers can choose this type of organizational pattern when they want to show the causes and effects of something. Remind students that writers decide on writing patterns depending on their topics, purposes, and audiences.

2. Describe Cause and Effect Writing by using the Organizational Pattern Outline that follows. Make an overhead transparency of the outline and point out the various components of the pattern. Remind students that Cause and Effect Writing will follow the outline in many respects but that writing can deviate from the outline.

3. Tell students that you will show them an example of Cause and Effect Writing. Locate an example written by a student at your grade level or, if appropriate, use the Student Example that follows.

4. Make a transparency of the Student Example. Identify the features that make the piece of writing a cause and effect pattern rather than a different organizational pattern.

 5. Locate additional pieces of writing that could be classified as Cause and Effect Writing. Have small groups of students read their writings and look for organizational features.

6. After students have seen how Cause and Effect Writing is organized, help them develop topics for writing that can be organized in a Writing Frame or on a Graphic Organizer. Young students and students who have little background with expository writing should begin organizing their ideas with a Writing Frame.

7. Provide students with a model of a Writing Frame as in the example that follows or develop your own piece of writing. Make a transparency of the example, share it with students, and explain how the example was developed from the Writing Frame. Duplicate and distribute the blank Writing Frame that follows. Tell students that they will be writing their ideas on the Writing Frame.

Writing Frame
Cause and Effect Example

Because of pollution it is no longer safe to swim in many lakes and rivers. The dumping of wastes from factories **has caused** lakes and rivers to become polluted. **Therefore,** swimmers can contract a variety of diseases if they swim in these waters. Motor oil **has also caused** pollution in lakes and rivers. The gasoline from motor boats spills into the lakes and rivers. **This explains why** the lakes and rivers are so polluted.

8. Students who are more independent writers can organize their ideas on Graphic Organizers. Once students have thought of ideas for writing, duplicate and distribute the Graphic Organizer that follows.

9. Have students map their ideas for their stories on the Graphic Organizers. Tell students that organizing their ideas before they write will improve their writing.

10. When students write their Cause and Effect papers, tell them that certain transition words help connect their sentences. Write the list of Cause and Effect Transition Words on the chalkboard or on an overhead transparency. Introduce one transition word at a time by writing it in a sentence. Encourage students to try to use transition words in their writing. Remember, though, that students will misuse words frequently. Encourage many attempts and help students learn from their mistakes.

Cause and Effect Writing
Transition Words

as a result
because
consequently
due to
for that reason
if
leads to
so
then
when

ORGANIZATIONAL PATTERN OUTLINE
CAUSE AND EFFECT WRITING

Introduction
◆ States the cause and its effects

Interior Paragraph #1
◆ Restates the *first* effect
◆ Gives examples that illustrate this effect

Interior Paragraph #2
◆ Restates the *second* effect
◆ Gives examples that illustrate this effect

Interior Paragraph #3
◆ Restates the *third* effect
◆ Gives examples that illustrate this effect

Conclusion
◆ Restates the cause with its effects

CAUSE AND EFFECT: STUDENT EXAMPLE

The Effects of Pollution

Pollution and abusing the natural environment are ruining the earth. Too many people drive by themselves and don't car pool or take public transportation. Because of the exhaust from these extra cars, there is more car exhaust in the air than there should be. Car exhaust, in turn, has caused acid rain which pollutes water, and has caused damage to buildings like the Statue of Liberty. The amount of exhaust in the air may also be responsible for the hole in the ozone layer. Burning trash has also caused pollution by contaminating the air we breathe.

> Cause and effect introduced

> Cause and effects described

There are many ways to change the increasing amounts of pollution in the earth. If each town collected everything that needed to be burned once a month and took the trash to a place where no one lived and burned it there, we wouldn't be hurt as much by contaminated air.

If people would car pool, take buses, planes, and taxis, we wouldn't have near as much car exhaust which in turn would mean less acid rain.

> Conclusion

Changing the way we look at our environment can make important changes in our earth's environment.

Josh Wurmnest
Seventh Grade

Name _____ Date _____

Writing Frame
Cause and Effect Writing

Because of _____

_____ .

_____ **has caused** _____

_____ .

Therefore, _____

_____ .

_____ **has also caused** _____

_____ .

_____ .

This explains why _____

_____ .

Name_____ Date_____

Graphic Organizer
Cause and Effect Writing

_____
Topic

Causes	Effects
_____ → _____
_____ → _____
_____ → _____
_____ → _____
_____ → _____

_____
Conclusion

 **Ideas and Activities**

1. Tell students that they read and hear expository writing at home and at school. Read nonfiction books and remind students that these books are expository writing similar to the kinds of writings they do. To choose books that are the most valuable for your class, use the criteria that follow (Moss, Leone, & Dipillo, 1997).

   • authority of the author
   • accuracy of text content
   • appropriateness of the book for children
   • literary artistry
   • appearance of the book

2. Help students learn the various organizational patterns of expository writing by Text Tapping (Turbill, Butler, Cambourne, & Langton, 1991). Text Tapping is a verbal modeling strategy that prepares young students for writing expository texts as they learn more about writing. Text Tapping "taps" into students' existing knowledge and links what students have read and heard with what they can write. Text Tapping is an important strategy to use with young students. Students rarely hear expository writing. To use Text Tapping, select a piece of writing that illustrates the kind of expository writing that you want students to learn. (You may have to write one yourself or use the example that follows.) Write the passage on the chalkboard or on an overhead transparency. Read the passage with students several times. Have students read the passage with you. Point out the features of the text to students reminding them that writers use this type of pattern at times. For example, for the pattern main idea-details, use the following sentences.

   > I saw two new animals at the zoo yesterday. One of the animals that I saw was a bear. He was sleeping in the sun. Another animal I saw was a giraffe, who was eating leaves from a very tall tree. I loved seeing these two beautiful animals.

   Explain to students that the first sentence is the big idea, or main idea. Tell students that writers sometimes begin their writing with a main idea sentence. Then read the next sentences with students. Help students understand that the sentences that follow the main idea relate to the first sentence. Point out the transition words "one" and "another." Tell students that these words connect the sentences. Tell students that writers use this kind of pattern at times.

3. Word Sorts (Gillet & Kita, 1979) can help young students learn how to organize and classify ideas. The object of a Word Sort is to group words into categories according to some shared feature. Select 12 to 15 words that are related. Some words should be categories and others should be details. Write the words on sets of note cards. Divide the class into groups of three or four students. Tell students that they will be participating in Word Sorts and that they are to sort the words according to the categories you have established. Distribute a set of note cards to each group. Allow 10 minutes for students to sort the words. Ask a student from each group to share one of their group's lists of words. Continue until all of the categories have been discussed. Invite students to explain why they sorted the words as they did.

4. Young students can learn the concept of main ideas and details by using an umbrella picture such as the one that follows. Draw an umbrella on the chalkboard or on an overhead transparency. Under the umbrella draw two or three raindrops. On the umbrella write a main idea or a topic such as teachers in the school. On the raindrops write the names of two or three teachers. Tell students that sometimes when writers write they begin with the main idea and then write details.

Model a paragraph using the information on the umbrella picture, such as "We have three kindergarten teachers in this school. One kindergarten teacher's name is Mr. Fremley. Another kindergarten teacher's name is Mrs. Mason. The third kindergarten teacher's name is Ms. Wetzel. All of our kindergarten teachers are nice."

Have students repeat the paragraph with you. Having students repeat sentences organized in the main idea-detail pattern helps them develop background knowledge about the organizational patterns of expository writing.

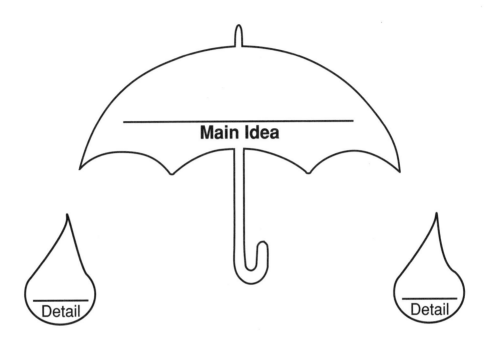

5. Introduce the concept of Magnet Words to your students by telling them that magnets attract metal objects to them and magnet words attract information or details to them (Lenski, Wham, & Johns, 1999). Have students read a nonfiction passage or read it to them. Help students understand that most of the details in the passage "stick to" the topic. Identify one or more words in the passage that are crucial to the meaning of the passage. List the words on the chalkboard or on an overhead transparency. Explain to students that these words are Magnet Words. Have students generate additional important words from the passage. List the student-generated words under the Magnet Words. Then have students write a new passage using the Magnet Words. Remind students that this type of informational writing is called expository writing and that it "sticks to" the topic.

6. Tell students that expository writing often uses a Known-New pattern of sentences (Kolln, 1999). Write a sentence on the chalkboard or on an overhead transparency about a topic that all students know. Under that sentence invite students to write something new. Tell students that the new sentence does not mean it is information that no one else knows but that the new sentence is generated from the first sentence. The following pair of sentences illustrates a Known-New pattern.

1. (Known) Most of the students in our class have computers at home.
2. (New) Students with computers prefer playing computer games to video games.

7. Encourage students to write brief messages and postcards using the form main idea-detail. Model an example for students such as the message that follows. After students have created messages or postcards, have them post their writings on the WRAL Postcard Shop web site that follows.

> I spent Saturday at the ballpark playing soccer.
> My team lost, but I made three excellent plays.

Technology Tip

WRAL Postcard Shop

Students can design, send, and receive postcard messages with this web site.

www.wral.tv.com/mall/cards/

▷ Will this young student learn main idea and detail concepts from the umbrella model?

Persuasive Writing

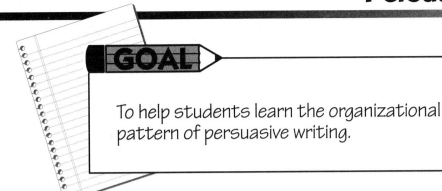

GOAL

To help students learn the organizational pattern of persuasive writing.

5.4

Background

The art of persuasion and creating effective arguments is not a natural human ability but must be learned (Fulkerson, 1996). Frequently, students come to teachers with requests or opinions with little substantiating rationale. For example, a student may say to a teacher, "We need a hamster in our class." When queried about the reasons for this opinion, a student may respond, "Because." In general, students haven't had experience forming opinions that are based on sound reasoning.

Some types of persuasion, such as the kinds of advertising campaigns we see on television and the Internet, use visual cues to transform viewers' opinions. Often the picture "sells" more than the text does. Creating an effective argument in writing, however, is much more difficult. Writing persuasive essays requires instruction and practice.

Persuasive writing is written in an organizational pattern that is similar to expository writing. To persuade, writers must:

- make a claim,
- offer reasons for that claim, and
- provide examples or details that illustrate the reasoning.

Students rarely have had these types of experiences in their lives. In addition, they rarely have read the type of persuasive essays they are expected to write in schools. For that reason, students need extra time to learn the organizational pattern of persuasive writing so they can learn to think and write using logic and reasoning. Once students have become comfortable with persuasion, watch out! They will have persuasive reasons for getting that class pet. This section provides resources, teaching strategies, ideas, and activities to help students learn how to organize and write persuasive essays.

The art of persuasion and creating effective arguments is not a natural human ability but must be learned.

TEACHING STRATEGY 1 ▶ ▶ ▶ ▶ ▶ ▶ **Organizational Pattern**

Persuasive writing has a specific organizational pattern: subject, reasons, and examples. Students often are unfamiliar with the organizational pattern of persuasive writing because it is a form that is used only in a certain type of writing. There are two basic steps to teach the structure of persuasive writing.

1. Tell students explicitly the organizational pattern of persuasive essays.
2. Show them an example of a persuasive essay that was written by a student at their grade level.

Students can identify patterns in essays that were written at their own developmental level easier than they can in essays that were written by professional authors. Writings that are too complex can discourage students and keep them from learning how to organize their own pieces of persuasive writing.

 ## Directions

1. Tell students that they hear persuasive arguments frequently but that they may not have read persuasive essays. Explain to students that when they hear commercials on television, read them on the Internet, or see advertisements, they are experiencing an author trying to persuade a listener or a reader. Tell students that these modes of persuasion can use pictures, sounds, and words. Explain that when writing persuasive essays students will be using words only.

2. Duplicate and distribute the Organizational Pattern Outline that follows. Tell students that persuasive writing usually follows the outline.

3. Divide the class into groups of three or four students. Have students read the Organizational Pattern Outline or read it with them. Discuss the components of persuasive writing with students.

4. Tell students that you will show them an example of persuasive writing. Locate an example of persuasive writing written by a student at your grade level or, if appropriate, use the Student Example that follows.

5. Make a transparency of an example of student writing. Identify the features that make the piece persuasive writing.

6. Locate additional pieces of writing that could be classified as persuasive writing. Have small groups of students read the stories and look for the organizational features of persuasive writing.

Organizational Pattern Outline
Persuasive Writing

Introduction
- States the subject and the purposes for writing
- Gives three reasons that support the view
- States the opinion in one sentence

Interior Paragraph #1
- Restates the *first* reason that supports the point of view
- Gives examples and details that support this reason

Interior Paragraph #2
- Restates the *second* reason that supports the point of view
- Gives examples and details that support this reason

Interior Paragraph #3
- Restates the *third* reason that supports the point of view
- Gives examples and details that support this reason

Conclusion
- Restates the subject of the paper
- Summarizes how the reasons support the point of view
- Concludes with a summary of the opinion

PERSUASIVE WRITING: STUDENT EXAMPLE

The Best Grandpa in the World

I have the best Grandpa in the world because he loves me. He makes a lot of things for me, he lets me do things that I can't do at home, and we have a lot of fun together.

Opinion and three reasons

First, Grandpa makes a lot of things for me. For example, he made my brothers and me a tire swing and an inner tube for the creek. I can climb to the top of the swing. Another example is that when there's something wrong with our go-cart, he fixes it.

Reason #1 and example

Next, Grandpa lets me do things I can't do at home. Once I got to drive his truck around their drive. I wrote my name on the floor of his shed when the concrete was still wet. After he's done using his skid steer, I get to drive it around.

Reason #2 and example

Last, we have a lot of fun together. He always makes me laugh. Sometimes he pretends he's going to run me over. One year after my birthday he told me he had next year's present already. I had to wait a whole year for it.

Reason #3 and example

My Grandpa is the best Grandpa ever. He makes a lot of stuff for me, he lets me do things I can't do at home, and we have a lot of fun together. What a wonderful man!

Conclusion

Koree Larimer
Sixth Grade

TEACHING STRATEGY 2 ▶▶▶▶▶▶▶▶▶▶ **Opinion Charts**

Before students can begin writing persuasive arguments, they need to know their opinions and the reasons for those opinions. Students can be very opinionated, but often they have not thought through their opinions. Having students complete Opinion Charts can help students discover their opinions, understand what they would like to change, and think of reasons to support their opinions.

 ## Directions

1. Tell students that they will be developing their own opinions with Opinion Charts. Explain to students that opinions are one person's viewpoint and that opinions are not necessarily shared by others.

2. Give an example of an opinion statement, such as "Hot weather is more comfortable than cold weather." Write the statement on the chalkboard or on an overhead transparency. Ask students how many agree with the statement and how many disagree. Tell students that there is not one right answer—an opinion expresses one person's ideas.

3. Read *If I Were in Charge of the World* (Viorst, 1981). Tell students to think about themselves as in charge of the world, the school, their family, or any other institution. Have students imagine what it would be like if they were in charge. Give students time to think, possibly more than one day.

 4. After students have thought about being in charge, divide the class into groups of three or four students and have them discuss their opinions with the members of their groups. Have students share several opinions with the entire class.

5. Tell each student to choose one opinion to write on the Opinion Chart. Explain that forming opinions is the basis for persuasive writing.

6. Duplicate and distribute the Opinion Chart that follows. Have students think through their viewpoints by deciding how it is now, what changes could be made, who is in charge, and the reasons for those changes.

7. Develop one row of an Opinion Chart yourself and share it with students or use the example that follows. Then give students time to complete at least one row of their Opinion Charts. Have students place their Opinion Charts in their writing folders for use when they want to write a persuasive argument.

How is it now?	What changes do I picture?	Who is in charge?	What reasons do I have for the change?
Students go to school 180 to 185 days each year.	I think students should go to school at least 200 days per year.	The school board, the parents, and the teachers.	Students would learn more if they were able to attend school more days per year.

Opinion Chart
Persuasive Writing

How is it now?	What changes do I picture?	Who is in charge?	What reasons do I have for the change?

TEACHING STRATEGY 3 ▶▶▶▶▶▶▶▶▶▶ Writing Frame

Persuasive writing has an organizational structure that is similar to expository writing. The key difference between persuasive writing and expository writing is that persuasive writing expresses an opinion rather than stating facts or explanations. Writing Frames help students understand how persuasive writing is organized. After students have generated opinions and reasons for those opinions, they should organize their ideas into the organizational pattern of persuasive writing. Students can organize their ideas in many ways. Young students generally are more successful when they organize their ideas with Writing Frames. Writing Frames give students experience writing with a specific organizational pattern without having to know how to write the transitions. They also give students important background knowledge about ways different pieces of writing can be structured.

✦ Directions

1. Tell students that once they have an opinion they need to organize their ideas using the organizational pattern of persuasive writing. Remind students that persuasive writing should have a subject or opinion, reasons for that opinion, and examples to support the reasons.

2. Young students and students who have little background with persuasive writing should begin organizing their ideas with a Writing Frame. Duplicate and distribute the Writing Frame that follows. Tell students that they will be writing their ideas on the Writing Frame.

3. Develop a Writing Frame example or make a transparency of the example that follows. Share the Writing Frame example with students and explain how the essay was developed from the Writing Frame.

4. Have students write their own pieces of persuasive writing using a Writing Frame.

Writing Frame
Persuasive Writing Example

I think that we should have a class pet **because** a class pet would be a great learning experience. **I think this because** pets need care, they are good topics for observational logs, and pets are lovable. **First**, to care for a pet would be good for us. We would learn responsibility because we would need to feed it and give it water. **Second**, a pet would be interesting to watch and write about. We could record how much it eats, when it sleeps, and how it plays. **Third**, it would be good for us to have something else in the class to love. Some students are shy and they could love and talk to the pet. **I believe that** a class pet would be a good decision **and I** hope you do too.

Writing Frame
Persuasive Writing

I think that _____

because _____ .

I think this because _____

_____ .

First, _____

_____ .

Second, _____

_____ .

Third, _____

_____ .

I believe that _____

and _____ .

TEACHING STRATEGY 4 ▶ ▶ ▶ ▶ ▶ ▶ ▶ ▶ **Graphic Organizer**

Graphic Organizers are another way to organize information before writing. Graphic Organizers are similar to outlines, but they form a visual representation of the writing's organization. Graphic Organizers can be used before, during, and after writing. Before writing, students can plot their ideas on Graphic Organizers and refer to them when they write. Students also can use Graphic Organizers during writing. As writers complete sections of writing, they can refer to their Graphic Organizers to remind themselves of the pattern of their writing. After writing, students can map out the ideas from their writing on Graphic Organizers to verify that they have all of the components of the writing pattern. Older students especially will find Graphic Organizers useful for learning the organizational patterns of different writing structures.

▶ Do you have copies of the Graphic Organizer ready to help students organize their writing?

✛ Directions

1. Remind students that Persuasive Writing has a specific organizational pattern. Tell students that a Graphic Organizer is a visual representation of the writing pattern.

2. Students who are independent writers can organize their ideas on Graphic Organizers. Once students have thought of an idea for a persuasive essay, duplicate and distribute the Graphic Organizer that follows.

3. Have students map out their ideas for their essays on Graphic Organizers. Provide guidance as necessary. Tell students that organizing their ideas before they write will help them organize their writing.

4. Allow students time to plot their ideas on Graphic Organizers. If students have not generated enough ideas before writing, have them partially complete their Graphic Organizers and begin writing.

5. Tell students that they also can assess their writing organization by using Graphic Organizers after writing. Have students place several copies of the Graphic Organizer in their writing folders. After students have written persuasive essays, have them use their Graphic Organizers to determine whether they organized their writing according to the writing pattern.

Name _____ Date _____

Graphic Organizer
Persuasive Writing

Opinion
_____
Opinion

Reason #1 _____
Examples _____
_____
_____

Reason #2 _____
Examples _____
_____
_____

Reason #3 _____
Examples _____
_____
_____

_____
Conclusion

Ideas and Activities

1. Tell students that each person has his or her own opinions. Explain to students that what one person believes may be different from what other people believe. Tell students that in order to persuade others they need to understand that other people will have different opinions. Choose a topic, such as animals. Write the name of the topic on the chalkboard or on an overhead transparency. Ask students individually to develop a series of statements about animals. Write on the chalkboard or on an overhead transparency an example of a statement, such as "I like animals such as bears that have stubby tails." Give students 10 minutes to write at least seven statements. After students have finished their lists, divide the class into groups of two or three students. Have students read to each other their lists of statements about animals. Tell students to notice how their lists are similar and how they are different.

2. Tell students that when they write persuasive essays they should try to predict the counterarguments of their readers. Counterarguments are other persons' points of view. Tell students that they can practice understanding other points of view by thinking about the opinions of fairy tale characters. Read *The True Story of the Three Little Pigs* (Schieska, 1989), which is the classic three little pigs tale told from the point of view of the wolf. Explain that even villains have a point of view and that villains may consider themselves to be in the right. Read another well-known tale that has a villain and play the game Who Me? Write on the chalkboard or on an overhead transparency the words "Who Me? The villain? You must be kidding." Have students list statements from the villain's point of view under the heading. For example, after reading *Little Red Riding Hood*, have a list of statements from the wolf's point of view, such as "Of course I ate Grandma. Wolves have to eat too. And Grandma thought nothing about eating animals." Have fun with the statements and encourage students to think beyond the typical point of view.

3. Tell students that they need to have a variety of valid reasons that support their opinions. Often students have difficulty thinking of reasons to support their thinking. To practice generating reasons, have students play I Have My Reasons. Think of an opinion that would be of interest to students, such as "Students should have longer recesses." Write the opinion on the chalkboard or on an overhead transparency. Divide the class into groups of three or four students. Tell students to discuss reasons that support the statement. Give the groups 10 minutes to generate their reasons. After students have thought of several reasons, have each group share one reason with the class. Write the reasons under the statement. As students share their reasons, guide them into giving valid reasons that support the statements.

4. To be persuasive, students need to learn how to defend their opinions. To help students practice defending their opinions, play the game Let's Vote (McCarthy, 1998). List on the chalkboard or on an overhead transparency the major qualities of characters in well-known tales as in the example that follows. Divide the class into groups of three or four students. Have each group choose one quality from the chart. Instruct students to choose the character from the chart who they think best exemplifies this quality and to list examples to support their claims. After students have generated examples have them write persuasive paragraphs defending their positions. Then have students vote on which paragraph is most persuasive.

Quality	Characters
Clever	The third pig in "The Three Little Pigs" Jack in "Jack and the Beanstalk"

5. Persuasive writing frequently includes certain words that make transitions between sentences. Write on the chalkboard or on an overhead transparency the list that follows. Explain to students that these transition words help readers understand how their ideas are connected. Model an example of a sentence that uses one of the words. Have students practice using that transition word in a sentence. Remind students to use that transition word in their writing. Teach additional transition words over a period of several weeks. Remember that students will need much practice using these words before they will use them correctly.

Persuasive Writing Transition Words
although but however in contrast nevertheless on the other hand though while yet

6. Encourage students to write essays that are sincerely persuasive. To provide students with a persuasive writing experience, create a radio broadcast similar to the *War of the Worlds* radio broadcast but with a different topic. Record some music that the class would want to hear. In the middle of the music, record a broadcast that applies to students, such as a news broadcast stating that the school board voted to require all students to wear uniforms to school. (You might want to have someone else record the broadcast in case students recognize your voice.) Play the tape of music for the class. Tell students to relax and listen to the music. When the broadcast comes on the tape, alert students. Tell them that this is current news and that they should respond to the news in writing. Have students write a persuasive essay either in favor of or opposed to the idea presented in the broadcast. After students have finished writing, explain that the broadcast is not real. Tell them it was an activity designed to prompt them to write persuasive essays. Then enjoy the students' reactions.

Organizational Pattern Outline
Persuasive Writing

Introduction
- States the subject and the purposes for writing
- Gives three reasons that support the view
- States the opinion in one sentence

Interior Paragraph #1
- Restates the *first* reason that supports the point of view
- Gives examples and details that support this reason

Interior Paragraph #2
- Restates the *second* reason that supports the point of view
- Gives examples and details that support this reason

Interior Paragraph #3
- Restates the *third* reason that supports the point of view
- Gives examples and details that support this reason

Conclusion
- Restates the subject of the paper
- Summarizes how the reasons support the point of view
- Concludes with a summary of the opinion

PERSUASIVE WRITING: STUDENT EXAMPLE

The Best Grandpa in the World

I have the best Grandpa in the world because he loves me. He makes a lot of things for me, he lets me do things that I can't do at home, and we have a lot of fun together.

Opinion and three reasons

First, Grandpa makes a lot of things for me. For example, he made my brothers and me a tire swing and an inner tube for the creek. I can climb to the top of the swing. Another example is that when there's something wrong with our go-cart, he fixes it.

Reason #1 and example

Next, Grandpa lets me do things I can't do at home. Once I got to drive his truck around their drive. I wrote my name on the floor of his shed when the concrete was still wet. After he's done using his skid steer, I get to drive it around.

Reason #2 and example

Last, we have a lot of fun together. He always makes me laugh. Sometimes he pretends he's going to run me over. One year after my birthday he told me he had next year's present already. I had to wait a whole year for it.

Reason #3 and example

My Grandpa is the best Grandpa ever. He makes a lot of stuff for me, he lets me do things I can't do at home, and we have a lot of fun together. What a wonderful man!

Conclusion

Koree Larimer
Sixth Grade

7. Some forms of writing, such as movie reviews and letters to the editor, are written to persuade. Have students write reviews and letters to editors to express opinions and to persuade readers. Encourage students to publish their reviews and letters on the Internet on web sites such as "Little Planet Times."

Technology Tip

Little Planet Times

An interactive online newspaper for students in grades K–5 that publishes letters to the editor, movie reviews, stories, and other creative activities.

www.littleplanet.com

Assessing Writing Organization

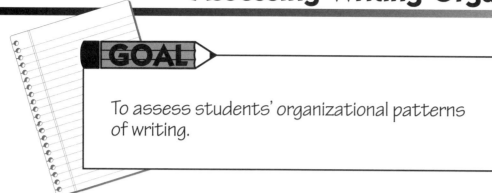

GOAL

To assess students' organizational patterns of writing.

Background

Students' writing can be assessed in a number of ways. The purpose of assessment should dictate which type of assessment strategy is used.

PRIMARY TRAIT ASSESSMENT. To assess students' organizational patterns of writing, you need to remember that you are looking only for the organization of the papers. To assess organizational patterns, you can use a primary trait assessment such as the game What's the Structure? When using a primary trait assessment strategy, assess only the organizational patterns of the writing.

HOLISTIC SCORING. Teachers frequently like to assess more than one trait of a piece of writing. Because teachers' time is limited, they frequently assess many aspects of a piece of writing at the same time. One way to look at the entire piece of writing, the organization as well as the content and mechanics, is through holistic scor-

> ### Organization Assessment
>
> - **Primary Trait Assessment (What's the Structure?)**
> - **Holistic Scoring (Anchor Papers)**
> - **Assessing with Rubrics**

ing. When you assess a piece of writing in its entirety to get a general sense of the quality of the writing, you are engaging in holistic assessment. Anchor papers can provide a helpful basis for assessment when you use holistic assessment (Wolcott & Legg, 1998). An anchor paper gives you an example of the quality of writing that you expect from students.

ASSESSING WITH RUBRICS. A final way to assess students' ability to organize writing as well as other writing skills is through a rubric. A rubric details the criteria you will use in assessment. You can use a rubric to assess one aspect of students' writing, or you can use a rubric to assess several aspects of their writing. A rubric can be tailored to your assessment expectations.

This section provides three assessment strategies to help you assess students' organizational patterns of writing.

What's the Structure? is a game to introduce and assess students' ability to identify and write different organizational patterns in writing (Richards & Gipe, 1995). You can use this game with students' writings, textbook passages, or teacher-written passages. Students can use What's the Structure? to review writing organizational patterns before they are assessed by the teacher.

Directions

1. Collect examples of the different kinds of writing: personal experience stories, fictional writing, expository writing, and persuasive writing. You can use examples from students' writings, textbooks, passages from literature books, and other sources.

2. Number the passages and place them on a large table. Place 12 passages on the table.

3. Give students a sheet of paper numbered from 1 through 12. List the names of the writing organizational patterns you used for the game. For example, if the passages are personal experience stories, persuasive writing, steps-in-a-process, and explanation, write these names on the paper.

4. Tell students that you will be giving them time during the day to go to the table, read the passages, and write on their papers the various types of writing organizational patterns used in the passages.

5. After students have finished writing the names of the organizational patterns, collect and assess their papers. Notice the types of writings that students were able to identify and unable to identify. Review the types of writings with which students had difficulty.

ANCHOR PAPERS

Anchor Papers are examples of writing that can be scored using holistic scoring methods (Wolcott & Legg, 1998). An Anchor Paper can be an exemplary paper, or it can be a typical paper done by students at your grade level. Anchor Papers help you determine the quality of your students' writings compared with writings done by other students.

Directions

1. Determine whether you want to assess students' personal experience stories, expository writing, or persuasive pieces. Tell students that you will be assessing a particular type of writing.

2. Give students a writing prompt from the lists that follow. Choose a writing prompt about which you believe students will have some background knowledge.

3. Tell students to write one draft responding to the prompt. Give students from 30 to 45 minutes to write.

4. Collect students' writings. Read the papers and divide them into three stacks: excellent writing, typical writing, and poor writing. From each of the three stacks choose four papers that seem typical for your class. Take the 12 pieces of writing and arrange them from excellent to poor. From the 12 papers, delete five papers that seem to overlap in quality with the other papers. You should now have seven papers to arrange in order of quality. Number the papers from seven for the best paper to one for the poorest paper. These are your Anchor Papers.

5. As students write new pieces, occasionally score them using the Anchor Papers as benchmarks. Read students' writings and decide the quality of the paper by assigning it a number from one through seven depending on which Anchor Paper is the most similar to students' writings.

Personal Experience Writing Prompts

1. Your class has just read a selection from the book *Rufus M.* by Eleanor Estes. As you read about Rufus's childhood, you learned that he was persistent in getting what he wanted. The editor of your local newspaper has been advertising for citizens to submit personal life stories that show determination. The top three winning stories will be published in the paper. Write a narrative paper that describes three instances in your life when you were determined to get or do something. For each of the three instances, include your own definition of determination and be sure to describe where, when, why, and how you were determined.

2. Think about a family trip you took to a special place. It might have been a trip to a forest preserve, a park, a relative, a zoo, or anything you thought was special. Write a story about going on that special trip. Tell how and why you remember the trip. Describe how you felt before, during, and after the trip. We will place all of the stories in a class book.

3. Think about a specific time when you felt awkward or embarrassed. It could have been at school, at home, or with friends. Write about that time. Explain the situation, what happened, and why you felt awkward or embarrassed. Give details surrounding the situation and be sure to explain how you felt during this experience. After you finish writing your stories, we will read them in the class writing groups.

4. Think about a special time when you celebrated a holiday or event. It could have been with your family or your friends. Choose only one event or holiday about which to write. Identify the occasion in the beginning of your paper. Tell when, where, and why the event occurred. Give specific details. Explain the feelings you experienced at that time. Give the reasons why it was special. After completing the stories, you will place them in your portfolios to show your family.

5. Think about a time when you celebrated your birthday in a special way. Identify which birthday you have selected in the beginning of your paper. Explain why it was special. Give specific details or events that led to that special birthday and explain how those events made you feel. Describe the importance or significance of your experiences. You may want to include other people who helped make this birthday special. After you finish the papers, we will include them in a class book.

6. Tell about a time when you and your family, friends, or classmates spent the day together. Perhaps it was on a special holiday or maybe a day when you planned an activity together. Identify one time about which to write. Describe your activities that day. Write who was included in the event and exactly what you did that day. Explain how you felt and why this particular day stands out in your memory. After you finish writing, you will give the stories to family or friends who were involved in the activities.

7. Think about an experience you have had that you will never forget and tell how or why it was memorable. It might have been when you saw a particular person or went to a special event or place. It might be a time when you felt that you were treated unfairly or a time when you were frightened. Choose one experience that you will never forget. Identify that special experience and tell why it was memorable. Tell what happened by giving details about the people, the situation, and how you felt. We will place the completed papers in a class book.

From Susan Davis Lenski and Jerry L. Johns, *Improving Writing: Resources, Strategies, and Assessments.* Copyright © 2000 by Kendall/Hunt Publishing Company (1-800-247-3458). May be reproduced for noncommercial educational purposes.

8. Think about a time when you learned a new skill. It may have been learning to ride a bike, learning how to read, or learning how to Rollerblade. Choose a skill that took some practice before you were able to learn it. Think of a specific skill that you learned. Include events that helped you learn the skill. Tell how you felt as you were learning. Include things you learned about yourself as a learner. After you complete the papers, you will read them to younger students.

9. Think about a time when you were a good friend or someone was a good friend to you. It could be a time when you were nice or did a special favor for someone. It could be a time when someone helped you out with a problem. Identify what you did to be a good friend. Explain the situation fully. Tell what happened during the situation and how you felt about what you did. Explain what you learned from the situation. We will put all the papers in a friendship book.

10. Think about things you have done or things that have happened to you that make your life interesting. It could be a place you have lived, an interest you have, or something you have done. Choose one aspect of your life that could be considered interesting. Describe that one situation by writing about how you felt, what you said, and who else was present. Explain why you think this situation is interesting. We will place the papers in our class museum.

11. Think about a time when you were scared. It could be a time when you were afraid as a young child, or it could be a more recent time. Identify the time when you were scared. Be sure to tell what scared you, what happened, and how you felt during and after you were scared. Use images that will help the reader feel what you felt. We will read these papers on Halloween.

12. Think about your favorite or best day at school this year. It could be a day you learned something new, a day you were recognized for an accomplishment, a day someone did something nice for you, or a day something special happened. Write about your special day by identifying the event that made the day your favorite day. Fully explain why this day was your favorite. Include the other people who were involved, your feelings about the event, and the details of the day. After you finish the papers, we will compile a classroom book about the memories of the class.

13. Think about your best Saturday ever. It could be a time when you went someplace special, when you relaxed, or when you were involved in a particular sporting event or activity. Identify the Saturday that was excellent for you. Tell why it was so special. Tell about the activities of the day in the order they occurred. Explain in detail what happened and why it happened. Tell how you felt about all of the things that happened and explain why it was your best Saturday. After you complete the papers, we will send them to the director of the park district to read.

14. Think about a time when you watched a terrific television program, played a video game, or found something interesting on the Internet. It could be a time when you were alone, with family members, or with friends. Identify a time when you really enjoyed viewing something. Describe the situation, who was there, and why you found it interesting. Explain how you felt. We will put all of the papers in our class media book.

Expository Writing Prompts

1. In science class, you have just finished learning about the different biomes that are found on Earth. The local newspaper recently has added a new travel section and has asked for your help in writing the first column. That column is titled "Biomes of the World: A Visitor's Paradise." Select a biome that you think would be an interesting place for a visitor to see, and write a news article about it.

2. Your community is planning an Earth Day celebration. Your classroom teacher is requesting that all students in the class write a paper explaining how people can help conserve the resources of our Earth. You are asked to include several things that people should or should not do to help conserve our Earth's resources. The community newspaper will print the three best papers.

3. You have been studying about health care for cats and dogs. One of the local veterinarians has expressed a need for an easy-to-read brochure that he can give to new dog and cat owners. Based on the knowledge you have gained from learning about caring for animals, write an essay explaining three important components of a pet care program for either a dog or a cat. Discuss in detail what parts of the program will provide an appropriate environment, good health care, and proper training in order to have a healthy, happy pet. Two veterinarians will pick the essays that they believe will be easy to understand and the most helpful to pet owners.

4. Families who live in the country are used to open spaces, trees and grass, fields of corn and wheat, and many different animals. Families who live in the city have buildings, trucks, buses, playgrounds, and many different kinds of people. Write an essay about the differences between city and country living for a group of city students who are going to spend a week on a farm.

5. You have been learning in school about the structure of the federal government in Washington, D.C. As part of a Global Government Awareness Program, the President requests that students in schools across the country write to their foreign classmates and explain to them as accurately as possible the structure of the United States government. Write a letter explaining what you know about the United States government.

6. The cafeteria recently has hired a new head cook who is looking for student input on menu planning. Using your knowledge of nutrition, suggest three general nutritional guidelines to follow while planning school lunch menus. Consider, also, foods students enjoy that meet these guidelines. Write a paper explaining the guidelines the new head cook should use to prepare menus.

7. You have been learning in school about dental health. The school nurse is holding an assembly for children who don't know how to care for their teeth. The nurse wants to know how children who are informed about dental health care for their teeth. Write a paper about how people can keep their teeth healthy, including examples of things to do to keep teeth healthy, and explain how each example helps maintain dental health.

8. We have been learning about fire safety. The fire department is having a writing contest for students. Think about what you would do if there were a fire at your house. Tell the fire fighters step by step what you would do to safely get out of your burning house. Be sure to include the safety rules we have learned. We will enter our work in the fire department contest.

9. You have just moved to a new town and have returned home from your first day at your new school. Your parents asked you what your new school is like. Write a paper comparing your old school with your new one. In the beginning of your paper, state whether you believe that your old and new schools are very alike or very different. Give three examples to support your belief.

10. Your science unit has been about matter. Your teacher asked you to write a paper that includes everything a classmate who has been on vacation needs to know about matter to pass the science test. Include the definition of matter, describe the three kinds of matter, and give examples of the different kinds of matter.

11. An out-of-town builder has decided to build houses where a local woods is right now. In order to build the houses, the builder must cut down over 200 trees. In class we have learned about the importance of trees in the environment. The city council doesn't seem aware of the importance of the trees; they just want the new homes in the town. Write the members of the city council a letter telling them at least three ways trees help the environment.

12. In science class, you have been learning about relationships in ecosystems. A zoologist is coming to our school to present a program on harmful and helpful relationships in ecosystems. She has requested that you become experts on the topic so that you can help her during her presentation. Write an expository paper that describes three harmful or three helpful relationships within ecosystems. Include the importance of relationships in ecosystems, the animals in each ecosystem relationship, and the names of the relationships you will discuss.

13. A member of your family recently has received some money and wants to spend some of it on a three-week family vacation to one of the fifty states. You were asked to give your opinion about where you should go, because this family member knows you have been studying the United States. Think about which state you would like to visit, why it would be a good choice, and how you could persuade your family to choose that state for your family vacation. Write a paper telling which state you want to visit, why it would be the best state to vacation in, and give examples to support your reasons.

14. Your teacher is new to your school. This teacher would like to know more about the school and would appreciate information about school traditions, school stories, and school rules. Write a paper explaining what you know about your school. State how your school has developed an identity and explain the types of things that your teacher should know. Give specific examples to support your ideas.

Persuasive Writing Prompts

1. The superintendent of our school recently asked the parents of our district whether the children should have an additional 40 minutes of school each day. Now the superintendent wants to know the students' opinions on lengthening the school day. The superintendent will read the students' papers to help her decide whether school will last 40 minutes longer next year. Write an essay for your superintendent in which you try to get the superintendent to agree with you about whether the school day should be longer.

2. Your principal is thinking about eliminating lunch recess because many discipline problems occur at that time. Think about all of the reasons for keeping or eliminating lunch recess and how you could persuade your principal to keep or eliminate it. Write an essay explaining the reasons for your position.

3. Your parents have agreed to talk to you about whether you may have a pet for your birthday. Write an essay to convince them that you will take care of your pet. In the essay, state the kind of pet you want, give reasons why you should have a pet, and explain how you would take care of your pet.

4. Your class has earned an extra field trip. Each student will vote on whether the class goes to the zoo, the park, or the YMCA to do activities. Decide which place you would like to visit and write an argument to persuade your classmates to vote your way.

5. Pretend you are living in the 1860s. You and your family spent your entire fortune starting a new homestead. A plague of locusts destroyed the crop that your family planted and planned to live on for the next year. Write a letter to a distant family member to plead for help and money to get your family back on its feet again. Decide to whom you want to write, describe the details of the event, make reasonable requests, and provide details about repayment.

6. Our classroom pet, a Russian dwarf hamster, unexpectedly gave birth to six babies. Your teacher has offered a baby hamster to those children who can convince their parents to let them have one as a pet. Write a letter to your parents to convince them that you can take care of this new pet. In your letter, give at least three reasons for your parents to let you have a hamster, give examples of how the pet would be good for you and your family, explain how you would take care of it, and conclude by summarizing the reasons you have given.

7. Your reading class has just finished reading the book *Tuck Everlasting*. The book discussed the topic of living forever. Some of the characters in the book believed they would live forever if they drank the spring water. Others believed that people were not destined to live forever and shouldn't drink the water. Write a paper for your reading teacher that tells your view. Explain why you would or would not drink the water. Support your belief by giving three reasons for it and support each reason with three details.

8. The mayor has decided to cancel the annual Halloween parade. The mayor believes the parade takes time away from school children to learn in class. We need to write the mayor a letter to explain why we should have the Halloween parade. We need to include three reasons why we should have the parade, and we need to give examples to support our reasons. Write that letter.

From Susan Davis Lenski and Jerry L. Johns, *Improving Writing: Resources, Strategies, and Assessments.* Copyright © 2000 by Kendall/Hunt Publishing Company (1-800-247-3458). May be reproduced for noncommercial educational purposes.

9. NASA has decided it will let one student ride to the moon on the next space shuttle mission. The panel in charge of the expedition has recommended asking you to be that person. Write an essay convincing NASA to let you ride the space shuttle.

10. Your city leaders have banned in-line skating from downtown sidewalks and from shopping centers. The city leaders feel that sidewalks should be solely for people who want to walk and that skaters are dangerous to walkers, especially in crowded city areas. Decide whether you agree or disagree with a law about banning skates from sidewalks. In the beginning of your paper, state your opinion clearly. Give reasons for your opinion and examples for each reason. Be sure to conclude your paper so that the reader clearly understands your opinion. We will give these essays to the city leaders to read.

11. Your parents are having a garage sale and have informed you that they would like to sell your stuffed animal collection. Think about whether you agree with this idea. State your opinion in the beginning of the paper. Then explain your feelings about your stuffed animals and their importance to you. Give specific examples that describe your feelings. Conclude your paper so that your parents understand your opinion.

12. Your school is having a spring concert. The music teacher thinks that everyone should attend the event to support the musicians and to learn more about music. Think about whether you agree with this decision. State your opinion in the beginning of the paper. Then tell why you think as you do. Be sure to give specific examples.

13. The governor of your state has decided that a large bike path will run through your state. Thousands of people will be able to enjoy this path while biking, jogging, or walking. You have just learned that this path is scheduled to run through your backyard and will eliminate your favorite soccer field. Think about whether you agree that a bike path should be developed. State your opinions and give detailed reasons for your opinions.

14. Chocolate was first manufactured in the United States in 1765. Now the people in the United States consume about half of the world's production of chocolate. In recent years, doctors have been concerned that too much fat from chocolate in our diets is harmful and that chocolate should be eliminated from our diets. Decide whether you agree or disagree with the doctors. Think about specific reasons for your opinions and give examples that support your reasons. Conclude your paper by restating your opinions.

Assessing with Rubrics

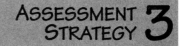

Rubrics are becoming the most popular method of assessing students' writings. Rubrics clarify teachers' expectations and guide students' writings by detailing criteria for assessment (Hill, Ruptic, & Norwick, 1998). Rubrics assess specific aspects of students' writings according to a predetermined set of criteria. These criteria can be set by the teacher or in partnership with students. Rubric assessment can inform teachers about the ability of students to write, and they also can help students self-assess their writing.

Directions

1. Determine the areas you want to assess and list the criteria. Arrange the criteria on a four-point table as in the example that follows. Make sure the criteria match your assessment goals and your instruction.

2. Duplicate and distribute copies of the rubric of your choice. Tell students that their writings will be assessed using the criteria on the rubric. Give students time to discuss the rubric with each other.

3. Ask students whether they have questions about the criteria stated on the rubric. If students have questions about the criteria, take time to teach the information that students need.

4. After you are certain that students understand the criteria, tell them that their next piece of writing will be assessed using the rubric. Remind students as they become immersed in writing to remember the criteria on the rubric.

5. After students have finished writing, have them self-assess their own writings using the rubric. Then assess students' writings using the rubric. Use a different color of ink to note your assessment. Then compare similarities and differences between the students' assessments and your assessments.

Name _____ Date _____

Writing Rubric

Title _____

	Ideas & Content	Organization	Mechanics & Style
4	Stays on topic Many examples Interesting	Organized logically Evident sequence Opening and closing	Excellent word choice Fluent Standard English
3	Mainly on topic Some examples Fairly interesting	Organized loosely Some sequence Opening or closing	Good word choice Fairly fluent Mostly Standard English
2	Topic evident A few examples Attempt at interest	Some organization Sequence attempt Attempt at opening or closing	Fair word choice Somewhat fluent Some Standard English
1	Topic confusing Few examples Little interest	Organization poor Sequence confusing No opening or closing	Poor word choice Not fluent Many mechanical errors

Chapter 6

Writing Style and Mechanics: Rewriting

"Everyone needs an editor."—Tim Foote

Overview

The purpose of writing is to express ideas for an audience. The degree to which readers are able to construct meaning from a piece of writing, however, depends on the way the piece is written. Clear writing written in a lively style that conforms to standard usage is easier to read than writing that is unclear, dull, and full of errors. In order for writers to make their meanings clear, they must pay attention to the details of writing and learn strategies for rewriting, revising, and editing.

Not all papers that students write should be revised and edited (Graves, 1994). Students should

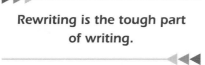

Rewriting is the tough part of writing.

write so much in schools that they simply don't have time to take every piece of writing to the sharing stage. If students are writing every day (sometimes writing for self-discovery, sometimes writing to learn, and sometimes writing to communicate with an audience), most of their writing should not be rewritten. However, when students are writing for an audience or when their writing will be read by someone else, they need to make their writing as clear and readable as possible. That's when they need to rewrite.

Writing for an audience usually needs to be

completed over a period of days. Rewriting doesn't mean that students merely recopy their papers; it means that they use their initial drafts as a lens to make clear what they really want to say (Calkins, 1994). Rewriting is the tough part of writing; it takes time, attention, and instruction.

Finding the right words to express thoughts is not always easy for writers. Even though there are times when writing flows, there are other times when writers need to rely on the craft of writing. Writing is a craft as well as an art. When words don't come easily, writers can rely on strategies such as rethinking, varying sentences, creating images, and using writers' tools. These strategies help writers shape ideas so that their meanings are clear.

In the past, writing instruction has emphasized editing rather than the craft of rewriting. Editing is only a small part of the rewriting process.

Teaching strategies can help students learn how to rewrite.

✓ Teachers can help students learn the craft of writing beyond getting words correct.
✓ Teachers can help students imagine their audiences so they write with the appropriate style.
✓ Teachers can help students learn how to write engaging first sentences and powerful conclusions.
✓ Teachers also can help students learn how to use writers' tools so that the writing conforms to Standard English usage.

Rewriting doesn't take place at a certain time during the writing process. Even though the bulk of rewriting generally takes place after drafting, the writing process is recursive (Lenski & Johns, 1997). Rewriting takes place all of the time. When students begin pieces of writing that will be read by audiences, they need to be conscious of crafting sentences that fit their writings. As students draft ideas, for example, they might stop and rewrite a phrase, sharpen an image, or check the spelling of a word.

> ### Writing Strategies
> - Rethinking
> - Varying Sentences
> - Creating Images
> - Using Writer's Tools

▶▶▶ ─────────────────

"Good writing is largely a matter of rewriting."

───────────────── ◀◀◀

Students can learn how to stop and think while writing to find a concise noun or a strong verb. Rewriting can take place throughout the writing process.

Before students' writings are given to their audiences, they need to be edited with a careful eye. Students are novice writers who do not know all of the rules that govern the English language. Therefore, students need to spend time polishing their writing by making sure all of the conventions of language are correct. To produce writings that are correct, students will need their teachers' assistance. Teachers can be copy editors and proofreaders for students who have not yet learned all of the conventions of language.

"Good writing is largely a matter of rewriting" (Britton, 1996, p. 323). Rewriting turns a string of sentences into a stirring piece of prose or an engaging story. This chapter contains resources, teaching strategies, ideas, and activities to teach students how to rewrite papers so that their writing expresses their ideas in ways that are readable for audiences. Ideas for assessment also are included.

▶ Are your students writing every day?

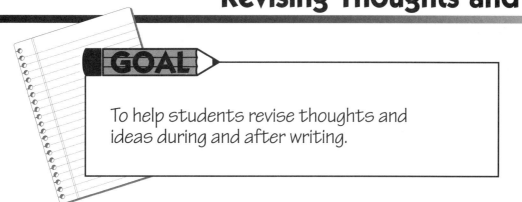

Revising Thoughts and Ideas

GOAL

To help students revise thoughts and ideas during and after writing.

6.1

Background

Revision is revisioning or rethinking a piece of writing. During writing, writers often put down words that do not completely capture their thoughts and ideas. Instead, these initial drafts reflect the surface thoughts of the writer. After writing an initial draft, writers often reread their original sentences and change them to make the words express their intentions more clearly.

Revision is labor intensive. That means revision takes a lot of time, thought, and work. Since revision is so time-consuming, not every piece of writing that students do in school should be revised (Graves, 1994). Students in school should be writing so much that only a portion of their work, not every piece of writing, should be placed in the revision cycle.

Revision is labor intensive.

Revision, however, is an important part of writing. Students need to write often to increase their writing fluency. Students also need to learn about the organizational patterns of writing, but if they are to grow as writers, students need to revise some of their pieces of writing. It is through revision that students learn the craft of writing and the recursive nature of the writing process (Dahl & Farnan, 1998).

In a model of the revision process, Hayes (1996) suggests that rereading during revision is essential. Writers reread their work during drafting to make decisions about words, events, spelling, and ideas. Writers also revise their work after the completion of a first draft. They reread and rethink their pieces on many levels, examining their logic, ideas, sentences, grammar, words, and sequence. Revision is necessary to produce high-quality writing.

Even writers in kindergarten need to learn about revision. Young students should learn that written words can be changed. Students in first grade and beyond can learn how to rework, or revise, their writings. They should think of revision during drafting and after drafting. Students should revise independently and with writing partners. While they are revising, though, students need to learn to think about their writing and follow where their minds lead.

Donald Murray (1991, p. 85) wrote, " I believe that if I attend to the draft, read it carefully, and listen to what it says, the draft will tell me what a reader needs." His words are good advice. This section contains resources, teaching strategies, ideas, and activities to help students learn how to revise, during and after writing, the thoughts and ideas they have.

TEACHING STRATEGY 1 ▶ ▶ ▶ ▶ ▶ ▶ ▶ ▶ ▶ **Grow a Sentence**

Young students can learn to revise sentences by participating in the strategy Grow a Sentence. When you Grow a Sentence, you show students that writing can be changed even after you have finished writing a sentence. Young students often think that once they have written something it should not change. Your instructional purpose in using the strategy Grow a Sentence, therefore, is to show young students that writing can be changed. When students learn that writing can be changed, they are more likely to understand the principles behind revision.

✛ Directions

1. Write a simple sentence on the chalkboard or on an overhead transparency. Use only a simple subject and a simple predicate, such as the example "Dogs run."

2. Tell students that you will Grow a Sentence by adding one word or phrase at a time. Stress the idea that after writers finish parts of writing they read over what they have written and decide whether or not they want to make any changes.

3. Tell students that you will add one word to the sentence, such as "Big dogs run." Explain that when you were thinking about the sentence you were not thinking about all dogs, only *big* dogs. Write the new word in a different color or underline the word so that it stands out.

4. Read the new sentence aloud to the class. Tell the class that you want to change the sentence some more. Have students volunteer words and phrases that would change the sentence. Write the new sentence under the second sentence as in the example that follows.

5. After revising the sentence three or four times, draw a triangle around the sentences. Point out to students how the first sentence was changed to become the final sentence. Remind students that when writers write they can make changes to their writing.

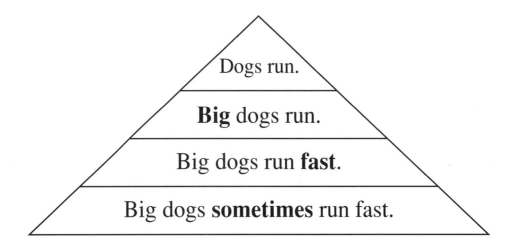

Dogs run.

Big dogs run.

Big dogs run **fast**.

Big dogs **sometimes** run fast.

TEACHING STRATEGY 2 ▶ ▶ ▶ ▶ ▶ ▶ ▶ ▶ ▶ **Stop and Think**

Writers do not revise their writing only after a piece is complete; they revise as they go. Stop and Think is a strategy to remind students to revise during writing and to monitor their revision. Teachers can model the Stop and Think strategy for young students. Older students should revise their work independently.

✛ Directions

1. Introduce the revision strategy Stop and Think by explaining to students that when they write they need to frequently stop what they are doing and make writing decisions. Tell students that the brief pauses they make while writing in order to choose just the right word or to reread a sentence to see if it makes sense are part of writing and revision. Remind students that *writers revise as they write*—not only after a draft is complete. Tell students that the Stop and Think strategy makes explicit some of the writing decisions they are making during writing.

2. To use the Stop and Think strategy, have students make a tally mark each time they stop and think during the drafting process. Ask them to jot down a word or phrase that will help them remember what made them stop and what they were thinking. Discuss these stopping points and develop a classification scheme using ideas such as the ones that follow.

   • stopped to figure out the spelling of a word
   • stopped to think what happens next
   • stopped to think of a million dollar word
   • stopped to decide if what I wrote made sense

▶ Are you encouraging your students to "Stop and Think" while writing?

3. Create a grid or a table for students to use the Stop and Think strategy on their own. See the example that follows. Duplicate the grid and distribute it to students. Have students use the Stop and Think grid while they are writing their next pieces.

4. Every few weeks, revisit the Stop and Think grid. Ask students whether the categories on the grid should remain the same or if they should change. Make changes suggested by students and create a new Stop and Think grid.

Stop and Think		
Stopped to figure out the spelling of a word	Stopped to think about what happens next	Stopped to think of a million dollar word
Stopped to see if the words made sense	Stopped to admire a sentence	Stopped to think about a conclusion

TEACHING STRATEGY 3 ▶ ▶ ▶ ▶ ▶ ▶ ▶ ▶ ▶ ▶ ▶ ▶ **Self-Revision**

One of the crucial parts of revision is Self-Revision. Writers need to read their own writing to decide whether their purpose was achieved. As writers revise, they need to find value in their writing, thinking about what they did well (Hansen, 1996, 1998). As writers reflect on their writing, they also can set new writing goals by determining in what ways this particular piece of writing exemplified "good writing" and in what ways they want to improve their next piece of writing.

✛ **Directions**

1. Tell students that writers revise their writing during writing, as in the previous Stop and Think strategy, but that writers also revise their writing after they have completed a draft. Tell students that after drafting a piece of writing they should reread their writing, looking for substantive ways to make the writing clear and compelling.

2. After students have finished drafting a piece of writing, tell them that you will give them the opportunity to revise this writing by using the Revision Suggestions that follow. Duplicate and distribute the Revision Suggestions so that all students have a copy.

3. Model the revision process using your own piece of writing. Make a transparency of a piece of writing you have drafted, place it on the overhead projector, and read the piece for students.

4. Read each of the Revision Suggestions on the following page. Apply the suggestions as appropriate to your own writing. Tell students that only some of the Revision Suggestions should be used for each piece of writing, not all of them. Model changes to your writing.

5. Have students use the Revision Suggestions to make changes to their own writing. Provide ample time for students to reread their pieces, read the Revision Suggestions, and make appropriate changes. Tell students that you expect them to apply at least one or two of the Revision Suggestions.

REVISION SUGGESTIONS

- ☐ Read your paper aloud. Listen for places that are awkward. Rewrite sections that caused you to stumble while reading.

- ☐ Picture your audience. Think about whether your reader could understand your message or story.

- ☐ Think about your purpose for writing. If your purpose is not clear, revise sections so that a reader will understand your purpose for writing.

- ☐ Reread your paper, looking for passages that are confusing because you need more information. Add more explanation or details if needed.

- ☐ Look for places in your writing that don't fit the topic. Delete sections that wander from your main point.

- ☐ Make sure your paragraphs are in logical order. If the events in the paper do not make sense in the order in which you wrote them, change the order.

- ☐ If necessary, revise your first sentence to grab the reader's attention.

- ☐ Underline words that have punch. Replace overused words with Million Dollar Words.

- ☐ Add figurative language where you can. Think of comparisons, similes, metaphors, and examples that help your reader understand your message.

- ☐ Read each sentence individually, looking for errors in grammar and usage. Use your writing tools to find out how to write words and sentences in Standard English.

Writing is a social activity. Writers need readers, and readers need writers. Both reading and writing are dependent on others. Since writing will be read by an audience of one or more readers, it helps writers to have a writing partner to give advice on the piece during the revision process. There are generally four functions of writing partners (Mohr, 1984). Writing Partners can offer writers choices. They also can give writers responses, show writers different possibilities, and speed up revision by their suggestions. Writing Partners are very useful for improving students' writing.

 ## Directions

1. Tell students that a valuable resource for revision is a Writing Partner. Explain that Writing Partners can offer useful suggestions during a writer's revision process. You may want to model the process for students.

 2. Have students choose a Writing Partner or divide the class into groups of two students. Tell students that the Writing Partners will change in three or four weeks.

3. Duplicate and distribute the Questions to Ask Writing Partners that follow. Tell students that the questions are designed to help the writer discuss a piece of writing and make decisions about ways to revise the piece.

4. Tell students that Writing Partners sometimes are at a loss for things to say about a piece of writing. Duplicate and distribute the list of Comment Ideas for Writing Partners. Tell students that they can use an appropriate comment from the list if they don't know what to say.

5. Have students move to various parts of the room with their Writing Partners, their pieces of writing, and their handouts. Tell Writing Partners that one of them will begin reading his or her piece of writing. Explain that the other partner should listen carefully during the reading. After the reader is finished, the second student should ask at least three questions, make at least three positive comments, and offer one suggestion. The Writing Partners then should trade roles.

▶ Do these students know the "Questions to Ask Writing Partners"?

QUESTIONS TO ASK WRITING PARTNERS

▲ How do you feel about your writing so far?

▲ Are you finished? If you want to write more, what do you plan to write?

▲ Which part is your favorite? Why?

▲ Could you tell me more about . . .?

▲ What do you mean by . . .?

▲ Why did you choose this topic?

▲ Does your first sentence grab the reader's attention?

▲ Did you say what you wanted to say in this piece?

▲ Who is your audience?

▲ What is your purpose for writing this piece? Did you accomplish your purpose?

▲ Does the piece end the way you want it to end?

I Don't Know What to Say!
Comment Ideas for Writing Partners

Positive Comments	Suggestions
Style	
Excellent first sentence.	You might try a different first sentence.
Many interesting sentences.	Vary sentence length.
Many interesting words.	Use Million Dollar Words.
Transitions apparent.	Add transitions.
Imagery used.	Add similes or metaphors.
Conversation natural.	Omit or revise some conversation.
Content	
Logical order of events.	Change the order of events.
Interesting situation or problem.	Strengthen the main situation or problem.
Clear plan.	Make the story plan more clear.
Interesting events.	Add details to events.
Ending solves the problem.	Change the story's ending.
Characters seem real.	Add details to the characters.
Setting is vivid.	Add details to the setting.
Mechanics	
Capitalization mostly correct.	Revise capitalization.
Punctuation mostly correct.	Revise punctuation.
Spelling mostly correct.	Revise spelling.
Grammar mostly correct.	Revise grammar.
Handwriting easy to read.	Write more neatly.

 # Ideas and Activities

1. Contact adults who write at their jobs. Ask them to describe the types of writing they do and to explain how they revise their writing. Over the course of the year, invite several people to come to your classroom to discuss writing in the real world. If you cannot arrange in-person visits, ask several people to tape record or videotape their use of writing and revision. Play the tapes for your class to illustrate the writing that adults do at their jobs. The following are examples of some jobs that require writing and revision.

   > Attorneys revise legal briefs.
   > Principals revise reports to the superintendent.
   > Managers revise memos.
   > Teachers revise letters to parents.
   > Scientists revise findings from experiments.
   > Pastors revise sermons.
   > Police officers revise reports of crimes.
   > Journalists revise stories.
   > Parents revise notes to the teacher.

2. Encourage young students to use Cue Questioning as a strategy for revision (Johns, Lenski, & Elish-Piper, 1999). Tell students that when they read they look for meaning, sound, and visual cues to decide whether they have read a word correctly. Remind students that as they write they also should look for the same cues. Have students write a sentence on their own. Then ask students to read and reread their sentences to determine whether the words make sense. If any words don't make sense, tell students to change the words so they do make sense. Then have students read their sentences so they sound correct. Have them make appropriate changes. Finally, have students reread their sentences to determine whether the words look correct. Have them make changes if necessary. Be sure students realize that they have revised their sentences.

3. Tell students that they can hear what they have written by reading their work into a tape recorder and then listening to it. Explain that sometimes writers inadvertently leave out words that they later insert while reading. Tell students that they can "catch" some of these errors if they listen to themselves read their own papers. Have students tape-record a piece of writing. After recording the writing, have students listen to the recording while looking at their hard copy. If students hear something different on the recording from what is written on the paper, have them put the tape player on pause and decide whether or not to make changes on the paper. Then have them continue listening to the recording until it is completed.

4. Distribute index cards to each student and tell them that they will be revising their writing using a Hot Tips for authors card. Tell students that readers can share ideas and suggestions for writers in the form of Hot Tips. Explain that writers frequently receive Hot Tips more positively than they do advice or suggestions. When students have finished a draft of a piece of writing, have them exchange their writing with another student. Ask students to read the piece of writing and write two suggestions for the author on the Hot Tips card. Then have a second student read the same piece of writing and write two more Hot Tips. Return the writing and the two Hot Tips cards to the author to use during revision.

5. Occasionally, role-play the part of a student in a writing conference. Tell students that they will be taking on a teacher's role during a writing conference and that you will be taking a student's role. Have a student who has recently completed a piece of writing volunteer to be part of the role-playing scenario. Sit in front of the class and have the student read his or her paper. Using the list of Questions to Ask Writing Partners, ask probing questions as you take on the role of a student during a writing conference. Model asking questions that are especially appropriate for that particular piece of writing. Then switch roles. Read a piece of your writing and have the student ask you questions.

6. Introduce the strategy Tell-Read-Revise by telling students that often writers can tell a more complete story than they can put in words. Explain to students that when others listen to a story, they can help the author include essential parts of the story that may be missing in a written draft. After students have written the first draft of their work, have them put the paper under a book and tell the story to a partner. The partner should ask questions or ask for more details. Then the author reads the actual paper to the partner. The partners can remind the authors of things they didn't write in the stories that they told. Then have students revise their drafts.

7. Sometimes students can find Writing Partners on the Internet. Some web sites, such as "Inkspot," include bulletin boards for finding Writing Partners. Access the web site in the classroom. Show students how to post a message on a bulletin board. Explain that comments from Writing Partners on the Internet might be insightful or they might be useless. Encourage interested students to use the Internet for finding readers to respond to their writing.

➤ Technology Tip

Inkspot

Bulletin board for posting writing-related questions and for locating peer-critique partners.

www.inkspot.com/

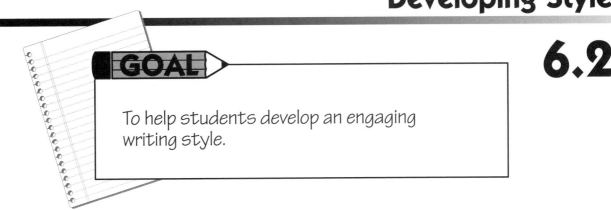

Developing Style

6.2

> **GOAL**
>
> To help students develop an engaging writing style.

Background

"I love Avi's writing style." This comment refers not to the content of Avi's books but to the way he uses language. Style is the way writers craft sentences and paragraphs in fresh, unique ways. Writing style, however, is elusive and subtle (Harris & Hodges, 1995). It's hard to pinpoint what style actually is.

Because writing style is hard to define, we tend to ignore the teaching of style. Some teachers believe that each writer's writing style is inherent, fixed, and unchangeable. Teachers who believe writing style is a part of writing talent tend to give their students opportunities to write and let style take care of itself. It's very likely that some of our writing style is part of our personality, part of our verbal talent. But there are other aspects of writing style that are amenable to instruction. The part of writing style that consists of word choice and sentence arrangement can be taught to students throughout the grades.

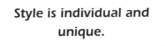

▶▶▶ **Style is individual and unique.** ◀◀

Good style is subjective. Writing style that appeals to some readers is abhorred by others. For example, some readers love Charles Dickens's writing: the long flowing sentences, the use of semicolons. Other readers prefer Hemingway's short, abrupt sentences. We can't legislate style. But we can help students select appropriate language for the purpose of a piece of writing (Beaver, 1998).

Style is individual and unique. It is like voice, the imprint of ourselves on our writing (Graves, 1994). Teachers can motivate students to use words in new ways; they can help students write with crisp, clear prose; and they can teach students how to vary words and sentences so that their writing expresses their personality. This section provides resources, teaching strategies, ideas, and activities for you to use as you help your students develop an engaging writing style.

TEACHING STRATEGY **1** ▶ ▶ ▶ ▶ ▶ ▶ ▶ **Million Dollar Words**

The words writers choose to use as they write are a large part of their writing style. Million Dollar Words can make the difference between ho-hum writing and writing with verve. Some writers seem to have a talent for using colorful words. Other writers need to use writing tools such as a thesaurus as they search for strong verbs and precise nouns. When students are aware that they need to try to write with Million Dollar Words, their writing can become much more exciting.

 ## Directions

1. Tell students that when they write they should try to use words that capture the images they have in their minds. Explain that sometimes writers need to search for the right word, because not just any word will do in a given situation. Tell students that they need to try to use Million Dollar Words when they write.

2. Write the following groups of sentences on the chalkboard or on an overhead transparency. Have students read the sentences independently.

   1. He **held** the bat tightly.
   2. He **gripped** the bat tightly.

   1. She stared in **surprise** at the Grand Canyon.
   2. She stared in **awe** at the Grand Canyon.

3. Ask students to identify the differences between the two sentences in each pair. Encourage students to discuss the more vivid words in the second sentences.

4. Create several Million Dollar Word Posters to display in the room so students have Million Dollar Words easily accessible. To create Million Dollar Word Posters, duplicate and distribute the list of words on the following page. Tell students that all of these words could be used in lieu of the word "said." Explain to students that each word has a slightly different connotation and that the words cannot necessarily be used interchangeably. Instead, the Million Dollar Word Posters list words that have different shades of meaning for the targeted word.

5. Divide the class into groups of three or four students. Have each group develop a Million Dollar Word Poster. You can use the following list of ideas for posters or have students think of the topics for their posters. Tell students that Million Dollar Words can be found in thesauruses and, if possible, secure several for your classroom library.

   Million Dollar Words for "nice."
   Million Dollar Words for "good."
   Million Dollar Words for "went."
   Million Dollar Words for "fun."

6. Encourage students to use Million Dollar Words as they write and share examples of students' use of Million Dollar Words in their writing.

Million Dollar Words for "Said"

added
admitted
agreed
announced
answered
asked

badgered
barked
begged
bellowed
blabbered
broadcasted

cackled
chattered
chuckled
coaxed
commented
complained
confessed
congratulated
cried

declared
decreed
demanded

echoed
exclaimed

gasped
giggled
grinned
groaned
grumbled

hectored
hinted
hollered
howled

informed
inquired
intimated

jabbered

laughed

mentioned
moaned
mumbled
murmured
muttered

nagged

ordered

persuaded
pleaded
proclaimed
prompted
proposed
protested

questioned

recited
remarked
reminded
repeated
replied
responded

screamed
shouted
shrieked
sighed
snarled
sniveled
stated
stormed
stuttered
suggested

taunted
teased
told

urged
uttered

wheedled
whined
whispered

yelled
yelped

TEACHING STRATEGY 2 ▶ ▶ ▶ ▶ ▶ ▶ ▶ Opening Sentences

Opening sentences can be a killer. They can make or break a piece of writing. The first sentence of a story can invite a reader to continue, or it can throw up a roadblock that hinders the reader. Many writers prefer short openers; others use a variety of different first sentences to grab the reader's interest. Most writers, however, don't automatically know how to write a first sentence. Many young writers begin their writing with sentences that tell the entire story in one fell swoop. All writers, however, can learn how to write catchy first sentences. Learning how to write good opening sentences is a part of style that can be learned.

 Directions

1. Tell students that the first sentence in a piece of writing can either invite readers to continue reading or keep them from reading more of the piece.

2. Write the following sentence on a chalkboard or on an overhead transparency.

   It was a dark and stormy night.

3. Many students have heard this famous opening sentence. Ask students to discuss what makes that sentence interesting or boring.

4. Read to students several opening sentences from familiar books or write the first sentence of *Drummond* (Odgers, 1990) on the chalkboard or on an overhead transparency. Read the sentence with students. Discuss why this sentence is a good opening. Explain that writers consciously determine how to begin a piece of writing.

   Sarah Jordan and her brother Nicholas were perfectly ordinary people until the day they met Drummond.

5. Ask students to find other opening sentences that they like, either from published books or from their own writing. Have students share these sentences with the class.

6. Tell students that writers can choose to use a variety of opening sentences. Explain that there are ten types of opening sentences that writers most frequently use. Duplicate the list of Opening Sentences on the following page and distribute it to students.

 7. Read and discuss the ten opening sentences with the class. Then divide the class into groups of three or four students. Have each group choose two types of opening sentences. Ask each group to write a sample sentence for the two types of opening sentences they chose.

8. Invite students to share their sample opening sentences. Post the sentences along with the sentence type on a display in the room. Encourage students to use the display as they compose opening sentences for their next piece of writing.

OPENING SENTENCES

1. **Ask a question.**

   Example: Where did all of these ants come from?

2. **Use a lively quotation.**

   Example: "Eating carrots will grow hair on your chest," Grandpa boomed.

3. **Create a sense of drama.**

   Example: The solitary figure limped along the rocky trail.

4. **Mention a strange or interesting detail.**

   Example: The temperature can drop to 50 degrees below zero on the summit of Mount Everest.

5. **Begin with action.**

   Example: The basketball circled the rim and wobbled maddeningly before dropping through the hoop.

6. **Use exclamations.**

   Example: Fifty dollars! You must be kidding!

7. **Use humor.**

   Example: He emptied his pocket: a few loose coins, a house key, a handkerchief, and a dead mouse.

8. **Present a problem.**

   Example: As the warriors crossed the narrow bridge, they spotted their enemies shooting fire arrows.

9. **Present an opinion.**

   Example: All students should do one hour of homework a day.

10. **Start with a single word.**

    Example: Lice. How I hate lice. Six of the students in my class have lice. It was only a matter of time.

TEACHING STRATEGY 3 ▶ ▶ ▶ ▶ ▶ ▶ ▶ ▶ ▶ Sentence Variety

Sentences have rhythm just like music does. When writers vary their sentences, the writing takes on a rhythm, a beat. A piece of writing that is full of sentences that begin with a simple subject and end with a simple predicate, such as "The kind woman gave us some candy," can lead to very monotonous reading. Reading is more enjoyable when some sentences are long, some are short, and some are in-between. Varying sentence length is another aspect of writing style. As with other stylistic components, some writers naturally vary sentence length while others need to learn that sentence variety adds spice to writing.

✦ Directions

1. Tell students that the flow of words in a piece of writing is like music; sentences have rhythm. Ask students to discuss their viewpoints about sentence rhythm. Then tell students that the length of sentences and the way sentences are organized can create a rhythmic piece of writing.

2. Duplicate the Student Example on the following page and distribute copies to students in the class. Point out the various types of sentences in the writing.

3. Tell students that they can vary sentences by using different types of sentences and by varying sentence beginnings. To help students vary types of sentences, show students how to combine two short sentences into sentences of different lengths, as in the following example.

   Sentences: The clouds began to move in. The day suddenly turned cold.
   Variation 1:   Suddenly, the clouds began to move in, and the day turned cold.
   Variation 2:   The clouds began to move in, and the day suddenly turned cold.
   Variation 3:   When the clouds began to move in, the day suddenly turned cold.

4. Have students combine the following groups of sentences in different ways. Then discuss their groupings.

   I'll never forget that day. We went to the circus.
   I admire my father. He is a wonderful man.
   We thought we were going to lose. The score was 7 to 3.

5. Tell students that they also can vary sentences by writing sentences with different beginnings and lengths. The following list provides examples of a variety of sentences. Duplicate the list Sentence Variety and distribute it to students. Remind students to vary sentences as they write.

SENTENCE VARIETY: STUDENT EXAMPLE

The Magic Lizard

Once upon a time a lizard was born. Soon the mother found out that it was

no ordinary lizard. It was a magic lizard that had no name. So the mother

thought it was time to name him. She thought and thought, and it finally came

to her. She named him Gex. Well, when Gex was six, he had no friends, so he

made friends with his magic, imaginary friends anyway. When Gex was eleven,

he had a few real friends. He learned new magic, such as how to fly, breathe

fire, and change colors. When Gex was twenty, he knew every magic trick.

Gex had a lot of friends now. There were small friends, fast friends, sly friends,

smooth friends, and even slick friends. Gex was the most popular lizard in

school. One day Gex got married. His wife's name was Gexalena. A few years

later they had a baby lizard. They named it Gex Jr., and, well, you know what

happened next.

Mark Watson
Third Grade

Fairy tale opening

Compound sentence

Short sentence

Complex sentence

Million Dollar Words

Circular ending

Sentence Variety

1. **Begin with an adverb.**

   Example: Slowly, Bobby backed away from the creaking door.

2. **Use words in a series.**

   Example: Last night Jason got a short, stand-up, wild hair cut.

3. **Add at least one adjective to a noun in your sentences.**

   Example: Amanda hiked up the rugged mountain trail.

4. **Include one simile.**

   Example: Although Wanda was a great grandmother, she felt as young as a spring chicken.

5. **Write a compound sentence.**

   Example: Crissy lost her ring, but she didn't tell her boyfriend about it.

6. **Write a complex sentence.**

   Example: When Jerry retires, he's going to go on four cruises each year.

7. **Write a partial sentence.**

   Example: I love ice cream. Really love it.

8. **End with a dependent clause.**

   Example: Fran traveled to Papua New Guinea because he wanted to see the Birds of Paradise.

 # Ideas and Activities

1. Explain to students that the rhythm of words can be pleasing or displeasing to different people. There are some words that are Fun Words. Think of a word that you enjoy, such as the word "amiable." Tell students that you simply like to say the word because you like how the word sounds and that you like the way the word flows from your lips. Provide students with a variety of examples of words you like. Some examples of Fun Words could be extemporaneous, kookaburra, or verisimilitude. Then ask students to think of a fun word by giving them the prompt, "I like the way _____ sounds." Provide students with several minutes to think of a word. Then have students tell the class their Fun Words. Write the Fun Words on a poster. (You may have to use a dictionary to help with the spellings of some of these words.) Display the words on a bulletin board so students can remember the words their classmates thought were Fun Words. Encourage students to add words to the display throughout the month.

2. Tell students that some books use recurring lines or phrases for emphasis. Young students are familiar with recurring lines because pattern books frequently are used in the early grades to teach reading. Begin the lesson on recurring lines by reading a pattern book such as *Brown Bear, Brown Bear, What Do You See?* (Martin, 1970). Then have students think of several pattern books that they remember hearing or reading. After students have suggested pattern books, have them think about the reason authors repeat phrases or sentences. Guide students to understand that authors use recurring lines in a piece of writing for emphasis. Then write the following quotation on the chalkboard or on an overhead transparency.

    "A recurring line is like rolling a snowball—it gains power and weight as it gets repeated"
    (Fletcher & Portalupi, 1998, p. 86).

    Ask students whether they agree that repeating a phrase or line in a story is an effective authoring technique. Encourage students to agree or disagree with this technique. Then suggest to students that they try to incorporate recurring lines in some of their writing.

3. Tell students that they should be on the lookout for words, phrases, and sentences that they think will make their writing sing. Explain that writers often keep idea files to use during writing. Tell students that they can have files that contain interesting words for their possible use while writing. Provide students with a file folder. Have students name and label the file using a term such as Way Cool Words folder. Model the activity by finding an example of an interesting sentence from your own reading. For example, the following sentence can be found in the novel *The Most Wanted* by Jacquelyn Mitchard (1999).

    "I had to work in the morning, though I was as sick as a dog eating grass"(p. 125).

    Write the sentence on the chalkboard or on an overhead transparency. Explain the reasons why the sentence appeals to you. Then have students actively look for interesting words, phrases, and sentences and copy them in the Way Cool Words folder. Tell students that they can look for Way Cool Words in dictionaries, thesauruses, and in their reading. They also can ask other readers to recommend Way Cool Words. After students have actively looked for words for a week or so, have them share some of their Way Cool Words.

4. Tell students that closing sentences may be the most important part of their writing (Fletcher & Portalupi, 1998). Help students realize that, just as an opening sentence can grab the attention of the reader, the closing sentence is what readers remember. Explain that writers often have difficulty knowing how to end their writing and that they need to try a variety of endings before deciding which ending they really want to use. Explain to students that before writers choose an ending they need to decide which emotion they want their readers to feel about the writing. For example, do they want to surprise readers, leave readers feeling encouraged, or have readers relieved? Or does the writer want readers to finish the piece by saying, "Boy, did I learn something." To help students understand the effect of ending sentences, read a variety of short books to the class over a period of time. Encourage students to notice how stories end and to identify which emotion the ending evoked in them. Discuss how different endings affect different students. Then encourage students to experiment with ending sentences when they write.

5. Explain to students that interesting writing is as sticky as a caramel, that language can stick in your mind as caramel sticks to your teeth. Tell students that using a comparison such as "writing is as sticky as a caramel" is imagery, in this case a simile. Tell students that writers often use similes to help readers visualize the images they want to present and that similes frequently can be found in our language. Tell students some of the well-known similes that you know, such as "hungry as a bear" or "sly as a fox." Have students try to write similes using the following prompts. Tell students to notice other similes as they read and listen to conversations.

> As loud as a _____.
> As soft as a _____.
> As slow as a _____.
> As fast as a _____.

6. Tell students that writers need to carefully observe the world around them for images that they can use in their writing. Explain to students that writers often carry an Image Journal (Grant, 1992) where they record images that impress them. These images can create ideas that students can use as they craft new stories. Identify an image that you have seen that you thought was interesting. For example, think about the last time you were in a grocery store. Let your mind remember the images that you captured as you pushed the grocery cart. Did you see a senior citizen who was packing groceries adjust his hearing aid as he asked you, "Paper or plastic, ma'am?" Choose an image to share with your students. Tell students to identify images that strike them as intriguing and to write them in their Image Journals.

7. Tell students that using details in writing is a way to make their stories more vivid. Provide students with the following example by writing it on the chalkboard or on an overhead transparency.

> The young man, muscles straining, heaved the kayak into the swiftly flowing river.

Explain that although this sentence is vivid readers will respond more directly if the man and the river are named. Ask students to suggest names for the man and the river. Then rewrite the sentence using students' suggestions. Tell students to add specific names to their writing whenever they can.

8. Remind students that playing word games is a good way to improve their writing styles. Inform students of sources that you know that have word games, such as the newspaper crossword puzzles. Ask students for sources of word games that they have seen. Then tell students that there are many sources for word games on the Internet, such as "Vandelay Games: Word Gamer's Paradise." Encourage students to access web sites that have word games that increase their vocabulary and help them see words in new ways.

Technology Tip

Vandelay Games: Word Gamer's Paradise

Play a variety of word games on this web site.

http://www.inxpress.net/~lnp/

GOAL

To help students edit their writing so that it conforms to Standard English.

Background

"Poor spelling in the midst of a good piece of writing is like attending a lovely banquet but with the leavings of grime and grease from the previous meal still left on the table" (Graves, 1983, p. 18). Editing is polishing a piece of writing, putting the piece of writing into its final form by correcting its surface features, or mechanics. Correct mechanics, such as spelling, usage, punctuation, capitalization, paragraphing, sentence structure, and handwriting/typing, can make the difference between a banquet and a dirty table.

Writers need to attend to the mechanics of writing. Published words require precision because writing doesn't offer the second chance that spoken words do (Horner & Lu, 1999). Written words need to express as clearly as possible what the author means. Usually after a writer gives a piece of writing to a reader, the writer loses control of the meaning of the text. It is then the responsibility of the reader to construct meaning, and if the writer hasn't been specific, the reader could misinterpret the author's point.

Most students tend to be poor editors. One of the reasons students aren't very good at cleaning up a piece of writing is that students have had very few chances in their lives to edit writing. The ratio of time students spend speaking and listening is three times greater than the time students spend writing. Most students, therefore, have few opportunities to edit their writings so that they conform to conventional language (Block, 1997).

The best way to teach the conventions of language has been debated for over two decades. Writers such as Donald Graves (1983) encourage teachers to teach students the mechanics of language in the context of their writing. Others suggest that the explicit teaching of conventions also is important. For example, Lisa Delpit (1988) suggests that the ability to write with conventional language can be a gatekeeper for students who do not know the language of power, Standard English. Delpit (1988) recommends that teachers of language minority students should explicitly teach students Standard English. Naguchi (1991) agrees that grammar, as one

▶ Do you agree that most students tend to have a difficult time editing their writing?

aspect of conventional language, should be taught, but not in the ways that we have taught it in the past. Short, direct lessons of grammar and other conventions can invite students of all backgrounds into the land of power, where Standard English is the norm.

Teaching students to edit their writing and helping them learn how to write in conventional language are important components of a writing program. Teachers should remember, however, that students need to write so much that only a small percentage of their writing should be edited. This section presents resources, teaching strategies, ideas, and activities to help teach students to edit their writing.

Most students tend to be poor editors.

TEACHING STRATEGY 1 ▶ ▶ ▶ ▶ ▶ ▶ ▶ ▶ ▶ Editing Bubbles

Young students can learn how to edit with Editing Bubbles. Editing Bubbles are bubbles placed over words that give directions for editing changes. When young students use Editing Bubbles, they learn that writing can be changed and corrected before it is read by an audience. Since producing any written text is difficult for young students, students do not have to rewrite entire texts when they use Editing Bubbles. Editing Bubbles also can help teachers emphasize the conventions of English in short instructional lessons.

Directions

1. Tell students that sometimes writers make mistakes that they need to correct. Explain that when writing for an audience writers need to write as clearly as possible so their readers understand what they are trying to say.

2. Tell students that words themselves can call out for changes if they are not correct. Write a sentence on the chalkboard or on an overhead transparency with one or two errors in mechanics. Over the errors, draw an Editing Bubble as in the example that follows. Write the words "Please change me!" in the bubble.

My dog had plaque on his tooths, so I brush his teeth yesterday.

3. Divide the class into groups of three or four students. Have students discuss how to change the words that need to be changed. Ask students to volunteer with the answers. When students have suggested the correct answers, change the words in the Editing Bubbles as in the example that follows.

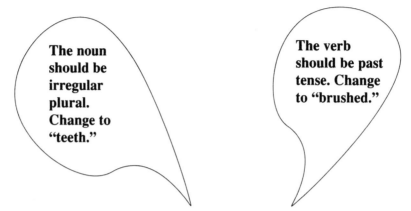

My dog had plaque on his teeth, so I brushed his teeth yesterday.

4. Create sentences with Editing Bubbles several times a week. After students have become familiar with Editing Bubbles, write sentences with an error or two and have students find the errors and draw their own Editing Bubbles. Occasionally, write a sentence with no errors.

Teaching Strategy 2 ▶ ▶ ▶ ▶ ▶ ▶ ▶ Edit: Ready or Not?

It takes a while before students reach the editing stage of a piece of writing. Because not every piece of writing students complete will be revised and edited, editing should be reserved for those pieces of writing that will make their way to an audience, who expects to read Standard English. Students need to be given multiple opportunities to revise their writing. Only when they have revised as much as they are capable of doing should they begin to edit. With the strategy Edit: Ready or Not? students monitor their progress on a piece of writing to determine whether they need to keep revising, or whether they are ready to edit it.

⟁ Directions

1. Tell students that editing is usually the last stage of the writing process before writers share their work with an audience. Stress the idea that writers often revise their writings several times before they are ready to edit them.

2. Duplicate and distribute the page Am I Ready to Edit? that follows. Give each student one copy.

3. Read the questions with students. Make sure all students understand the meanings of the words and phrases on the checklist.

4. Model editing readiness with a revised draft of your own. Choose a piece of writing that is near completion but not quite ready to edit. Make an overhead transparency of your writing, or if you have written it on a computer, project the copy on a screen using an LCD panel. Read the writing with your students and discuss whether you are ready to edit it.

5. Divide the class into groups of three or four students. Have students discuss whether their writings are ready to edit.

6. Answer the questions from the sheet Am I Ready to Edit? Explain why you believe you are ready to edit in some respects and not ready in others.

7. Tell students that because you could not answer all questions with a "yes" you need to revise your writing before you are ready to edit it.

8. As students finish revising their writings, have them use the questions on the Am I Ready to Edit? sheet before moving to the editing stage. Set the cutoff point for the number of answers that are "yes" and the number of answers that are "no" based on the writing level of your class, the time you want to devote to this piece of writing, and your expectations of your students.

Name _____ Date _____

Am I Ready to Edit?

Title _____

1. I read the writing to myself and it makes sense.   Yes   No

2. I read the piece to a writing partner and used some of the suggestions.   Yes   No

3. The purpose of the writing is clear.   Yes   No

4. My writing style fits my audience.   Yes   No

5. The writing is focused on one event or idea.   Yes   No

6. I have enough details to make my writing interesting.   Yes   No

7. I have included Million Dollar Words.   Yes   No

8. I have an interesting first sentence.   Yes   No

9. The title for this writing fits the piece.   Yes   No

10. The ending has punch.   Yes   No

11. I corrected as many mistakes as I could find during revising.   Yes   No

12. I am satisfied with this piece of writing.   Yes   No

TEACHING STRATEGY 3 ▶ ▶ ▶ ▶ ▶ ▶ ▶ Editing Conferences

There are a number of ways you can approach editing conferences (Danielson & LaBonty, 1994). Students should edit their own writing first. After students have edited their own writing, they should take part in Editing Conferences. Editing Conferences can be held with other student writers, or they can be with you, the teacher. If you choose to hold Editing Conferences with students, you can hold on-the-spot conferences where you walk around the room helping students edit. A second type of conference is an instructional conference, where you bring several students who have the same kinds of writing needs together for small group editing. A third type of conference is an individual Editing Conference where you work with one student to conform the writing to conventional English. The purpose of Editing Conferences is to help students make their revised writings conform more closely to conventional language.

⬦ Directions

1. After students have determined that they are ready to edit, they should be assigned to an Editing Conference. Tell students that at an Editing Conference a partner will help them edit their writing. Explain that writers often miss some of their own surface errors and that having a second reader often helps the writer make additional corrections to the paper.

2. Tell students that you will use an Editing Checklist at their Editing Conference. Duplicate and distribute the Editing Checklist that follows. Give a copy to each student.

3. Make a transparency of a piece of writing prepared by a former student or use the Student Example that follows. Project the writing onto a screen. Read the Editing Checklist, answering the questions as you go. After answering the questions, sign your name in the space for the editor's name and write one or more positive comments about the piece of writing. Explain that you will be using the same process in Editing Conferences.

4. When students have a piece of writing to edit, have them come to an Editing Conference with you. Use the Editing Checklist to help students conform their writings to conventional language. After you have used the Editing Checklist, have students make the appropriate changes to their writings.

▶ Which type of Editing Conference do you prefer?

Editing Checklist

Author _____ Date _____

Title _____

1.	Spelling is accurate.	Yes	No
2.	Capitalization is correct.	Yes	No
3.	Punctuation is correct.	Yes	No
4.	Subjects and verbs agree.	Yes	No
5.	Paragraphs are indented.	Yes	No
6.	Margins are appropriate.	Yes	No
7.	Sentences are complete.	Yes	No
8.	Sentences are clear.	Yes	No
9.	Words are used correctly.	Yes	No
10.	Writing is legible, or typing is without typos.	Yes	No

Comments: _____

_____

_____

Editor's Name _____ Date _____

EDITING: STUDENT EXAMPLE

In the Field

In the feild thar was a farm. And in that farm thar was a barn.

And in that farn thar was a stabole. In that stabole thar was a cow.

In that cow thar was a fle. And . . . The cow want Moooo!

That skard the fle that wat our of the . . . Stabol. out of the barn

and out of the farm out of the felde and OUT OUT OUT !!!

Coté Anne Tracy
First Grade

TEACHING STRATEGY 4 ▶ ▶ ▶ ▶ ▶ **Teacher as Copy Editor**

Writers rarely compose totally correct text. That's why copy editors play a crucial role in the writing process. Even though writers struggle to write correct copy, they often fall short of the mark. Professional writers know this. They also know that copy editors bring a fresh "read" to a piece of writing and are able to find surface errors that the writer missed. In classrooms, the teacher should be the copy editor for the class. The teacher knows the most about correct writing mechanics, so after the writing process is complete and students have edited their writings, the teacher can put on a copy editor hat and take the writings to their final form.

⊹ Directions

1. Tell students that you will copy edit their final writings but that they need to have every possible correction made before you will act as copy editor.

2. Duplicate and distribute the Editing Marks sheet that follows. Give each student a copy of the Editing Marks sheet. Explain that you will copy edit their writings using the symbols on this sheet.

3. Make a transparency of the Editing Marks sheet. Using an overhead projector, show students the editing symbols and discuss each of their meanings. Remind students that you will be using these symbols as you copy edit.

4. Make a transparency of the Unedited Writing Example that follows and display it on a screen. Show students the first copy of the writing, the one without marks. Have students read the text to find errors. Encourage students to correct errors using editing marks. Then display a transparency of the Edited Writing Example. Explain each symbol and why it was used.

5. Have a special tray or box in your room marked "For the Copy Editor." Tell students to place their finished writings in the copy editor's tray. Copy edit students' writings as they place them in the tray. You may decide to use different colored pencils for the different editing marks. If you find that you make an exceptional number of editing marks on a student's writing, monitor the student's editing before the future piece of writing goes to copy editing.

6. Tell students that after their writings are copy edited they should make the changes specified by the editing marks before sharing their writing with an audience.

Editing Marks

Mark	What It Means	Example
sp.	Correct spelling	I went (fowrard.) *sp.*
≡	Change a lower case letter to a capital letter.	I went to new york. ≡ ≡
/	Change a capital letter to a lower case letter.	In May, I went to the Ẑoo.
ℓ	Delete or take out letters, words, sentences, lines, and punctuation marks.	I/went to my friend's house after I went school.
∧	Add or insert letters, words, or sentences.	My trip ∧ fun. *was*
˅	Add an apostrophe.	I am Doug˅s friend.
¶	New paragraph.	¶ My friend and I were ready to go.
⊙	Add a period.	The dogs were barking⊙
∧	Add a comma.	I ran, jumped∧and played at the park.
#	Add space between two words.	The dog/was mine. #
‿	Combine two words.	The dog‿house was huge.

UNEDITED WRITING EXAMPLE

Wolves are found in cold areas throughout the Northern Hemisphere. Because people have pushed wolves farther into the wilderness they are common only in canada and Alaska. Some wolf species can also be found in Europe and Asia.

Wolves prey on rabbits, game birds, and deer. Some times they eat livestock. Hunters and farmers often object to wolves living in ranching areas because wolves can eat livestock. Many people think that wolves also eat humans, but they don't. Wolves have a bad name, probably because they frequently play the villains roll in fairy tales. Wolves, however, are not bad. They are clever animals that are a part of the natural environment. Wolves are fascinating wild animals.

EDITED WRITING EXAMPLE

¶ Wolves are found in cold areas throughout the Northern Hemisphere. Because people have pushed wolves farther into the wilderness, they are common only in canada and Alaska. Some wolf species can also be found in Europe and Asia.

¶ Wolves prey on rabbits, game birds, and deer. Some times they also eat livestock. Hunters and farmers often object to wolves living in ranching areas because wolves can eat livestock. Many people think that wolves also eat humans, but they don't. ¶ Wolves have a bad name, probably because they frequently play the villains roll *sp.* in fairy tales. Wolves, however, are not bad. They are clever animals that are a part of the natural environment. Wolves are fascinating wild animals.

 # Ideas and Activities

1. Tell students that when writers work on a piece of writing they tend to lose their objectivity about the piece during the drafting and revising stages. Remind students that after revising a piece of writing they need to let the writing "rest" before editing it. Make the comparison to students who have played all day and need to sleep at night to have energy for the next day. Tell students that writing can be energized if it has a rest. Place a tray in the classroom. Label the tray Writing at Rest. After students have revised pieces of writing, have them place their writings in the Writing at Rest tray. Keep the pieces of writing in the Writing at Rest tray for two or three days. After the writings have "rested," tell students their pieces of writing are ready to edit.

2. Tell students that they will be going on a Punctuation Hunt. Emphasize that writers need to be aware of the ways language is used and that reading is an excellent way to learn how to use punctuation. List on the chalkboard the punctuation marks that students have learned. For example, if students recently have learned how to use commas, list the word "comma" on the chalkboard with its symbol. During independent reading time, have students look for the ways commas are used in their reading. Allow 10 to 15 minutes for reading and the Punctuation Hunt. After the time is up, have students discuss the ways they noticed commas were used in their reading. Repeat this activity with other mechanics, such as the use of capital "I," subject-verb agreement, or other language skills that you have taught.

3. Different types of books have a diverse range of words, sentence patterns, and dialects (Barnitz, 1998). Using literature as a model for different types of writing can help students learn how writers use language in real books. Read a book with a different dialect to students. Point out the ways conventional language is replaced with dialect. Explain that authors use dialect to make writing more realistic. Have students write a short passage using a dialect with which they are familiar. Explain the difference between the dialect and conventional language.

4. Have students keep track of the errors in their writing using an Error Chart. After you have copy edited a piece of writing, have students record the errors they made. Develop the list into a chart similar to the one that follows. As students complete additional pieces of writing, have them keep track of the errors they made. Explain that, by knowing the types of errors they are prone to make, students can become more aware of their trouble spots as they revise and edit.

ERROR CHART			
Spelling Errors	Punctuation Errors	Usage Errors	Capitalization Errors
chose then its further	comma before "and" colon	The boy with the basket of golf balls **sell** them at the stand.	National Park

5. Tell students that they should have Nitty-Gritty Writing Goals. Nitty-Gritty Writing Goals are goals about the fundamentals of writing: punctuation, capitalization, usage, and spelling. Tell students that they should have many types of writing goals and among those goals that they set for themselves are goals about the conventions of language. Provide an example that is appropriate for your class, such as the correct use of commas in a series. Give students time to look through their copy edited writing to find the types of errors they tend to make. If students have used an Error Chart, they can refer to the chart. Ask students to list three Nitty-Gritty Writing Goals for their next piece of writing. Remind students as they write to refer to their goals.

6. Many students write on computers and use a spell-check program. Tell students that a spell-check program will not identify words that are spelled correctly but are used incorrectly. Write the following sentence on the chalkboard or on an overhead transparency.

Trevor found three peddles in his shoe.

Explain that the correct word is "pebbles," not "peddles." Because the word "peddles" was not misspelled, the spell-check program did not highlight it as incorrect. Remind students that a spell-check program will find typos but not all misspelled words.

7. Remind students that the purpose of editing is to produce a readable text. For students who make many errors in Standard English, use the strategy Choose Three. In Choose Three, students ask you to find three errors at a time for them to correct. Tell students that you will be editing their writing in stages. Have them choose a number of items for you to find. For example, tell them that if they Choose Three you will find three errors. If they Choose Four, you will look for four errors. Explain that after you find the errors students will correct the writing and return it to you for another round of Choose Three. Read and return papers as many times as it takes to conform the papers to conventional writing.

8. Tell students that the rules for writing may be broken, but only occasionally. Explain that writers break the rules at times for emphasis. Tell students that they can break the conventional rules if they have a good reason. To show students that sometimes writing does not follow rules, read an example of writing from a noted author who breaks the rules, or use the example that follows (Kane, 1997).

"Nobody could make Ramona pick up her crayons. Nobody. Not her father nor her mother. Not even the principal" (Cleary, 1968, p. 174).

Explain that the author used sentence fragments for emphasis. Have students occasionally try to write so that their writing breaks the rules.

9. When students see how real editors work, students understand the necessity of editing. Tell students that they will be submitting a piece of their writing to an Internet publication. Access an Internet site such as "Stone Soup." Project the web site on an LCD panel so all students can see the web site. After accessing the web site, have a piece of student writing ready for publication. Go through the process of making the writing ready for publication in the electronic journal. Emphasize the need for self-editing if the editor requires writings to be copy ready.

Stone Soup

This web site contains an international magazine where students up to age 13 can submit stories, poems, and book reviews.

www.stonesoup.com

Assessing Writing Style and Mechanics

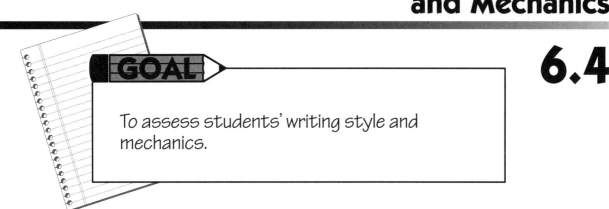

6.4

GOAL

To assess students' writing style and mechanics.

Background

Writing style and mechanics are small, but important, components of writing. Writing that is full of errors is difficult to read. Certainly, young students who are experimenting with writing will write with "invented spelling" and will not use the accepted mechanics of English. However, even young students can learn to rewrite words, sentences, and passages to make their writing more readable. Older students can learn to rewrite so that their writing is clear, interesting, and written in conventional English.

Not all of the writing students complete needs to be rewritten. However, students should learn to rewrite when they have written for an audience. As students rewrite, they need to look for the value in their writing, or what they do well (Hansen, 1996, 1998). Students also can be assessed on how well they have learned to use an interesting writing style

(Beaver, 1998) and how well they have learned to write with conventional English (Bratcher, 1994).

There are a number of ways you can assess students' growth as writers. You can use an Analytic Writing Scale such as the one exemplified in Assessment Strategy 1. Using an analytic scale, you can help students pinpoint areas in which they have improved and in which they need to concentrate (Wolcott & Legg, 1998). You also can have students assess their own writing growth as in Assessment Strategy 2, Fix-It. Finally, Assessment Strategy 3 emphasizes Portfolio Assessment, or ways you can assess students' growth using a collection of writings. Each of these assessment strategies should be used as you assess students' growth in developing an engaging writing style and the proper use of the mechanics of writing.

WRITING SCALE FOR STYLE AND MECHANICS

As students grow as writers, one of the most visible ways in which they improve is through their use of an engaging writing style and the use of conventional mechanics in writing. When students learn how to write with their own unique voice using the conventions of Standard English, their writing becomes increasingly more refined. Teachers and students can use a Writing Scale for Style and Mechanics to assess these components of a single piece of writing.

Directions

1. Collect a piece of writing that students have written for an audience. Tell students that this piece of writing should be a finished product, one that has been written with an engaging writing style using Standard English.

2. Duplicate the Writing Scale for Style and Mechanics that best matches your students' writing development or adapt the scale so it fulfills your purposes.

3. Complete the Writing Scale for Style and Mechanics for each student's writing. After you have completed the scale, conference with students to discuss the strengths and weaknesses of their writing samples.

Name _____ Date _____

Writing Scale for Style and Mechanics
Younger Students

1. Name and date are correct.	Yes	Mostly	No
2. Title is appropriate.	Yes	Mostly	No
3. Margins are clear.	Yes	Mostly	No
4. Spaces between words are even.	Yes	Mostly	No
5. Capital letters are correct.	Yes	Mostly	No
6. Punctuation is correct.	Yes	Mostly	No
7. Sentences are complete.	Yes	Mostly	No
8. Words are spelled correctly.	Yes	Mostly	No
9. Handwriting is legible.	Yes	Mostly	No
10. Voice is apparent.	Yes	Mostly	No

From Susan Davis Lenski and Jerry L. Johns, *Improving Writing: Resources, Strategies, and Assessments.* Copyright © 2000 by Kendall/Hunt Publishing Company (1-800-247-3458). May be reproduced for noncommercial educational purposes.

Writing Scale for Style and Mechanics
Older Students

1. Name and date are legible.	Yes	Mostly	No
2. Title is appropriate.	Yes	Mostly	No
3. First sentence is engaging.	Yes	Mostly	No
4. Margins are even.	Yes	Mostly	No
5. Capitalization is correct.	Yes	Mostly	No
6. Punctuation is correct.	Yes	Mostly	No
7. Spelling is correct.	Yes	Mostly	No
8. Sentences are fluent and varied.	Yes	Mostly	No
9. Words are precise and interesting.	Yes	Mostly	No
10. Figurative language is used.	Yes	Mostly	No
11. Paragraphing is correct.	Yes	Mostly	No
12. Handwriting is legible or typos are minimal.	Yes	Mostly	No
13. Voice is evident.	Yes	Mostly	No
14. Concluding sentence is powerful.	Yes	Mostly	No

Students can assess their own growth in writing style and mechanics using the Fix-It assessment strategy (Hill, Ruptic, & Norwick, 1998). With the Fix-It strategy, each student saves one or more writing samples that were written early in the year, compares the samples with writing composed at a later date, makes corrections on the earlier drafts, and reflects on his or her learning. Many students are amazed at their growth as writers with these before and after writing samples. Fix-It pairs of writing also can be placed in students' writing portfolios.

✛ Directions

1. Photocopy writing samples from students early in the school year. Save the writing samples in a folder titled Fix-It samples.

2. Write "Fix-It" on a calendar or in a lesson plan book for a time at least four months in the future. Plan to spend a class period at that time for students to participate in the Fix-It assessment strategy.

3. After four or more months, take out the Fix-It folder and distribute the writing samples to students. Ask students to read their writings.

4. Tell students that they have learned many writing skills and strategies during the intervening time period. List two or three of the skills and strategies that students have learned in the past four months, such as writing an engaging first sentence. Have students share other writing skills and strategies that they have learned. Write the list on the chalkboard or on an overhead transparency.

5. Ask students to rewrite their original pieces of writing. Remind students to use the skills and strategies that they have learned in the ensuing months. Tell students that they can write on their original drafts or they can rewrite their entire pieces.

6. After students have completed "fixing" their early writing, ask them to reflect on the ways they have grown as writers. Ask students to write in their personal journals about their writing growth.

7. Save the writing samples for students' portfolios.

Portfolios are a collection of students' writings. With a collection of writings, you can assess students' writing growth over time. In order to determine whether students' writing is improving, you need to have more than one piece of writing. Students might have difficulty writing with style or writing in conventional English on a specific writing sample. However, using a collection of students' writings, you can assess students' growth as writers (Murphy, 1999).

Directions

1. Tell students that you will be saving several of their writing samples during the year. Explain that these pieces of writing will not be returned until the end of the year.

2. Provide students with expandable writing file folders. Have students put their names on the files, give their portfolios names, and decorate their files.

3. Every two or three weeks, have students choose a piece of writing to place in their Writing Portfolios. You can choose some pieces of writing to include as well. Label the pieces of writing that your choose "Teacher's Choice."

4. After several months, have students gather their writing portfolios to assess their growth as writers. Duplicate and distribute the list of skills and strategies on the Portfolio Assessment that follows to assess students' writing growth.

5. Have students assess their writing growth using the Portfolio Assessment statements by circling the answers that best describe their growth. Then meet with students in small groups or individually to discuss their responses to the statements. Congratulate students on areas of growth and encourage students to continue to improve as writers.

Portfolio Assessment

1. I read my own writing and notice areas to revise.	Often	Sometimes	Rarely
2. I notice areas of strength and weakness in my writing.	Often	Sometimes	Rarely
3. I seek feedback for troublesome passages.	Often	Sometimes	Rarely
4. I use writers' tools such as dictionaries and thesauruses during writing.	Often	Sometimes	Rarely
5. I incorporate suggestions from Writing Partners.	Often	Sometimes	Rarely
6. I incorporate suggestions from Writing Conferences.	Often	Sometimes	Rarely
7. I provide suggestions for other writers.	Often	Sometimes	Rarely
8. I show an interest in improving my writing.	Often	Sometimes	Rarely
9. I revise my drafts several times.	Often	Sometimes	Rarely
10. I use interesting language in my writing.	Often	Sometimes	Rarely
11. I vary my sentence structures.	Often	Sometimes	Rarely
12. I use Million Dollar Words.	Often	Sometimes	Rarely
13. I write in a variety of formats.	Often	Sometimes	Rarely
14. I use conventional English.	Often	Sometimes	Rarely

Comments: _____

_____

_____

A
Professional Organizations and Agencies

B
Audiences for Student Writing

C
Basketball Teams' Addresses

D
549 Writing Formats

Appendix A

Professional Organizations and Agencies

American Library Association (ALA)
50 East Huron
Chicago, IL 60611
Phone: 800-545-2433
Fax: 312-440-9374
Web site: http://www.ala.org
Publications: *Choice Magazine*

Association for Supervision and Curriculum
　Development (ASCD)
1703 Beauregard Street
Alexandria, VA 22311
Phone: 800-933-ASCD
Fax: 703-575-5400
E-mail: info@ascd.org
Web site: http://www.ascd.org
Publications: *Educational Leadership*,
　Educational Bulletin

Children's Book Council
568 Broadway, Suite 404
New York, NY 10012
Phone: 212 966-1990
Fax: 212-966-2073
E-mail: staff@cbcbooks.org
Web site: http://www.cbcbooks.org

International Reading Association (IRA)
800 Barksdale Road
P.O. Box 8139
Newark, DE 19714-8139
Phone: 302-731-1600
　　　800-336-7323
Fax: 302-731-1057
E-mail: ubinfo@reading.org
Web site: http://www.reading.org
Publications: *Reading Research Quarterly*, *The Reading
　Teacher*, *Journal of Adolescent & Adult Literacy*,
　Lectura y vida (Spanish)

National Association of the Education of
　Young Children (NAEYC)
1509 16th St., N.W.
Washington, DC 20036
Phone: 800-424-2460
Fax: 202-328-1846
Web site: http://www.naeyc.org
Publications: *Young Children*, *Early Childhood
　Research Quarterly*

National Council of Teachers of English (NCTE)
1111 W. Kenyon Road
Urbana, IL 61801
Phone: 217-328-3870
　　　800-369-6283
Fax: 217-328-0977
E-mail: membership@ncte.org
Web site: http://www.ncte.org
Publications: *Language Arts*, *Primary Voices*,
　English Journal

National Writing Project
University of California
5511 Tolman Hall #1670
Berkeley, CA 94720-1670
Phone: 510-642-0963
Fax: 510-642-4545
E-mail: nwp@socrates.berkeley.edu
Web site: http://www.gse.berkeley.ed/nwp

Appendix B

Audiences for Student Writing

Compiled by M. Kristiina Montero

The Acorn (ages 5–18)
Editorial & Ordering Address:
1530 Seventh Street
Rock Island, IL 61201
309-788-3980
(fiction, nonfiction, articles, poetry)

American Girl (ages 8 and up)
Editorial Address:
Pleasant Company Publications, Inc.
8400 Fairway Place
Middleton, WI 53562-0986
608-836-4848
Fax: 608-831-7089
E-mail: ageditor@ag.pleasantco.com

Ordering Address:
Pleasant Company Publications, Inc.
8400 Fairway Place
P.O. Box 62986
Middleton, WI 53562-0986
800-234-1278
(letters, comments, jokes, anecdotes, poems)

Barbie, The Magazine for Girls (ages 5–12)
Editorial Address:
Marvel Entertainment Group, Inc.
387 Park Avenue
New York, NY 10106
212-576-4042
Fax: 212-576-9286

Ordering Address:
Marvel Entertainment Group, Inc.
P.O. Box 10798
Des Moines, IA 50340
515-243-4543
(letters, art)

Black Belt for Kids (ages 5–16)
Editorial & Ordering Address:
Rainbow Publications
P.O. Box 918
Santa Clarita, CA 91380
805-257-4066
(letters, first person accounts, art)

Boodle (ages 6–13)
Editorial & Ordering Address:
Graphic Printing Co.
P.O. Box 1049
Portland, IN 47371
219-726-8141
Fax: 219-726-8143
(stories, poems, puzzles, artwork)

**Boomerang! The Children's Audio Magazine
  about Big Ideas** (ages 6–12)
Editorial & Ordering Address:
P.O. Box 261
La Honda, CA 94020
800-333-7858
415-747-0978
Fax: 800-333-7858
(letters, interviews, audio clips)

California Weekly Explorer (ages 9–11)
Editorial & Ordering Address:
285 E. Main Street, Suite 3
Tustin, CA 92780
714-730-5991
Fax: 714-730-3548
E-mail: cwex@aol.com
(area reports, geography, history)

Calliope (ages 8–15)
Editorial & Ordering Address:
Cobblestone Publishing, Inc.
7 School Street
Peterborough, NH 03458
603-924-7209
Fax: 603-924-7380
(letters)

Casper the Friendly Ghost (ages 5–9)
Editorial & Ordering Address:
Harvey Entertainment Company
100 Wilshire Boulevard, Suite 1400
Santa Monica, CA 90401-1110
310-451-3377
Fax: 310-458-6995
(letters, artwork)

Chickadee Magazine (ages 8 and under)
Editorial Address:
Owl Communications, Inc.
179 John Street, Suite 500
Toronto, ON
Canada M5T 3G5
416-971-5275
Fax: 416-971-5294
E-mail: owlcom@owl.on.ca

Ordering Address:
In the U.S.
Chickadee Magazine
25 Boxwood Lane
Buffalo, NY 14227-2780
(stories, poems)

Child Life (ages 9–11)
Editorial Address:
Children's Better Health Institute
1100 Waterway Boulevard
P.O. Box 567
Indianapolis, IN 46206
317-636-8881
Fax: 317-684-8094

Ordering Address:
Children's Better Health Institute
P.O. Box 7133
Red Oak, IA 51591-0133
317-636-8881, ext. 233
(stories, poems, jokes, photos, drawings)

Children's Digest (ages 10–12)
Editorial & Ordering Address:
Children's Better Health Institute
1100 Waterway Boulevard
P.O. Box 567
Indianapolis, IN 46206
317-636-8881
(original stories under 200 words, jokes, poems)

Children's Playmate (ages 6–8)
Editorial & Ordering Address:
Children's Better Health Institute
1100 Waterway Boulevard
P.O. Box 567
Indianapolis, IN 46206
317-636-8881
Fax: 317-684-8094
(drawings, poems, jokes, riddles)

Cobblestone (ages 8–15)
Editorial & Ordering Address:
Cobblestone Publishing, Inc.
7 School Street
Peterborough, NH 03458
603-924-7209
Fax: 603-924-7380
E-mail: http://www.cobblestonepub.com
(stories, poems)

Crayola Kids Magazine (ages 4–8)
Editorial Address:
Meredith Custom Publishing Services
1912 Grand Avenue
Des Moines, IA 50309-3379
515-284-2007

Ordering Address:
Crayola Kids Customer Service
P.O. Box 37198
Boone, IA 50037-0198
800-846-7968
(letters, artwork related to upcoming themes)

Creative Kids (ages 8–14)
Editorial & Ordering Address:
Prufrock Press
P.O. Box 8813
Waco, TX 76714-8813
800-998-2208
Fax: 800-240-0333
E-mail: Creative_kid@prufrock.com
(poems, stories, games, artwork, photography)

Daybreak Star Indian Reader (ages 9–12)
Editorial & Ordering Address:
United Indians of All Tribes Foundation
1945 Yale Place E.
Seattle, WA 98102
206-325-0070
Fax: 206-328-1608
(Native children's artwork, letters, stories, puzzles,
   legends)

Disney Adventures (ages 7–14)
Editorial Address:
Disney Adventures Magazine
114 Fifth Avenue
New York, NY 10011-5690
212-807-5821
Fax: 212-807-5499
E-mail: dazpc@aol.com

Ordering Address:
Disney Adventures Magazine
114 Fifth Avenue, Suite 101
New York, NY 10011-5690
212-973-4173
800-829-5146
Fax: 818-559-7353
(occasional contests for stories)

EarthSavers (ages 6–13)
Editorial & Ordering Address:
National Wildlife Federation
8925 Leesburg Pike
Vienna, VA 22184
703-790-4535
(letters)

Faces (ages 8–14)
Editorial & Ordering Address:
Cobblestone Publishing, Inc.
7 School Street
Peterborough, NH 03458
603-924-7209
Fax: 603-924-7380
E-mail: http://www.cobblestonepub.com
(stories)

Falcon Magazine (ages 8–12)
Editorial & Ordering Address:
Two Worlds Publishing
3060 Peachtree Road, NW, Suite 500
Atlanta, GA 30305
404-262-8921
(book reviews, columns)

Fantastic Flyer Magazine (ages 2–12)
Editorial & Ordering Address:
Delta Airlines, Inc.
Department 790, Admin. Bldg.
1030 Delta Boulevard
Atlanta, GA 30320
404-715-4813
(letters, art, jokes, stories)

Girls' Life (ages 7–14)
Editorial & Ordering Address:
Monarch Publishing
4517 Harford Rd.
Baltimore, MD 21214
410-254-9200
Fax: 410-254-0991
(some stories, poems, artwork)

The Goldfinch (ages 8–13)
Editorial & Ordering Address:
State Historical Society of Iowa
402 Iowa Avenue
Iowa City, IA 52240
319-335-3930
(letters, stories, artwork, poems)

Guide Magazine (ages 10–14)
Editorial & Ordering Address:
Review & Herald Publishing Association
55 W. Oak Ridge Drive
Hagerstown, MD 21740
301-791-7000, ext. 2433
Fax: 301-790-9734
E-mail: 74617.3100@compuserve.com
(stories)

Harambee (ages 7–14)
Editorial & Ordering Address:
Just Us Books, Inc.
356 Glenwood Avenue
East Orange, NJ 07017
201-676-4345
Fax: 201-677-7570
(stories)

Highlights for Children (ages 2–12)
Editorial Address:
803 Church Street
Honesdale, PA 18431
717-253-1080
Fax: 717-253-0179

Ordering Address:
P.O. Box 269
Columbus, OH 43272-0002
800-848-8922
(poems, drawings, stories, letters to the editor)

HiP Magazine (ages 8–14)
Editorial Address:
HiP Magazine
127 Seabridge Court
Alameda, CA 94502
510-523-4221
Fax: 510-523-4081

Ordering Address:
HiP Magazine
1563 Solano Avenue, #137
Berkeley, CA 94707
510-527-8993
(letters, stories, artwork, responses to magazine
    questions, personal profiles)

Hopscotch: The Magazine for Young Girls
    (ages 6–12)
Editorial & Ordering Address:
P.O. Box 164
Bluffton, OH 45817-0164
419-358-4610
Fax: 419-358-5027
(letters to the editor, contests)

Humpty Dumpty (ages 4–6)
Editorial & Ordering Address:
Children's Better Health Institute
1100 Waterway Boulevard
P.O. Box 567
Indianapolis, IN 46206
317-636-8881
Fax: 317-684-8094
(readers' drawings)

Jack and Jill (ages 7–10)
Editorial Address:
Children's Better Health Institute
1100 Waterway Boulevard
P.O. Box 567
Indianapolis, IN 46206
317-636-8881

Ordering Address:
P.O. Box 10003
Des Moines, IA 50340
(jokes, poetry, stories, drawings, special contests)

Junior Scholastic (ages 6–8)
Editorial Address:
Scholastic, Inc.
555 Broadway
New York, NY 10012
212-505-3071

Ordering Address:
Scholastic, Inc.
2931 E. McCarty Street
P.O. Box 3710
Jefferson City, MO 65102-9957
314-636-8890
(letters to the editor, junior reporter news stories)

KSE News (Kids for Saving Earth News) (ages 7–13)
Editorial & Ordering Address:
Kids for Saving Earth
P.O. Box 47247
Plymouth, MN 55447
612-525-0002
Fax: 612-525-0243
(artwork, letters, poetry)

Kids Today (ages 8–14)
Editorial & Ordering Address:
1000 Wilson Boulevard
Arlington, VA 22229-0002
703-276-3780
(letters, poems, jokes, recipes)

KIND News (Kids in Nature's Defense News)
    (ages 5–11)
Editorial & Ordering Address:
P.O. Box 362
East Haddam, CT 06423-0362
860-434-8666
Fax: 860-434-9579
Fax Orders: 860-434-6282
(letters, accounts of animals, environmental activities)

Merlyn's Pen (ages 10–15)
4 King Street
P.O. Box 910
East Greenwich, RI 02818
(stories, poems, plays, essays)

MetroKids Magazine (13 and under)
Editorial & Ordering Address:
KidStuff Publications, Inc.
1080 N. Delaware Avenue, Suite 702
Philadelphia, PA 19112
215-291-5560
Fax: 215-291-5563
E-mail: metrokids@family.com
(a kids' column each month)

National Geographic World (ages 8–14)
Editorial Address:
National Geographic
1145 17th Street N.W.
Washington, DC 20036
202-857-7000
Fax: 202-429-5712

Ordering Address:
National Geographic
P.O. Box 2330
Washington, DC 20013-2330
800-638-4077
800-548-9797
(artwork, letters)

New Moon (girls 8–14)
Editorial Address:
New Moon
P.O. Box 620
Duluth, MN 55806
(stories, poems, drawings)

Nickelodeon Magazine (ages 6–14)
Editorial Address:
Nickelodeon Magazine
1515 Broadway, 41st Floor
New York, NY 10036
212-258-7388
Fax: 212-846-1766
E-mail: nickeditor@aol.com

Ordering Address:
P.O. Box 0945
Des Moines, IA 50340-0945
515-280-8750
(letters, contests)

Nineteenth Avenue (ages 6–10)
Editorial & Ordering Address:
The Humphrey Forum
301 19th Avenue, S.
Minneapolis, MN 55455
612-624-5799
Fax: 612-624-6351
(essays, letters, fiction)

Odyssey (ages 8–14)
Editorial & Ordering Address:
Cobblestone Publishing, Inc.
7 School Street
Peterborough, NH 03458
603-924-7209
Fax: 603-924-7380
(letters, art, poems, contest entries)

**Otterwise: For Kids Who Are into Saving Animals
    and the Environment** (ages 8–13)
Editorial & Ordering Address:
P.O. Box 1374
Portland, ME 04104
207-283-2964
(stories, art, poems, letters)

Owl: The Discovery Magazine for Kids
    (ages 8 and up)
Editorial Address:
Young Naturalist Foundation
179 John Street, Suite 500
Toronto, ON
Canada M5T 3G5
416-971-5275
Fax: 416-971-5294
E-mail: owlcom@owl.on.ca

Ordering Address:
In the U.S.
25 Boxwood Lane
Buffalo, NY 14227-2780
(drawings, letters, stories, poetry)

Pockets (ages 6–12)
Editorial Address:
The Upper Room
1908 Grand Avenue
Box 189
Nashville, TN 37202-0189
615-340-7333
Fax: 615-340-7006
E-mail: 102615.3127@compuserve.com

Ordering Address:
Pockets
P.O. Box 37146
Boone, IA 50037-0146
800-925-6847
(letters, poems, stories, art)

Racing for Kids (ages 4–16)
Editorial & Ordering Address:
Racing for Kids, LLC
P.O. Box 192
Concord, NC 28026-0192
704-786-7132
Fax: 704-795-4460
Orders: 800-443-3020
(artwork, short stories, poetry)

R-A-D-A-R (ages 8–12)
Editorial & Ordering Address:
Standard Publishing
8121 Hamilton Avenue
Cincinnati, OH 45230
513-931-4050
Fax: 513-931-0904
(letters, stories)

Ranger Rick (ages 6–12)
Editorial & Ordering Address:
National Wildlife Federation
8925 Leesburg Pike
Vienna, VA 22184-0001
703-790-4000
Fax: 703-442-7332
(letters, questions)

Scholastic Math (ages 12–14)
Editorial Address:
Scholastic, Inc.
555 Broadway
New York, NY 10012
212-343-6435
Fax: 212-343-6333
E-mail: mathmag@scholastic.com

Ordering Address:
Scholastic, Inc.
2931 E. McCarty Street
P.O. Box 3710
Jefferson City, MO 65102-3710
800-631-1586
(puzzles, brain teasers, published math mistakes)

School Magazine (ages 8–12)
Editorial & Ordering Address:
Private Bag 3
Ryde, NSW
Australia 2112
02-9808-9598
Fax: 02-9808-9588
(letters)

School Mates (ages 5 and up)
Editorial & Ordering Address:
U.S. Chess Federation
186 Route 9W
New Windsor, NY 12553
914-562-8350
Fax: 914-562-2437
800-388-KING
E-mail: USCF@delphi.com
(letters, art, photos, puzzles, stories, poems, chess
  games students have won)

Signatures from Big Sky (ages 5–17)
Editorial & Ordering Address:
928 Fourth Avenue
Laurel, MT 59044
406-628-7063
(stories, poems, essays, black and white drawings)

Soccer Jr. Magazine (ages 8–16)
Editorial Address:
Triplepoint, Inc.
27 Unquowa Road
Fairfield, CT 06430
203-259-5766
Fax: 203-254-2966

Ordering Address:
Soccer Jr. Magazine
P.O. Box 420442
Palm Coast, FL 32142
(stories, artwork)

Sports Illustrated for Kids (ages 8 and up)
Editorial Address:
Time, Inc. Magazine Co.
1271 Sixth Avenue
New York, NY 10020
212-522-KIDS
Fax: 212-522-0120

Ordering Address:
Time, Inc. Magazine Co.
P.O. Box 830609
Birmingham, AL 35283-0609
800-334-2229 U.S. and Canada
(letters, artwork)

Stone Soup: The Magazine for Children (ages 6–13)
Editorial Address:
P.O. Box 83
Santa Cruz, CA 95063
(stories, poems, book reviews, artwork)

Storyworks Magazine (ages 8–10)
Editorial Address:
Scholastic, Inc.
555 Broadway
New York, NY 10012
212-343-6298
Fax: 212-343-6333

Ordering Address:
Scholastic, Inc.
2931 E. McCarty Street
P.O. Box 3710
Jefferson City, MO 65101-3710
800-631-1586
(children's book reviews, letters)

Surprises: Activities for Today's Kids and Parents
  (ages 5–12)
Editorial Address:
Children's Surprises, Inc.
275 Market Street, Suite 521
Minneapolis, MN 55405
612-937-8345

Ordering Address:
Children's Surprises, Inc.
P.O. Box 20471
Bloomington, MN 55405
(letters, artwork, activities)

Tapori (ages 6–13)
Editorial & Ordering Address:
Tapori/Fourth World Movement
7600 Willow Hill Drive
Landover, MD 20785-4658
301-336-9489
(stories about experiences and ideas on how to fight
  extreme poverty)

Troll Magazine (ages 6–12)
Editorial Address:
Marvel Entertainment Group, Inc.
87 Park Avenue
New York, NY 10016
212-687-0680
Fax: 212-986-1849

Ordering Address:
Marvel Entertainment Group, Inc.
P.O. Box 7346
Red Oak, IA 51591
515-243-4543
(letters, photographs)

U*S* Kids (ages 5–10)
Editorial Address:
Children's Better Health Institute
1100 Waterway Boulevard
P.O. Box 567
Indianapolis, IN 46206
317-636-8881
Fax: 317-684-8094

Ordering Address:
Children's Better Health Institute
P.O. Box 7133
Red Oak, IA 51591-0133
(art, poetry)

Winner (ages 9–11)
Editorial Address:
The Health Connection
55 West Oak Ridge Drive
Hagerstown, MD 21740
301-790-9734

Ordering Address:
The Health Connection
P.O. Box 859
Hagerstown, MD 21741
800-548-8700
(artwork, poems, posters on drug education themes)

Word Dance Magazine (ages 5–13)
Editorial & Ordering Address:
Word Dance Magazine
P.O. Box 10804
Wilmington, DE 19850
302-328-6834
(letters, poetry, short stories; special consideration
  given to unique group projects and work from
  mentally and physically challenged youths)

ZiNj Magazine (ages 7–14)
Editorial & Ordering Address:
The ZiNj Education Project
300 Rio Grande
Salt Lake City, UT 84101
801-533-3565
Fax: 801-533-3503
(articles, book reviews, questions for Dr. What,
  artwork, activities, photos)

Appendix C

Basketball Teams' Addresses

Atlanta Hawks
One CNN Center
South Tower, Suite 405
Atlanta, GA 30303
800-326-4000
www.nba.com/hawks

Boston Celtics
151 Merrimac Street
Boston, MA 02114
617-523-3030
www.nba.com/celtics

Charlotte Hornets
100 Hive Drive
Charlotte, NC 28217
704-522-6500
www.nba.com/hornets

Chicago Bulls
1901 W. Madison Street
Chicago, IL 60612
312-559-1212
www.nba.com/bulls

Cleveland Cavaliers
1 Center Court
Cleveland, OH 44115-4001
216-420-2000
www.nba.com/cavs

Dallas Mavericks
Reunion Arena
777 Sports Street
Dallas, TX 75207
214-939-2800
www.nba.com/mavericks

Denver Nuggets
McNichols Sports Arena
1635 Clay Street
Denver, CO 80204-1799
303-893-6700
www.nba.com/nuggets

Detroit Pistons
The Palace of Auburn Hills
Two Championship Drive
Auburn Hills, MI 48362
810-377-0100
www.nba.com/pistons

Golden State Warriors
Oakland Coliseum Arena
7000 Coliseum Way
Oakland, CA 94621-1918
510-638-6300
www.nba.com/warriors

Houston Rockets
The Summit
Ten Greenway Plaza
Houston, TX 77046
713-627-3865
www.nba.com/rockets

Indiana Pacers
300 E. Market Street
Indianapolis, IN 46204
317-239-5151
www.nba.com/pacers

Los Angeles Clippers
L.A. Memorial Sports Arena
3939 S. Figueroa Street
Los Angeles, CA 90037
213-745-0500
www.nba.com/clippers

Los Angeles Lakers
Great Western Forum
3900 West Manchester
P.O. Box 10
Inglewood, CA 90306
310-419-3100
www.nba.com/lakers

Miami Heat
The Miami Arena
Miami, FL 33136-4102
800-940-4400
www.nba.com/heat

Milwaukee Bucks
Bradley Center
1001 N. Fourth Street
Milwaukee, WI 53203-1312
www.nba.com/bucks

Minnesota Timberwolves
Target Center
600 First Avenue, North
Minneapolis, MN 55403
612-673-1600
www.nba.com/timberwolves/index.html

New Jersey Nets
405 Murray Hill Parkway
East Rutherford, NJ 07073
201-935-8888
www.nba.com/nets/index.html

New York Knicks
Madison Square Garden
Two Pennsylvania Plaza
New York, NY 10121-0091
212-307-7171
www.nba.com/knicks/index.html

Orlando Magic
One Magic Place
Orlando Arena
Orlando, FL 32801-1114
800-338-0005
www.nba.com/magic

Philadelphia 76ers
1 Corestates Complex
Philadelphia, PA 19148
215-339-7676
www.nba.com/sixers

Phoenix Suns
201 E. Jefferson Street
Phoenix, AZ 85004
602-379-7867
www.nba.com/suns

Portland Trail Blazers
One North Center Court, Ste. 200
Portland, OR 97227
503-234-9291
www.nba.com/blazers

Sacramento Kings
One Sports Parkway
Sacramento, CA 95834
916-928-6900
www.nba.com/kings

San Antonio Spurs
600 E. Market Street
Suite 102
San Antonio, TX 78205
210-554-7700
www.nba.com/Spurs

Seattle SuperSonics
190 Queen Anne Avenue, North
Suite 200
Seattle, WA 98109-9711
206-283-3865
www.nba.com/sonics

Toronto Raptors
Waterpark Place
20 Bay Street, Suite 1702
Toronto, ON M5J 2N8
416-366-3865
www.nba.com/raptors

Utah Jazz
Delta Center
301 West South Temple
Salt Lake City, UT 84101
801-325-2500
www.nba.com/Jazz

Vancouver Grizzlies
800 Griffiths Way
Vancouver, BC V6B 6G1
604-899-4666
www.nba.com/grizzlies

Washington Wizards
MCI Center
601 F Street, N.W.
Washington, DC 20001
301-622-3865
www.nba.com/wizards

Appendix D

549 Writing Formats

By Margaret E. McIntosh

abbreviation
ABCs of something
abecedarian
abridgment
absolution
abstract
acceptance speech
accolade
account of
acknowledgment
acronym
adaptation
address
address book
advertisement
advice column
agenda
agreement
aha!
allegory
alternative to counting sheep (for insomniacs)
amendment
analogy
anecdote
annotation
announcement
anthem
anthology
anything boustrophedonic
anything written in runic characters
aphorism
apologue
apology
appeal
application
article
ascription
assembly directions
assertion
assignment

assumption
astrological prediction
autobiography
award
axiom

baby book
baccalaureate address
ballad
ballot
banner
beauty tip
bedtime story
beginning
belief
billboard
bill of lading
bill of sale
biographical sketch
biography
birth announcement
blessing
boast
book
book jacket
book review
bookplate
brochure
bulletin
bumper sticker
business card

calendar
calendar quip
calorie chart
campaign speech
cantata
captain's log
caption
cartoon
case study
catalog description

censure
cereal boxes
ceremony
certificate
certificate of authenticity
chapter
character sketch
charter
checkbook register
cheer
children's book
choral reading
chorus
chronicle
church bulletin
cinquain
cipher
clue
code
collection notice
college application letter
comic strip
commemoration
commendation
comment
commentary
community notice
comparison
complaint
concatenation
confession
confutation
congratulatory note
conjecture
consequence
contest rules
contract
conundrum
conversation
convocation
correspondence (series of)
counterfeit document

couplet
covenant
cover letter
creed
critique
cumulative story
curse
customs

data sheet
date book
declaration
decree
dedication
deed
definition
denunciation
description
dialogue
diary
dictionary
diet
directions
directory
disclosure
ditty
docudrama
document
double-talk
drama
dream script

editorial
elogium
e-mail
emblem
encyclopedia entry
ending
epic
epilogue
episode
epistle
epistrophe
epitaph
epithet
epitome
essay
estimate
euphemism
evaluation
exaggeration
examination

exclamation
excuse
exhortation
expense account
explanation
expose

fable
fabrication
fact
fact sheet
fairy tale
fallacy
falsehood
falsity
family tree
fantasy
farce
farewell
fashion article
fashion show narration
feasibility study/statement
fib
fiction
figure of speech
filibuster
filmstrip
folderol
folktale
folklore
forewarning
formula
fortune
fraud

game rules
generalization
ghost story
gloss
goals
good news/bad news
gossip
grace
graffiti
greeting card
grievance
grocery lists
guarantee
guess
guess what? descriptions
guess who? descriptions
guide to watching TV

habit
hagiography
hagiology
harangue
headline
history
homily
horoscope
how-to-do-it speeches
hyperbole
hypothesis

idea
ideograph
impassioned statement
impromptu speech
impugns (something that . . .)
index
inflammatory statement
inscription
inspirational piece
insult
interview
introductions to books
introductions to people
invective
invitation
invoice
itinerary

jabber (the way it would look on
    paper)
jargon for a particular field or
    profession
job application
joke
journal
jump rope rhyme
junk mail
justification

kudos

l'envoi (or l'envoy)
lab report
label
labeled ichnography
lament
lampoon
lease
lecture
legend

letter
letter gram
letter of acceptance
letter of application
letter of condolence
letter of consent
letter of credit
letter of support
letter of surrender
letters of credence
letters of marque and reprisal
letters of resignation
letters to the editor
lexicon
lexiphanic writing
libel
license
lie
list
list of items for sale at an auction
long distance phone bill
love note
luscious words

magazine
magic spell
make a motion
manifest
manifesto
marquee notice
maxim
melodrama
memo
memoir
memory
menu
message
message in semaphore
message to send in a bottle
metaphor
minutes of a meeting
monograph
monologue
monument
motto
movie review
movie script
mystery
myth

news analysis
news release

newscast
newspaper
newspaper "fillers"
nonsense
note
notebook
notes for a debate
notice of employment
notification
nursery rhyme

oath
obituary
observation
ode
one liner
opinion
oration
oxymoron

pact
palindrome
pamphlet
pamphlet to aid sightseeing
parable
paradox
parody
party tips
pedigree
personal reaction
persuasive letter
phone survey
phrase
plaque
play
plea
pledge
poem
political announcement
postcard
poster
prayer
preamble
precis
prediction
preface
prescription
press release exposing malfeasance
probability
problem
problem solution
proclamation

product description
profile
proforma
profound saying
prologue
promotional campaign
propaganda sheet
proposal
protest letter
protest sign
proverb
public service announcement
pun
puppet show
purchase order
puzzle

querela
querimony
query
question
questionnaire
quip
quiz
quotation
quote

ransom note
rationale
reaction
real estate description
rebuttal
recapitulation
recipe
record cover
refrain
refutation
remedy
remembrance
renunciation
report
report card
report of an inquisition
request
requiem
resolution
response
resume
retrospective account
review
revision
rhapsody

riddle
rite
road signs
roast
Rolodex™ file
rondeau
rondel
rondelet
RSVP
rule
rules of etiquette
rumor

saga
sale notice
sales pitch
sandwich board
satire
schedule
script
secret
self-description
sentence
sequel
serenade
serialized story
sermon
service agreement
sign
silly saying
skywriting message
slide show
slogan
soap opera
society news
something that needs to be
    shredded
something to be stored on
    microfilm
something with a surprise ending
song
speech
speech balloon
spoof
spoonerism
sporting event rules
sports account
sports analysis
stage directions

statement
statute
study guide
style book
style sheet
subjective vs. objective account
    (of the same event)
suggestion
summary
summons
superlatives
superstition
supervisor's report
supply list
supposition
survival guide
suspense
suspicious note
syllabus
syllogism

tall tale
tautologism
tax form
technical report
telegram
telephone directories
test
testimony
textbook
thank you note
theater program
theorem
thumbnail sketches of content
    ideas
thumbnail sketches of famous
    people
thumbnail sketches of historical
    events
thumbnail sketches of places
title
toast
tongue lashing
tongue twister
traffic rules
transcript of a quarrel
transcript of a trial
transcript of an oral recollection by
    someone 10, 20, 30, or more
    years older than you

travel brochure
travel poster
treatise
treaty
tribute
trivia
true-false statements
TV commercial
TV guide
TV program

umpirage
untruth

validation
verse
vignette
vita
voucher
vow

wager
waiver
want ad
wanted poster
warning
warrant
warranty
watchword
weather forecast
weather reports
what you would do with an
    intercalary day each week(end)
while you were out
will
wise saying
wish
word
word problem
word search
words/sentences for spelling bee
written apology for maladroitness
written demonstration of
    know-how

yarn
yearbook inscription
yellow pages

References

Atwell, N. (1987). *In the middle: Writing, reading, and learning with adolescents.* Portsmouth, NH: Boynton/Cook.

Bajtelsmit, L. & Naab, H. (1994). Partner writers: A shared reading and writing experience. *The Reading Teacher, 48,* 91–93.

Barnitz, J.G. (1998). Revising grammar instruction for authentic composing and comprehending. *The Reading Teacher, 51,* 608–611.

Barone, D., & Lovell, J. (1990). Michael the show and tell magician: A journey through literature to self. *Language Arts, 67,* 134–143.

Beach, R.W. (1999). Evaluating students' response strategies in writing about literature. In C.R. Cooper & L. Odell (Eds.), *Evaluating writing: The role of teachers' knowledge about text, learning, and culture* (pp. 195–221). Urbana, IL: National Council of Teachers of English.

Beaver, T. (1998). *The author's profile: Assessing writing in context.* York, ME: Stenhouse.

Berger, L.R. (1996). Reader response journals: You make the meaning . . . and how. *Journal of Adolescent & Adult Literacy, 39,* 380–385.

Block, C.C. (1997). *Teaching the language arts: Expanding thinking through student-centered instruction* (2nd ed.). Boston: Allyn and Bacon.

Bouas, M.J., Thompson, P., & Farlow, N. (1997). Self-selected journal writing in the kindergarten classroom: Five conditions that foster literacy development. *Reading Horizons, 38,* 3–12.

Bouchard, D., & Ripplinger, H. (1995). *If you're not from the prairie.* New York: Simon & Schuster.

Bratcher, S. (1994). *Evaluating children's writing.* New York: St. Martin's.

Bright, R. (1995). *Writing instruction in the intermediate grades: What is said, what is done, what is understood.* Newark, DE: International Reading Association.

Brinkley, E.H. (1993). Passing on the joy of literacy: Students become writing teachers. In L. Patterson, C.M. Santa, K.G. Short, & K. Smith (Eds.), *Teachers as researchers: Reflection and action* (pp. 210–219). Newark, DE: International Reading Association.

Britton, B.K. (1996). Rewriting: The arts and sciences of improving expository instructional text. In C.M. Levy & S. Ransdell (Eds.), *The science of writing: Theories, methods, individual differences, and applications* (pp. 323–345). Mahwah, NJ: Erlbaum.

Britton, J., Burgess, T., Martin, N., McLeod, A., & Rosen, H. (1975). *The development of writing abilities.* London: Macmillan.

Bromley, K. (1999). Key components of sound writing instruction. In L.B. Gambrell, L.M. Morrow, S.B. Neuman, & M. Pressley (Eds.), *Best practices in literacy instruction* (pp. 152–174). New York: Guilford.

Calkins, L.M. (1994). *The art of teaching writing.* Portsmouth, NH: Heinemann.

Carroll, J., & Wilson, E. (1993). *Acts of teaching: How to teach writing.* Englewood, CO: Teacher Ideas Press.

Cleary, B. (1968). *Ramona the pest.* New York: Morrow.

Collins, J.L. (1998). *Strategies for struggling writers.* New York: Guilford.

Cooper, C.R., & Odell, L. (1999). Describing texts. In C.R. Cooper, & L. Odell (Eds.), *Evaluating writing: The role of teachers' knowledge about text, learning, and culture* (pp. 1–6). Urbana, IL: National Council of Teachers of English.

Craig, S.T. (1983). Self-discovery through writing personal journals. *Language Arts, 60,* 373–379.

Dahl, K.L., & Farnan, N. (1998). *Children's writing: Perspectives from research.* Newark, DE: International Reading Association.

Dakos, K. (1989). *What's there to write about?* New York: Scholastic.

Danielson, K.D., & LaBonty, J. (1994). *Integrating reading and writing through children's literature*. Boston: Allyn and Bacon.

Delpit, L.D. (1988). The silenced dialogue: Power and pedagogy in educating other people's children. *Harvard Educational Review, 58,* 280–298.

Dorn, L.J., French, C., & Jones, T. (1998). *Apprenticeship in literacy: Transitions across reading and writing*. York, ME: Stenhouse.

Downing, S.O. (1995). Teaching writing for today's demands. *Language Arts, 72,* 200–205.

Dyson, A.H., & Freedman, S.W. (1991). Writing. In J. Flood, J.M. Jensen, D. Lapp, & J.R. Squire (Eds.), *Handbook of research on teaching the English language arts* (pp. 754–774). New York: Macmillan.

Elbow, P. (1981). *Writing with power*. New York: Oxford.

Emig, J. (1971). *The composing process of twelfth graders*. Urbana, IL: National Council of Teachers of English.

Fletcher, R., & Portalupi, J. (1998). *Craft lessons: Teaching writing K–8*. York, ME: Stenhouse.

Fox, M. (1990). There's a coffin in my office. *Language Arts, 67,* 468–472.

Freedman, R. (1983). *Children of the wild west*. New York: Scholastic.

Freire, P., & Macedo, D. (1987). *Literacy: Reading the word and the world*. South Hadley, MA: Bergin & Garvey.

Fulkerson, R. (1996). *Teaching the argument in writing*. Urbana, IL: National Council of Teachers of English.

Fulwiler, T. (1987). *The journal book*. Portsmouth, NH: Heinemann.

Gambrell, L.B. (1985). Dialogue journals: Reading-writing interaction. *The Reading Teacher, 38,* 512–515.

Gambrell, L.B. (1996). Creating classroom cultures that foster reading motivation. *The Reading Teacher, 50,* 14–25.

Gardner, H. (1993). *Multiple intelligences*. New York: BasicBooks.

Gillespie, J.S. (1993). Buddy book journals: Responding to literature. *English Journal, 37,* 64–68.

Gillet, J., & Kita, M.J. (1979). Words, kids, and categories. *The Reading Teacher, 32,* 538–542.

Grant, J.E. (1992). *The writing coach: Strategies for helping students develop their own writing voice*. Ontario, Canada: Pembroke.

Graves, D.H. (1975). An examination of the writing processes of seven-year-old children. *Research in the Teaching of English, 9,* 227–241.

Graves, D.H. (1983). *Writing: Teachers and children at work*. Portsmouth, NH: Heinemann.

Graves, D.H. (1994). *A fresh look at writing*. Portsmouth, NH: Heinemann.

Graves, D.H., & Hansen, J. (1983). The author's chair. *Language Arts, 60,* 176–183.

Hansen, J. (1996). Evaluation: The center of writing instruction. *The Reading Teacher, 50,* 188–195.

Hansen, J. (1998). *When learners evaluate*. Portsmouth, NH: Heinemann.

Harris, T.L., & Hodges, R.E. (Eds.). (1995). *The literacy dictionary: The vocabulary of reading and writing*. Newark, DE: International Reading Association.

Harvey, S. (1998). *Nonfiction matters: Reading, writing, and research in grades 3–8*. York, ME: Stenhouse.

Hayes, J.R. (1996). A new framework for understanding cognition and affect in writing. In C.M. Levy & S. Ransdell (Eds.), *The science of writing: Theories, methods, individual differences, and applications* (pp. 1–27). Mahwah, NJ: Erlbaum.

Hayes, J.R., & Nash, J.G. (1996). On the nature of planning in writing. In C.M. Levy & S. Ransdell (Eds.), *The science of writing: Theories, methods, individual differences, and applications* (pp. 29–55). Mahwah, NJ: Erlbaum.

Hill, B.C., Ruptic, C., & Norwick, L. (1998). *Classroom based assessment*. Norwood, MA: Christopher-Gordon.

Hindley, J. (1996). *In the company of children*. York, ME: Stenhouse.

Horner, B., & Lu, M-Z. (1999). *Representing the "other."* Urbana, IL: National Council of Teachers of English.

Hubbard, R. (1985). Second graders answer the question 'Why publish?' *The Reading Teacher, 38,* 658–662.

International Reading Association & National Council of Teachers of English. (1994). *Standards for the assessment of reading and writing*. Newark, DE and Urbana, IL: Author.

International Reading Association & National Council of Teachers of English. (1996). *Standards for the English language arts*. Newark, DE and Urbana, IL: Author.

Johns, J.L., & Lenski, S.D. (1997). *Improving reading: A handbook of strategies* (2nd ed.). Dubuque, IA: Kendall/Hunt.

Johns, J.L., Lenski, S.D., & Elish-Piper, L. (1999). *Early literacy assessments & teaching strategies*. Dubuque, IA: Kendall/Hunt.

Kane, S. (1997). Favorite sentences: Grammar in action. *The Reading Teacher, 51*, 70–72.

Kellaher, K. (1999). Get kids' work published! Top tips on how to do it from children's magazine editors. *Instructor, 108*, 14–18.

Kolln, M. (1999). Cohesion and coherence. In C.R. Cooper & L. Odell (Eds.), *Evaluating writing: The role of teachers' knowledge about text, learning, and culture* (pp. 93–113). Urbana, IL: National Council of Teachers of English.

Laird, D.M. (1990). *The three little Hawaiian pigs and the magic shark*. Honolulu: Barnaby.

Lancia, P.J. (1997). Literary borrowing: The effects of literature on children's writing. *The Reading Teacher, 50*, 470–475.

Laster, B., & Conte, B. (1998/1999). Emerging literacy: Message boards in preschool. *The Reading Teacher, 52*, 417–420.

Learning Media. (1992). *Dancing with the pen: The learner as writer*. Wellington, New Zealand: Ministry of Education.

Lenski, S.D. (Ed.). (1997). *A closer look: Writings by teachers*. Bloomington, IL: Illinois Reading Council.

Lenski, S.D., & Johns, J.L. (1997). Patterns of reading-to-write. *Reading Research and Instruction, 37*, 15–38.

Lenski, S.D., Wham, M.A., & Johns, J.L. (1999). *Reading & learning strategies for middle & high school students*. Dubuque, IA: Kendall/Hunt.

Mackey, M. (1997). Good-enough reading: Momentum and accuracy in the reading of complex fiction. *Research in the Teaching of English, 31*, 428–458.

MacLachlan, P. (1985). *Sarah, plain and tall*. New York: Harper and Row.

Madigan, D., & Koivu-Rybicki, V.T. (1997). *The writing lives of children*. York, ME: Stenhouse.

Mallon, T. (1984). *A book of one's own: People and their diaries*. New York: Ticknor & Fields.

Martin, B., Jr. (1970). *Brown bear, brown bear, what do you see?* New York: Holt.

Martin, S.H. (1992). Using journals to promote learning across the curriculum (3rd ed.). In E.K. Dishner, T.W. Bean, J.E. Readence, & D.W. Moore (Eds.), *Reading in the content areas: Improving classroom instruction* (pp. 311–318). Dubuque, IA: Kendall/Hunt.

McCarthy, T. (1998). *Persuasive writing*. New York: Scholastic Professional Books.

McIntosh, M. (1997). 500 writing formats. *Mathematics Teaching in the Middle School, 2*, 354–357.

Mitchard, J. (1999). *The most wanted*. New York: Signet.

Mohr, M.M. (1984). *Revision: The rhythm of meaning*. Upper Montclair, NJ: Boynton/Cook.

Morrow, L.M. (1997). *The literacy center: Contexts for reading and writing*. York, ME: Stenhouse.

Moss, B., Leone, S., & Dipillo, M.L. (1997). Exploring the literature of fact: Linking reading and writing through information trade books. *Language Arts, 74*, 418–428.

Murphy, S. (1999). Assessing portfolios. In C.R. Cooper & L. Odell (Eds.), *Evaluating writing: The role of teachers' knowledge about text, learning, and culture* (pp. 114–135). Urbana, IL: National Council of Teachers of English.

Murray, D. (1982). *Learning by teaching: Selected articles on writing and teaching*. Upper Montclair, NJ: Boyton/Cook.

Murray, D.M. (1991). *The craft of revision*. Fort Worth, TX: Holt.

Naguchi, R.R. (1991). *Grammar and the teaching of writing: Limits and possibilities*. Urbana, IL: National Council of Teachers of English.

Newman, J. (1983). On becoming a writer. *Language Arts, 60*, 860–870.

Odgers, S. (1990). *Drummond*. New York: Holiday House.

Ollmann, H.E. (1991/1992). The voice behind the print: Letters to an author. *Journal of Reading, 35,* 322–324.

Ollmann, H.E. (1992). Two-column response to literature. *Journal of Reading, 36,* 58–59.

Ollmann, H.E. (1996). Creating higher level thinking with reading response. *Journal of Adolescent & Adult Literacy, 39,* 576–581.

Pike, K., & Mumper, J. (1998). *Books don't have to be flat!* New York: Scholastic Professional Books.

Pilkey, D. (1996). *The paperboy.* New York: Scholastic.

Portalupi, J. (1999). Learning to write: Honoring both process and product. *Primary Voices, 7,* 2–6.

Prain, V. (1995). Helping students identify how writers signal purpose in autobiographical writing. *Journal of Reading, 38,* 476–481.

Richards, J.C., & Gipe, J.P. (1995). What's the structure? A game to help middle school students recognize common writing patterns. *Journal of Reading, 38,* 667–669.

Rief, L. (1992). *Seeking diversity: Language arts with adolescents.* Portsmouth, NH: Heinemann.

Rief, L. (1999). *Vision & voice: Extending the literacy spectrum.* Portsmouth, NH: Heinemann.

Rogers, L. (1997). Using newspaper sports pages with an upper primary class. *Practically Primary, 2,* 6–11.

Root, R.L., & Steinberg, M. (1996). *Those who do, can: Teachers writing, writers teaching.* Urbana, IL: National Council of Teachers of English.

Rosenblatt, L. (1985). Language, literature, and values. In S.N. Tchudi (Ed.), *Language, schooling, and society* (pp. 64–80). Upper Montclair, NJ: Boyton/Cook.

Routman, R. (1994). *Invitations: Changing as teachers and learners K–12.* Portsmouth, NH: Heinemann.

Rubin, D.L. (Ed.). (1995). *Composing social identity in written language.* Mahwah, NJ: Erlbaum.

Rubin, D.L. (1998). Writing for readers: The primacy of audience in composing. In N. Nelson & R.C. Calfee (Eds.), *The reading-writing connection* (pp. 53–73). Chicago: University of Chicago.

Ryder, R.J. (1994). Using frames to promote critical writing. *Journal of Reading, 38,* 210–218.

Santa, C.M., Havens, L., & Harrison, S. (1989). Teaching secondary science through reading, writing, studying, and problem-solving. In D. Lapp, J. Flood, & N. Farnan (Eds.), *Content area reading and learning: Instructional strategies* (pp. 137–151). Englewood Cliffs, NJ: Prentice Hall.

Schmidt, B., & Buckley, M. (1991). Plot relationships chart. In J.M. Macon, D. Bewell, & M. Vogt (Eds.), *Responses to literature: Grades K–8* (pp. 7–8). Newark, DE: International Reading Association.

Scieszka, J. (1989). *The true story of the three little pigs.* New York: Viking.

Sharples, M. (1996). An account of writing as creative design. In C.M. Levy & S. Ransdell (Eds.), *The science of writing: Theories, methods, individual differences, and applications* (pp. 127–148). Mahwah, NJ: Erlbaum.

Smith, F. (1988). *Joining the literacy club.* Portsmouth, NH: Heinemann.

Smith, F. (1990). *To think.* New York: Teachers College Press.

Spandel, V., & Stiggins, R.J. (1997). *Creating writers: Linking writing assessment and instruction* (2nd ed.). New York: Longman.

Spaulding, C.L. (1992). The motivation to read and write. In J.W. Irwin & M.A. Doyle (Eds.), *Reading/writing connections: Learning from research* (pp. 177–201). Newark, DE: International Reading Association.

Stotsky, S. (1995). The uses and limitations of personal or personalized writing in writing theory, research, and instruction. *Reading Research Quarterly, 30,* 758–776.

Straub, R. (1997). Students' reactions to teacher comments: An exploratory study. *Research in the Teaching of English, 31,* 91–118.

Tchudi, S. (Ed.). (1997). *Alternatives to grading student writing.* Urbana, IL: National Council of Teachers of English.

Tompkins, G.E. (1994). *Teaching writing: Balancing process and product* (2nd ed.). New York: Macmillan.

Tower, C. (1998). Making room for laughter: The use of humor in the writing classroom. *New England Reading Association Journal, 34,* 11–16.

Turbill, J., Butler, A., Cambourne, B., & Langton, G. (1991). *Frameworks course notebook*. Stanley, NY: Wayne Finger Lakes Board of Cooperative Educational Services.

Viorst, J. (1981). *If I were in charge of the world*. New York: Atheneum.

Wham, M.A., & Lenski, S.D. (1996). Sharing the journey: Seven strategies for responding to literature. *Wisconsin State Reading Association Journal*, *40*, 29–34.

Williams, J.D. (1996). *Preparing to teach writing*. Mahwah, NJ: Erlbaum.

Wolcott, W., & Legg, S.M. (1998). *An overview of writing assessment: Theory, research, and practice*. Urbana, IL: National Council of Teachers of English.

Wray, D., & Lewis, M. (1997). Teaching factual writing: Purpose and structure. *The Australian Journal of Language and Literacy*, *20*, 131–138.

Zaragoza, N., & Vaughn, S. (1995). Children teach us to teach writing. *The Reading Teacher*, *49*, 42–47.

Index

Notes and Additional Strategies